LIVING
WITH
DEATH

by
HELMUT THIELICKE

Translated by
GEOFFREY W. BROMILEY

WILLIAM B. EERDMANS PUBLISHING COMPANY
Grand Rapids, Michigan

Copyright © 1983 by Wm. B. Eerdmans Publishing Co.
255 Jefferson Ave. S.E., Grand Rapids, MI 49503

Translated from the German edition, *Leben mit dem Tod*
© Helmut Thielicke/J. C. B. Mohr (Paul Siebeck) Tübingen 1980

Library of Congress Cataloging in Publication Data
Thielicke, Helmut, 1908-
Living with death.

Translation of: Leben mit dem Tod.
Bibliography: p. 202.
Includes index.
1. Death — Religious aspects — Christianity — Addresses,
essays, lectures. I. Title.
BT825.T4513 1982   236'.1   82-18221
ISBN 0-8028-3522-4

CONTENTS

Contents

ABBREVIATIONS

Anthrop. H. Thielicke, *Mensch sein —Mensch werden,* 3rd ed., 1980
CD   K. Barth, *Church Dogmatics,* T. and T. Clark, 1956ff.
EA   Erlangen Edition of Luther's Works
EF (EG) H. Thielicke, *The Evangelical Faith,* Vols. I– III, Eerdmans, 1974ff.
LW   *Luther's Works,* Concordia and Fortress
NT   New Testament
OT   Old Testament
TDNT   *Theological Dictionary of the New Testament,* Eerdmans, 1964ff.
ThE   H. Thielicke, *Theological Ethics,* Fortress, 1966ff. (German, Vols. I– III, Tübingen: Mohr)
WA   Weimar Edition of Luther's Works
ZThK   *Zeitschrift für Theologie und Kirche*

PREFACE

Some years ago I wrote a book on death. It was composed during the horrors of aerial bombardment and the dictatorship. Since I was forbidden to travel, speak, or write at the time, it could not be published in Germany. The manuscript was smuggled into Switzerland in a diplomatic bag. It was published anonymously by Oikumene (Geneva) and used for many courses set up for German prisoners of war in various parts of the world. After the war it was published in several editions by J. C. B. Mohr, Tübingen, under the title *Tod und Leben*. Fortress Press, Philadelphia, brought out an English version, *Death and Life*, translated by Edward H. Schroeder.

Since then many of the questions have changed with the changing situation. Hence one stone of the earlier book could not be left upon another. It has been completely rewritten. Only here and there will a short passage from the original text be found, and even then only with revision at essential points.

Yet I hope that in this new form there will still be many traces of my own brushes with death. I experienced these not only during the war but also in some dark periods of sickness. The book could hardly have been written without this background.

It is written for people who reflect on the end of life, and technical theological terms are avoided. Quotations in other languages are translated or put in the notes.

The extended manuscript is based on lectures given to an audience drawn from all the faculties at Hamburg. I refer to readers, not hearers, but otherwise the lecture style is for the most part retained.

Helmut Thielicke

Only as I die do I detect that I am.
     —*Hugo von Hofmannsthal*

We shall see when the light goes out.
     —*Ernst Jünger*

Life would not be worth a rap if there were no death.
     —*Bavarian Proverb*

God loves life; he invented it.
     —*Paul Tournier*

Hell? I believe it is the world in which there is no more love. We do not die in order to be dead or to become something dead. We die for life, we die according to a plan.
     —*Knut Hamsun*

It takes all of life to learn how to die.
     —*Seneca*

We can be lord of nothing so long as we fear death. When we no longer fear it, all things are ours.
     —*Leo N. Tolstoy*

Life; happy are those to whom it brings joy and children and daily bread; but the best that it brings is the knowledge that it ends, its outcome, death.
     —*Theodor Fontane*

LIVING
WITH
DEATH

Chapter 1

THE PROBLEM: A FIRST SURVEY

A. THE BEGINNING AND END OF HUMAN LIFE
Distinction between the Dimensions of Bios and the Humanum

I do not think I am under a false impression if I say that in our days the question of the beginning and end of human life is one of the most discussed ethical, or, one might say, existential, questions. However we put it, this question has explosive metaphysical force. It brings the horizon of human existence into view. In it the meaning of life becomes a problem.

As concerns the beginning of life, the discussion of abortion and its legalization in many parts of the world makes it clear to any thoughtful observer that in this matter we quickly leave purely hygienic, legal, and sociological criteria behind and press on to the question of the understanding of human life which forms the background to our decision.

No matter what that decision may be, we are confronted by the fact that developing life, being "human," stands under some kind of a taboo. To this extent it is protected against arbitrary disposition, or abortion at will. But the question that immediately arises is, *When* does what is developing become a specifically human life? Where does the break take place from a purely biological pre-existence of the humanum? Does conception itself mean the beginning of human life? Or implanting in the womb? Or the fashioning of the embryo in human form after the first months of pregnancy?

We remember Michelangelo's famous painting in the Sistine Chapel that symbolizes human creation: The man Adam appears already in perfect form, but he does not yet have life or breath; the next moment he gets up and stands on his own feet, and then God the Father comes to him and makes him a living image of himself by a touch of his finger and the imparting of his Spirit. Before this happens, Adam is not yet human; he is only a candidate for humanity.

The analogy to which I allude and the question which I see put by it is obvious. I am asking whether in the prehuman stage (we again think of the embryo) a person stands already under the taboo of the humanum, or whether at this stage we can dispose of this being like a mere thing, a non-Thou. If I am right, Michelangelo decides in favor of a taboo. For the candidate for humanity, although not yet awakened, is already invested with future dignity and is — expectantly — related to the Thou of the Creator. The goal of the humanum is already prefigured in the perfection of the form.

If there is already intimated here the distinction between purely biological life and life in the strictly human sense, the question naturally arises at once (and again) of when this specifically human phase begins in developing life. One might put it this way: When does the break come in the evolution? When does the taboo phase commence?

One should not think that this is a purely modern question or that it presupposes certain results of embryonic research. The specifically human element in being, and the question of when and how this comes to transcend the sphere of pure *bios*, was known to previous ages, too. This question is connected with their religious convictions. People who regard human beings as being made in God's image, as being separated from the rest of creation and sharing special privileges, obviously come up against this question. Naturally, it did not arise as a scientific question in the modern sense in antiquity and in the medieval period. Rather, it came to expression under the banner of a religious concern, namely, in the question of how and when the human seed acquires a "soul."[1]

This often led to strange speculations that can make us laugh today, but it should not prevent us from thinking historically and taking seriously the arguments of an age preceding scientifically oriented medicine. The issue is still that of the break between candidacy for, and the enthronement of, the humanum. This break is marked by the older idea of acquiring a soul and thus becoming human in the true sense. From the moment of acquiring a soul any attack upon the developing life is infanticide.[2] In Scholastic theology the question of the time when a soul is acquired was answered under Aristotle's influence as follows: The male embryo acquires a soul after forty days, and the female embryo (there is no equality of the sexes here) after eighty days. These theories are not normative for modern Roman Catholicism, but the idea of acquiring a soul still exerts an influence in fixing the time of fructification, or becoming human, which is put at forty-eight hours after conception. This point marks the break prior to which the pregnancy may in special cases be manipulated by flushing or injection.

The idea of acquiring a soul may today strike many people as mythological, but it should not prevent us from respecting the doctrinal intention behind it. The aim was to distinguish potential life from real life and to fix the different degrees of guilt in impermissible prevention of pregnancy on the one side and its termination on the other.

Fundamentally, the question has not changed today, at least so far as the principle behind the theory of acquiring a soul is concerned. We simply put the question in another way. To do so, we think in terms of humanity and its privileges. These privileges express that wherein the humanum transcends purely biological status. Can the question of the beginning of humanity be decided by purely medical means? At the very latest in matters of abortion, and therefore in the question of when human life has to be protected, it has become clear to everyone that medical categories are inadequate to provide the necessary criteria for this decision. The disagreement of doctors, their inability to say when this time is reached, is a sufficient sign of this inadequacy.

These controversies cannot be solved objectively, because we have here a metamedical problem. A simple illustration will suffice. Faced with this issue, we have to say (confessionally) what we understand by humanity. But we cannot do this so long as we merely describe in empirical fashion the phenomenon of human beings. It is amusing to see how Norbert Wiener in his pioneering work on cybernetics (*Mensch und Mensch-Maschine*, 1952) reduces this kind of description to absurdity: The most general empirical assertion, he thinks, might be that a human being is a creature with two feet and no feathers. But then, he adds, this puts it in the same group as a plucked fowl, a kangaroo, or a jerboa: an indication that what is distinctively human cannot be determined by phenomenological criteria of this kind.

Obviously there is something contained in humanity that cannot be described phenomenologically; its core is invisible. The essential thing is that humans can transcend themselves, and have to do so.

Herder (in his *Ideen*) says that we are not at all infallible machines in the hands of nature, but we become the goals and ends of our own activity. Not being puppets under external direction, but seeing ourselves as endowed by the Creator with the gift of being the center of our own deeds, we live at open risk. We can increase or squander this pound of responsible life that the Creator has loaned to us.

Schiller writes something of the same in his essay *Anmut und Würde*. In the case of plants and animals, nature not only gives the determination and fixes the goal of development but also executes it on its own. In the case of humans, however, nature gives the determination and then leaves us to achieve it. This means that the goal of existence is "given" us, and it is not in our own power to fix our determination, but the way to achieve it is a task that is set for us. We may fail at this task. The experiment of being human may not succeed; there is a possibility of "dehumanization."

All this means that we must *project* ourselves toward an end. We must become what we are. But to do this we must first ask what we are, wherein our identity consists. And this implies the further question of what our determination is, what is the meaning of our life, what values we are to actualize. The possibility also arises that we might fail to achieve our determination, that is, ourselves, whereas animals are not subject to this possibility of wrong decision and mistaken self-realization.

The degree of the relevance of this problem in our generation may be seen from the many discussions of identity crises and the various exercises in self-experience with which attempts are made to treat them therapeutically.[3] How, then, does it come about — I might ask in passing — that at medical conferences and legal discussions of penal reform there is a desire to hear the voice of philosophers and theologians? Is it not because human development raises metaphysiological and metalegal problems, and psychosomatic relations — as in the matter of "punishment" — bear an affinity to these problems of the identity and determination, or, finally, the meaning of human life?

This is why Ludwig Wittgenstein can say in his *Tractatus logicophilosophicus* (1969, 6.41) that the meaning of the world has to lie outside it. In the world everything is as it is and occurs as it occurs; but in it there is no value — and if there were, it would have no value. If there is a value that has value, it has to lie outside occurrence and existence. For all occurrence and existence is accidental. This describes exactly the transcendental element that I have in view.

These problems of the nature and meaning of human existence become really acute when the issue is its end and finitude, that is, human death. We can see this — provisionally — from some questions that confront us with the fact of our dying (and do so in such a way as to affect all of us, not merely those in what are called frontier situations).

The first question is whether in dying we pass from being into nonbeing, or being no more? Is death the mode of this nonbeing? If we interpret death in this sense, like all interpretations of death this influences our understanding of life. Epicurus offers a classical example of this in his letter to Menoikos[4] when he tells him to accustom himself to the thought that death does not affect us. For everything good and bad rests on perception; but death is loss of perception (and precisely to that extent a form of nonbeing). Hence the worst evil, death, does not affect us. For (in a famous statement) so long as we exist, death is not present, and when death is present, we no longer exist. It thus affects neither the living nor the dead, for it does not touch the former and the latter no longer exist. According to Epicurus, then, fear of death is nonsense. To be enlightened on this point, to see through the nonsense, automatically frees us from the absurd fear of death and restores to us unbroken life and enjoyment of life.

How does it come about, I might ask, that this very logically formulated antithesis of being and nonbeing, for all its apparent logic, has not been able to permeate the emotional sphere and free us from anxiety regarding our finitude? Yet this is obviously so — or is it? Might it be that the ridiculous anxiety persists and resists all enlightenment because we cannot conceive of our nonbeing, and the absurdity encamps in the unattainability of nothingness?

Jean Améry says something worth pondering about in his essay on suicide. He says that our thinking is dominated by the logic of life. He means a logic that works with the categories of being and thus relates constantly to our own existence and to the being that encounters us. Nonbeing cannot be grasped in these categories of the logic of life. In this framework it is absurd and unthinkable.

Because there is no bridge from being to nonbeing, we are helpless in thinking about death. Close to this is Wittgenstein's statement[5] that we cannot formulate an answer to a question that cannot be formulated. It is best to keep silent about matters on which we cannot speak. Related to our present problem, this means that because nonbeing is an answer that cannot be formulated, the question is invalid. To ask about something absurd is itself absurd. But this means that if nonbeing, or being no longer, is my destiny, then what causes me anxiety is the question itself. For the path that I enter with it is "potentially" pathless. Thus my destiny of life becomes one that itself has neither path nor being. In this way the consolation of Epicurus comes to an abrupt halt, for the nonbeing that eliminates all the anxiety of finitude escapes the reach of my thinking. My thinking, then, is defenseless when confronted by death.

The second question that death puts to life is that of meaning. I can illustrate this by a reader's letter that the atheistic monthly *Science and Religion* (published in Moscow) received among many others when it published a provocative article entitled: "What is the Point of Human Life?"[6]

To quote just a few sentences, this letter says that if life arises in our earthly frame, fills itself with understanding and emotion, and then everything vanishes (dissolving into mere nonbeing)..., life is an intolerable absurdity. Why should we develop our minds and emotions if we arise out of nothing ... and will be changed back into nothing? Why should we have a transitory consciousness of our existence, for a brief moment see myriads of stars, learn to add and divide..., experience pleasure and pain, rejoice in beauty..., and love unselfishly? Why — we ask — was all this given to us if we are not eternal but the next moment will vanish into nonbeing without even dreams remaining? Is not this life that is extinguished in death a fantastic nightmare?

The context of this letter was as follows. The editorial that triggered the correspondence answered the question of the point of human life along Marxist lines. From this standpoint the only possible reply is that we are here to serve specific goals, especially the goal of changing society. Since the goals are finite, the finitude of human life is obviously no problem on the pragmatic level. If we are only means to ends — to put it with intentional sharpness — the means can be destroyed without any problem when the function of serving the ends has been discharged. And this function can in fact be discharged. But the moment we humans are seen not as means to ends but as ends of our own (I am intentionally choosing a Kantian rather than a Christian formulation), the question of the point of human life can no longer be answered by referring to immanent goals. If we are ends ourselves, this implies a predication of human dignity that lifts us out of immanent functional relations. For this reason it is somewhat macabre to read in obituaries (in the Western press, too) that someone lived to produce fresh milk or, in the case of an engineer, to provide heating and ventilation.

The predication of human dignity puts meaning in place of a goal that life can fix and achieve. Meaning is a transcendental thing. It has to do with the destiny that is assigned to us and that we have not set for ourselves. But it is meaning that our end in death makes into a problem; *this* is what the writer of the letter wants to say. In virtue of meaning, my existence transcends itself; it points to something that is beyond its finitude. And is all this to be terminated?

This becomes a problem, then, once I am aware of the unconditional nature of my existence, or once I have come to see the accent of uniqueness or noninterchangeability that the meaning of my life gives me. To my knowledge no writer of the east has so clearly seen and stated the burden of the problem of death as Vitezslav Gardavsky in his book *God Is Not Yet Dead*. That I die, he says, means that I cannot complete my work, I will no longer see those I have loved, and I will no longer experience beauty or sorrow. The unrepeatable music of this world will no longer ring in my senses; never again will I anywhere or in any way move out beyond myself. Only this final thing remains for me (p. 229).

What moves us in this passage is the sincerity with which the author renounces all assumptions of a continuation of life after death, even though these are close enough to his thinking. He exposes the plight of unbelief while showing it, without any illusions, to be a real plight. For to live a human life is to live in a fullness of sensory relations, especially those of love and meaning. He refers to the unrepeatable music that sounds in our ears. And are these unique things, that can never be reproduced, to come to a final end? We cannot conceive of this (as Améry also said), but we accept the brute fact and cannot look beyond our bound eyes.

7

What evokes respect in the case of Gardavsky is that he puts forth questions — especially to himself — that have to remain open. Perhaps the worth of people is better measured by their questions than their answers.

Death confronts us with the question of meaning in a second form. A look at supraindividual history shows this. Guilt and expiation, wrongdoing and disaster, have a more implacable emphasis when we consider longer historical periods and larger areas. The accounting of history, as Bismarck once observed, is more exact and pitiless than the supreme audit office of Prussia. What is wrong usually avenges itself and guilt is usually expiated. Lying usually has a short life; the sun exposes it. Good also pays long-term dividends *if* (this is the condition) one can take a sufficiently long view.

In the limited sphere of personal individuality and the limited time between birth and death, this rule does not work out so well. The shorter the view and the time, the less can the statistical law of averages be claimed, and the more we are under the sway of chance and of that which is contrary to all logos.

No wonder if in existential crises we ask: "Why me?" No wonder if the subject of theodicy arises especially here. We think of people with multiple sclerosis or cancer, and the question arises: "How can God allow this?" (This is precisely the question that in Albert Camus opens the gate to absurdity, to the idea of a Sisyphus existence.) In Greek tragedy this question is the spur that constantly advances the tragic mystery. Sophocles' Oedipus is the classical example. Why does he have to be guilty of the double crime of incest and patricide, or better, why does it have to take place through him? This is a dark secret that cannot be solved in the limited time available. The question "Why?" — the question of meaning — remains an open one. It remains also an open wound through which faith in the gods threatens to bleed to death. The only way out of the torment of this question is that of the lonely and blinded Oedipus Colonneus when he gives up wrestling with the riddle of his destiny and becomes reconciled to it. Love of fate, acceptance of destiny, becomes his liberation. And what once raged as a lacerating inward battle now turns outward and becomes a struggle with his sons and his cursing of them. Those who are reconciled to their destiny become agents of fresh destiny. The limited time they have between birth and death, their finitude,

8

does not permit any solution of the question "Why?" within their present lifetime. The watchman over this finitude is death. Death forms the boundary or break that borders the light of existence with darkness — a darkness in which all beaten paths end and the unbounded begins. One can call this mysterious or absurd as one chooses.

The third question that death puts to life will occupy us more fully when we come to Nietzsche. I mention it here only for the sake of systematic completeness. It is the question of whether we ever have the right — or perhaps even the duty — not just to let death come upon us as our fate, but to bring it about, whether in the form of suicide or of euthanasia. Is not dying as a self-chosen act, an autonomous decision about ourselves, one of the privileges of humanity that animals do not enjoy? Are not suicide and euthanasia a sign of our freedom, a freedom that also makes us responsible for our continuing to live or not continuing to do so? To be our own judges in this way might be a special sign of our humanity and self-transcendence — or perhaps not? We shall leave this question for the moment and come back to it later.

B. THE PERSONAL NATURE OF HUMAN DYING

1. Death as the End of Something Unique, of All Relationships

All these questions that death puts to life can be understood only if we see that human dying differs from animal dying, that it involves more than a biological process, that it participates in the personal nature of my ego. Being personal here means, to put it negatively first, that my ego is not just an exchangeable specimen of a species but has the character of uniqueness. (What this character involves from a Christian standpoint we shall deal with later.) The problem of death does not arise for a mere specimen of a species, for example, a fly, for this continues to live on in the ongoing species. The accent of the unconditional that is placed on human life, however, gives it the character of uniqueness. Death becomes a problem because it ends something unique and is something more and other than a natural processs.

For this reason I think Carl Zuckmayer is right when he accuses

Bert Brecht[7] of losing what we here call uniqueness (or particularity) in the rhythm of purely natural processes; he is massively "pagan" in this regard. For, as Brecht puts it in a little poem, we are to praise the tree that grows joyfully up to heaven out of carrion, we are to praise the carrion and the tree that consumes it, and we are also to praise heaven. Are human birth and death really to be integrated into this creative sequence of carrion and tree, of tree and carrion?

I recall the diary of a young soldier who was killed. He tells how once, swept away and intoxicated by the spring, he parted a budding elder bush and found under it a corpse half rotted away. Why did he experience the shock of corruptibility that he goes on to depict very movingly? If he had merely found decayed bushes beside the blooms, this would not have seemed to him to be any antithesis, but simply a natural sequence in the rhythm of life, an expression of the established law that causes Bert Brecht to demand that we "also" praise heaven. But the dead soldier seemed to him to be a contradiction of this world of nature, something unnatural that gives death the mask of a stranger, a horror.

It undoubtedly belongs to this nature-transcending character of human death that it cannot be defined in terms of natural science, or, to put it more cautiously, that it cannot be fully defined in this way. In such terms we cannot appreciate the difference between the end of an experimental dog and the death of a patient in intensive care. The specific aspect of human dying is not expressed.

I shall now try to bring out this aspect by some models that will be taken for the most part from literature.

1. The truth of human death comes to light only when I can speak in the first person — "I die" — so that I understand the death to be mine, to belong to me. Only when the death at issue is mine does it cease to be a general and half-true phenomenon and become a personal experience in which I know the mystery of my being. Death, then, has to grow on me, or, as Rilke says, grow "in me."

Along these lines Karl Holl could say on his deathbed, when the doctor offered to help him over the last threshold with drugs: "I will not be deprived of *my* death." Naturally what moved him to say this was not the curiosity of a scientist wanting to know the extinction of vital life "from within" (as is reported, for example, of Hemingway). Rather, he was moved by the mystery of being

10

to which his own death belonged and which declared itself for this reason in what was most personal to him.

Martin Heidegger, too, drew attention to the personal nature of dying in his *Being and Time*. If I make death no more than an objective fact, as in the truth that "people die," I refuse to make it my own. To say that "people die" is simply to say that it only affects people in the mass. A general understanding of being says "People die," because this enables us to apply it to everybody but ourselves, and everybody is nobody. Hence we achieve a constant pacification in relation to death. But this ceases once I see that death is ontologically constituted by personal application and existence.[8]

In Tolstoy's story "The Death of Ivan Ilych," Pyotr Ivanovich masters death by generalizing it along these lines. He robs it of personal application in a way that illustrates very well what has just been said. Three days and nights of dreadful suffering and then death; it might strike him at any moment, he thought. But immediately, he did not know how, he was helped by the everyday thought that it had struck Ivan Ilych and not himself, and that it would not and could not strike him. . . . This consideration pacified him. . . , as though death were an event that was proper only to Ivan Ilych and alien to himself.

The Hungarian poet Gyula Illyes has something similar in his essay-story "The Beautiful Years of Old. In Charon's Boat" (1975), when he says that we can none of us conceive of our own death. We find it absurd, and this absurdity is obviously the presupposition for ending the other absurdity that we call life. If I understand this correctly, what he means is that that declaration of the absurd is a form of withdrawal, of not letting it touch us. What it signifies is taken out of the circle of the things that we worry about, or normally concern ourselves with, or organize rationally in constant procedures.

In contrast to this suppression by generalization, or by absorption into an observable physiological process, or by postulating the unreality of the absurd, there stands the real truth about human dying, namely, that it is a personal event that belongs inexchangeably to me.

2. The second model that we shall use to clarify the personal nature or particularity of human dying is to be found in some lines of Hölderlin's poem "Man." What is pointed out here is the dif-

ference between human death and the death of animals: the birds of the forest breathe freely, but we humans see the dark future and therefore are forced to look on death and fear it alone.

Hölderlin does not base the distinction in the awareness of death on the denial of a soul to animals — a belief one finds in antiquity in Homer, Plato, and Philo. Rather, he finds the distinction in different ways of knowing, or, better yet, in differences in self-consciousness. Birds breathe more freely and feel no threat of death (even though they are in fact in mortal peril), because the temporal dimension of the "future" has no place in their consciousness. They move in the moment, the now. Living like this, they are immortal. This immortality is simply ignorance of their mortality. Humans, however, have a knowledge of their mortality because they live in orientation to the future. In the language of Heidegger, their future is even now a concern. When I was in East Africa I came across some primitive tribes that had not yet reached this point in human development. They lived only for the moment. The wealth of the tropics, for example, relieved them of all care for winter. There was no such thing as winter. They lived from hand to mouth and maintained a kind of prehistorical existence. Their gaze was on the moment. Humanity develops historically and culturally only when human beings project themselves into the future and transcend the single moment. Only then do they begin to plan, to fashion, to work for what is to come. Only then do they become creative and set up civilizations. On this depends also whether they are politically efficient or remain passive.

As existence with this knowledge orients itself to the future, "it is forced to look on death and fear it alone." It thus lives and acts in a limited and finite span. Knowledge of the future that puts an end to it is a specific mark of humanity. For it is the condition on which we can (and must) transcend ourselves. I have shown — remember the quotations from Schiller and Herder — that we have to grasp ourselves, that we are summoned to an actualization of meaning, and that we wait for a determination that we can fulfill or fail to fulfill. We can make something of ourselves; we have to become what we are.

The need to ask about the "Why" and "Wherefore" of life is conceivable only on two conditions. The first is knowledge of the future as the possible time of self-actualization. The second is knowledge that this future is bordered by death. Death is the end of all possible self-actualization.

In the same way, we might know that on two conditions we are not called to self-actualization, so that the appeal to become what we are is irrelevant. The first would be if, like the birds of the forest, we had a sense only of the moment and moved only in the present. The second would be if we had a future that was not bordered by death, if we were immortal gods. We could then vegetate, continually putting things off and never coming to ourselves. (And as gods we should not need to!) There is self-actualization only when we are aware of our future and its limit. Our determination is always a determination by death.

3. A final model that holds out before us the personal nature of human dying is one that I can mention here only in passing. It has been given to us by Sigmund Freud. According to Freud, the only explanation for the fear of death as a form of melancholia is that the ego surrenders because it feels that it is hated and persecuted instead of loved by the super-ego — by father, providence, or fate. This is the basis of the fear of death. Also in Freud — at least to some extent[9] — worrying about death is a specifically human fate because it arises out of a conflict that animals do not know, namely, a wrestling with forces — described as the super-ego — to which we are necessarily related, by which we see ourselves questioned, and which drive us either to self-assertion and self-discovery or to self-abandonment in the entanglement of melancholia.

To state a first conclusion, then, we cannot understand human dying apart from the fact that the dying being is not just a thing that might be replaced by something else, that it is not, for example, an exchangeable specimen of a species as in animal life. The uniqueness of human existence is defined by the special character of its "individuality." Undoubtedly it would be impermissibly one-sided to find the particularity of this human individuality merely in its inner structure, as in Goethe's "entelechy" or Leibniz's "monad." What I mean by individuality here includes also the particularity of a fullness of external relations, a multiple correspondence with the surrounding world, especially with the history into which I am interwoven. Trans-subjective groups of relations also constitute individuality in this sense.

In spite of everything that links us to others of our kind, all of us are centers from which we see our own worlds,[10] and to that extent we really have "our own worlds" that relate all our life's encounters to us in a special and unique way. In this sense the psychiatrist Alfred E. Hoche says that it is a strange spectacle that, seeing the cessation of life around us and behind us at every level as the supreme and pitiless law of life, we find it hard personally to adjust to it; the thought seems intolerable to us that this vast subjective world that we carry within us, and that lives only once in this form, should simply be erased, that we should fall by the wayside while others move on talking as though nothing had happened.... The force of this feeling ... mocks all logic.[11] It is — the same word again! — "absurd."

Uniqueness of individuality means, then, uniqueness of the relations that bind me to the surrounding world in love, perception, and feeling. It means the "infinite subjective world" in which all this is reflected and imaged.[12]

Maupassant speaks to the same effect in the truly dreadful deathbed scenes of his story *Bel Ami*, when the dying Norbert of Varenne says that a being (like himself) will never, never return. We can take impressions of works of art and reproduce them, but *his* body, face, thoughts, and yearnings (what Hoche calls the "vast subjective world") will never come back. Millions of people will be born with noses, eyes, brows, and cheeks like his, and even a soul like his, but he himself will never return, nor will there be in them anything that is recognizably his. With his death the world will lose a central standpoint, and yet the unique nexus that is seen from this standpoint — inconceivably — lives on in its facticity, as we finally hear in Tolstoy's *War and Peace* when Prince Andrey, on the eve of the battle of Borodino, looked at the row of birches with their motionless yellow-green leaves, and their white barks glistening in the sun, and said: To die ... I may be killed tomorrow so that I will no longer be.... All this may continue, and only I shall no longer be.

One may say that precisely on the basis of this uniqueness we are more than purely natural beings that are simply equal specimens of the same species. This characteristic that transcends nature has always resulted in our being treated as "historical" (and not just natural) beings.

A further result is that epistemologically, too, our historical being has been methodically treated as more than a natural object.

14

Heinrich Rickert tried to express this when he ascribed a generalizing tendency to natural science and an individualizing tendency to history. What interests me in an egg is its egglike quality, that is, what it shares with other eggs. Only the odd head of a collection of curiosities and not a scientist would be interested in individual abnormalities and exceptions in this sphere. But the historian is interested in the uniqueness of a historical figure, in its individuality, in what distinguishes this figure from others of its kind. Paul de Lagarde once gave a generalized account of Moltke as though he were an object of natural science (how as a baby he soiled his diapers and cried at night, then reached puberty, etc.), but he did so with satirical intent, and could hardly flatter himself that he had hit on what was really "historical" in Moltke. By the law of grotesque contradiction, only a comic effect could be achieved.

The true root of the historical particularity of existence lies in one's quality as a "person." What we called "individuality" is simply an imprecise aspect of this deeper essence. Human beings are "persons." They have the responsibility of grasping their own destiny. They can win it or lose it. They have their own time in which this unalterable decision is made. The decision is unalterable because the stretch of time is irreversible. It has "direction."

In this temporality of existence that makes the basic decision unique and unalterable lies the deepest essence of the uniqueness and irreplaceability of existence as it is established by its personal character. This essence is to be located in an even more basic dimension than that which presents life as a plenitude of relations and a "vast subjective world."

Personhood denotes the final core of our humanity. It makes us ask what we are apart from our relations to the world around us, and what we can take with us over the threshold of death.

I can think of no better illustration of our ultimate personal substance than Jesus' parable of the rich farmer (Luke 12:16ff.) whose crops were so abundant that he had no room to store them. He thus decided to build bigger barns to provide for his future. Then he could say to his soul, "Eat, drink, and be merry." But God said to him, "You fool! This night your life is required of you. And then whose will those things be that you have stored up?" So it is with those who heap up riches and are not rich in God. To put it in modern terms, death was for the rich farmer a barrier that he could pass through only on his own and with no baggage. He could take nothing with him.

When he realized that he was rich and did not have to worry about the future, he was identifying himself, as it were, with his possessions. In this assumed identity he merged what he was and what he had into a single entity. (If you have a thing, you are that thing.) But death dispels this illusory identity. Surprising him with God's Word, it puts to him the question: What are you on this last night apart from your possessions, your functions, and your relations? What being remains, and will go with you, when you have to leave what you have? What is your ultimate identity? What are you as a person apart from these penultimate things and external attachments? What is left of you and your being when you are subjected to the subtraction of death?

This is, as it were, the most pointed of all the questions that death puts to us.

2. Different Forms of Our Awareness of Death

The Consciousness of Our Temporality

After these preliminary basic observations regarding the specific character of human dying, I should like to turn parenthetically to some empirical considerations.

We have seen that we humans are referred to the future and thus far are aware of death. The question that now concerns us is more the phenomenological one: In what forms does awareness of death concretely express itself? In this respect we come up against some surprising contradictions that call for explanation.

When Philo says in his *Phaedo* that the whole life of the philosopher is a commentary on death,[13] he certainly does not mean that the philosopher (or thinking person) is always thinking of his last hour. Daily experience refutes this. It may be different in a home for senior citizens in which one constantly faces the last hour. But in childhood, youth, and maturity the thought of one's end hardly surfaces above the ruffled flow of life except in time of war or among racing motorists and perhaps the pilots of high-powered aircraft — and seldom among these, either.

How, then, does our awareness of death manifest itself? We undoubtedly have to reckon with a concealed form of its presence. In a cautious approach to this question of the nature of our awareness of death, I will mention two literary testimonies and append to these some observations of my own.

The first testimony is from Thomas Mann's little-known *Fragment on the Religious*.[14] In this work he defines the religious as the permanent thought of death or remembrance of our mortality. Upon this definition, which is so surprising coming from this source, Mann then offers an autobiographical comment, which is even more surprising. He says that he saw his father die, and knows that he himself will die, and finds this thought the most intimate one of all, standing behind all that he thinks and writes. We are so hemmed in by the eternal puzzle that we would have to be animals to put it out of our minds. On no waking day does he not think of death and its riddle. What does Mann mean by saying he thinks about this puzzle? Does he really have in mind meditation on the fact that one day death will end things? We shall postpone this question for future discussion.

Jean Améry comes closer to the secret of this awareness when, in his *Discourse on Suicide*, he says that in moments of raw and unexpected awareness of our corruptibility, such as we all experience, we realize that we are creatures of time without needing to know anything about entropy. Someday the relatively irreversible time that we know day by day (each morning doing the same things, going the same ways, seeing the same faces) will be found by the dying to be absolutely irreversible.

Mann, like Améry, is saying that certain experiences of corruptibility such as the death of his father or the process of aging remind us of death. But what appearance does death take here? In what form will I experience it in the hour of death? We must probe this question more deeply.

Améry offers an important clue when he alludes to entropy (or the irreversibility of natural processes). This is an indication that our awareness of death is related to the realization of our temporality, and again to the specifically human character of this temporality. But how and in what sense are we aware of our temporality?

If I am right, we are so in two ways. First, no matter whether we are young or old, we constantly have to reckon with the finitude of the stretch of time at our disposal. Second, we have to do so in such a way that we constantly are aware of the orientation or irreversibility of this stretch of time.

What is meant by awareness of the finitude of this stretch of time?

When we do our work, whether choosing a vocation, or taking examinations, or fulfilling our professional duties, or setting up a family with its obligations, we are always aware that something has to be achieved before the hour for it passes. Thus athletes know that around the age of thirty the curve of their achievements will pass its peak and their day will soon be done.

Young people can say quite unphilosophically and unreflectingly that youth passes and they must not miss out on anything. They mean that they realize that only a limited time is at their disposal for life and action and that they cannot put off things as they choose. Our life is a gaining of time, as Shakespeare puts it somewhere in *Julius Caesar*. In this awareness that time is limited, it is plain that a knowledge that death is our destiny constantly accompanies us.

This is not so much the thought of our last hour; it is the thought of the fleeting present. The future of our end presents itself in the qualification of the present moment — even for the young who are still a long way from their end.

Only when we think of it this way do we understand Pascal's profound statement in *Pensées* that death when one does not think about it is more bearable than the thought of death when one is not in danger. What makes death so terrible, as Pascal sees it, is not its quality as a physical moment, as the final point — for this may carry me off without any terror, either cheating my consciousness or even depriving me of it. Nor does the terror of death consist in the preceding moment of disintegration, such as in a serious wound or sickness. All this can be just as alarming even without a fatal outcome. No, Pascal finds the horrible thing about death in death as a *thought*: in the thought that lies like a shadow over the whole of life and impresses upon it the stamp of a being for death. Luther can relate death similarly to life when he interprets fear of corruptibility as a kind of anticipation of death, saying that the fear of death, despair, terror, is *itself* death.[15]

For this reason I regard it as an open question, which I cannot finally answer, whether the almost fashionable literature on the process of dying, on the last hour, really hits the point of what worries us in the thought of death. This applies even to serious authors who seek to avoid as far as possible the incipient mystifi-

18

cations and speculations.[16] Most of the relevant works are books of comfort that try to counteract the anxious fear of death by recounting the subjective impressions that those who have been resuscitated received in their fragmentary experience of dying. These stories are usually happy ones, recording the nearness of benevolent spirits and radiant beings (e.g., in the form of angels) or the severing of the ego from the dying body, which is already seen at a distance and in triumph. In relation to the self there can also be experiences of judgment, but only at the level of subjectivity and therefore having no connection with the Christian concept of the judgment of the last day (cf. Moody's *Life after Life*).

The French physician Barbarin, in his book with the arresting title *Death as a Friend* (1938), had already tried to prove statistically from those who had been condemned to death, who had survived air crashes, and who had been rescued from drowning at the last moment, that the final moments before death are uplifting and liberating, and that only the period leading up to death is marked by pain and shock and anxiety and terror. Thus death itself comes as a friend and an emancipator and is always accompanied by a state of euphoria.

What seems to me to be dubious about the subject matter of these works on the experience of death is the effort to reduce the problem of dying to the last hour of life and therewith to rob it of its character as a sign of our finitude. Awareness of the destiny of death as the constant companion of the whole of life is here suppressed. One might say that the existential character of our dying and our awareness of mortality are eliminated. Whereas death is relevant here only as an event of the last hour, the Christian understanding of death as the "last enemy" has always regarded it as the shadow cast over the whole of existence and as a power that accompanies existence over its whole temporal length.

The second point is connected with this presence of awareness of death. I mean awareness of the orientation of this stretch of time, its irreversibility.

We could not experience the present as the qualified moment, as the representative of our finitude, if we were not aware at the same time, if we were not necessarily sure, that it will not return. Our stretch of life is like a garden with open doors but not even the smallest opening at the back. It is a one-way street — though this does not have to mean, as we shall see, that it is a dead end.

The unrepeatability of the moment, the irreversibility of the time line, is manifested, for example, in the fact that we cannot relive our past, or can do so only to a very limited extent. We are riveted to our past and in some sense even identical with it. This uniqueness of the phases of life is connected with what we have called the uniqueness of the person. If the person is oriented to its determination, and time is the medium in which it is to become what it is and what it is meant to be, then each point on the time line has its own unconditional weight, and to that extent it is as unexchangeable as the person itself. The oriented stretch of time is thus the temporal form of personality.

Furthermore, the biblical concept of judgment is constitutively connected with this temporal form. History is here an oriented stretch of time between the fall and judgment; its individual points cannot be revised. We cannot make ourselves new or become other than what we have received and perceive ourselves to be. As Nicodemus says in his talk with Jesus, we cannot reenter our mother's womb and achieve a new birth, beginning all over again (John 3:4). There can be new birth only as a creative miracle of the Spirit (3:5).

That this understanding of time is not just a dogma which we have to believe but corresponds to everyday forms of our experience of time may be shown from many instances of this experience. I will give only a few by way of example.

Every firm or institution hiring a new employee wants a resumé from the applicant. It does so because this offers essential information about the candidate's person. The unexpressed and often unrealized principle of anthropology that lies behind this procedure may be stated in the thesis that people are what they have behind them, that they *are* their past. It will hardly be expected that their future will not be in continuity with their past, that it is not already pre-formed in it.

This fixation on the past that we presuppose in our understanding of time can be a great hindrance. We see this in the great difficulties experienced in resettling people released from prison. These difficulties are grounded in a prejudgment on the part of the society that ought to accept such people and find regular work for them in some calling. A stubborn mistrust usually stands in the way of this acceptance. In the eyes of what is called society, those who have once been sentenced to prison are always identified with their past, even when they have experienced a change of mind or a conversion. Often the resultant alienation produces a vicious circle. One-time criminals who are now shunned find that their only option is to rejoin their old associates and thus relapse into a life of crime.

In my experience, French existentialism has achieved the sharpest literary profiling of this understanding of time, and I ask myself whether some recollection of the Christian awareness of oriented time has not been at work here under its atheistic cover. I will give just one example. In Sartre's *Les Mouches*, Orestes, returning from Corinth to his home in Argos, encounters a situation of general paralysis through shock. A dreadful sense of collective guilt burdens the city. Clytemnestra and her lover, King Aegisthus, have killed her husband Agamemnon on his return from Troy, and this crime in the immediate past has led to a fixation on the event that was of uncanny intensity. People find they cannot rid themselves of the sense of doom; they are gripped by terror; there is no longer any path to an open future; the whole city is riveted to the past. Orestes passionately rejects this fixation and climaxes his resistance in the saying: "I am my freedom." Typically he does not say that he *has* freedom but that he *is* freedom; he identifies his whole being with it. In our terms this means: "I am a person, and as such a being that must grasp itself and its destiny, that must achieve its identity. But now that the past of the house of Argos tries to seize me, I am totally alienated from myself. I have become a mere object of this past when I ought and want to be the subject of a future that I myself seize."

When the flies encircle him and as avengers try to imprison him in the collective guilt — they are the goddesses of the past — he strides through them and thus breaks free from their dominion. Where does he go? To the land Nowhere, called Utopia, where he can shake off the past and achieve an abstract future, where he can begin again from scratch without the mortgage of the past.[17]

What Sartre's Orestes does here is a Promethean act of self-fulfillment, namely, an attempt to actualize himself in absolute freedom and thereby to emancipate himself from his past. This attempt is Promethean because he dismisses his past in assumed omnipotence. A hidden, unexpressed irony accompanying the attempt might be that he conceals from himself its impossibility. It can lead only to Nowhere; the goal that is sought does not exist. For wherever he might go after escaping from the Furies, the new place will heap new guilt upon him and help to give the avengers a new claim over him. Only an abstract moment, a kind of mathematical point, can be thought of as without a past. As he moves on to the next moment, he takes the first step toward the formation of a new past.

Precisely because this concept of the irreversible stretch of time is originally related to the biblical understanding of the uniqueness and unconditionality of our personal worth—we shall return to this later—that which the Christian faith understands by *redemption* can be expressed only in the scheme of this view of time. Since the irreversibility of time, "historical" time, does not allow us either to create ourselves or to re-create ourselves, the new birth and new creation rest on the miracle of the experience of the Spirit. In this context the event of redemption is to be expressed precisely in the categories of time. Thus forgiveness can be defined as an event by which my past is expunged and the accusation is nailed to the cross (Col. 2:14). Forgiveness means that a new future is assigned to us—not one that is grasped in arrogant Promethean fashion, but one that is given.

We may say in conclusion that awareness of the orientation of time always signals its end as well. Whereas the mythical view of time with its great and little year[18] (the rhythm of the constellations and the alternation of the seasons) proclaims cyclical recurrence, the biblical understanding of time makes it clear to us that history is the way from the fall to judgment, and therefore that time is oriented and to that extent limited.

The same applies to individual life. The attempt to grasp eternity, to break out of finitude and become a superman, is a mark of the fall. Genesis 3 expressly points out that Adam's revolt is an attempt to break out of temporality. Having to die is here a warning reminder that he is only human and that the boundary of time separates him from God's eternity. Paul's statement, which we shall have to discuss later, that "the wages of sin is death," is related to this complex of the order of finitude and the attempt to escape it. At any rate, the orientation of our stretch of time implies an encoded awareness of our death.

Repression of This Awareness
Everyday phenomena. In opposition to these basic aspects of life
we make an astonishing discovery. The implicit awareness of death
is constantly hampered in its explication, in its coming to consciousness. In psychoanalytical terms, it is repressed.

To see this one need not go to the famous cemetery at Holly-
wood where the peace of the dead is banished by operatic melodies
from hundreds of loudspeakers hidden in the shrubbery, and where
the graves are expertly rendered insignificant and almost invisible.
Nor need one have experienced the burials there in which special
cosmetics are applied to give the color of life to the corpses. It is
enough to look at what goes on in our own immediate environs.

In considering the everyday phenomena of the repression of the
awareness of death it would be as well to bear in mind certain
things that will protect us against misinterpretation.

Let it be stated first that in an age of general secularization it
is not thoughts of the last judgment or ideas of hell that cause us
to banish death from our field of vision. Worrying about what
might follow death we now regard as medieval. For most of our
contemporaries death is no longer a colon that announces the
continuation of the text of life in new dimensions. Rather, it is an
absolutely conclusive and definitive period. Even fear of the process
of death will hardly ever have much weight, or only in exceptional
cases, such as in old age or when there is acute danger of death.

What basically causes anxiety and mobilizes the forces of repression is to be sought predominantly in what we have called the
personal character of death, namely, that it is a sign of our finitude,
of our being for death, that it ends all the relationships in which
we live and move and have our being, that it plunges us into total
unrelatedness, that it annuls our "vast subjective world," as Hoche
has put it, while others live on, talking and going about the business
of life as though nothing had happened. It is this descent into a
nothingness which defies the logic of life that causes anxiety and
triggers the impulse of repression that meets us on every hand. As
we have already seen, it leads us to speak about death in an impersonal way: it is people that die, not I myself. Death is thus
pushed back into a region outside the I.[19] Our collective life-style
is oriented to this repression of the awareness of death.

1. Sickness as a symptom of mortality is essentially confined to
clinics. This is particularly true of marginal phenomena like mental

illnesses. These are isolated and withdrawn from public view. Public pressure against such things takes the primary form of the extolling of the healthy life, especially in the young. This feeds the illusion that health is life. In consequence of this repressive illusion it is possible (when the symptoms are exaggerated, as under the Third Reich, when the religion of vitality ran riot) to take an ideal figure as the symbol of life and to play it off against the disturbing form of, for example, Friedrich von Hohenlohe, the bishop of Bamberg, whose emaciated frame bears witness not only to physical suffering but also to the pain of the overpowering knowledge acquired therewith.

2. The same repression may be seen in the events of birth and death, which are removed from sight and hearing and again isolated in clinics. Burial processions no longer traverse the streets. Interment takes place behind the cemetery walls. In many cities hearses are no longer black, and an effort is made to make them as similar as possible to the automobiles of the living. Death is made anonymous. Many of the ways in which this is done may not be intentional but are connected with commercial, hygienic, and economic concerns. Nevertheless — a remarkable trick — in and in spite of this indirectness they express the ignoring of death, and help to cause it.

How are we to understand these circumstances? Do they express a genuine triumph of life no longer recognizing death? Or do they express a frantic attempt to ward off death by refusing to accept it because there is no longer any courage to meet the fear of death[20] and there is therefore a desperate resort to the processes of repression just described?

3. Furthermore, uncommitted people diligently try to evade the situation of loneliness into which dying puts them. Loneliness thrusts them back upon their primal personhood and robs them of the illusion of being simply "people." The more empty and lost they know themselves to be in their personhood, the more they flee to anonymity, to the overflowing charms by which the voices of emptiness — not finally without technical aids — can be overcome. This type of occupied and possessed person who opens the door to the powers that invade the ego, this *homo occupatus*, as Seneca calls him, uses life for every kind of purpose except that of gaining an awareness of mortality and learning about death.[21] "Those who are harassed by the pace of modern life will find

relaxation and refreshment on a vacation only when they do not feel the pressure of loneliness," I read in the advertisement for a trip. Even in collapsible boats, portable radios and two-way systems buoy such people up with the illusion of communication. The whole misery of man, as Pascal points out in his *Pensées*, arises from a single cause; he cannot stay still in a room.

This life-style is significant for the attitude toward death inasmuch as it cannot accept the situation of personal loneliness that has such a bearing on dying (cf. Heidegger), and it thus deceives us as to our indelible character as persons and our being subject to a being for death. This life-style is also significant for the attitude toward death because it hardly leaves any place for the remembrance of death in the brutal physical sense. Death does not exist; it *must* not exist.

If we were to try to reduce the repressive restlessness of this life-style to a formula that would also do justice to the theological character of this flight from the self, and therefore to death itself, one might put it as follows:

The rejuvenating and upbuilding of those who are in relationship with God has always had the typical character of gathering or concentration, of reflection on the basis, goal, and meaning of existence, and therefore of the holding together and girdling of the self, of protecting it against outward loss.[22]

In contrast to this gathering or concentration, the recreation of uncommitted people rests typically on scattering or dissipation.[23] (To guard against misunderstanding I should observe that I am contrasting concentration and dissipation as types that can be opposed to one another only in principle, there being many mixed forms and fleeting transitions in practice. Thus when I speak about dissipation I have in view a style of recreation but do not intend to pass any judgment on the need for dissipation and mental unfocusing.)

Recreation as thus understood rests on an inability to accept the self and its emptiness. A synonym for dissipation is diversion. As a specific form of recreation this is obviously not so much diversion from something uncomfortable that causes anxiety as diversion from the self which is already gripped by anxiety, which is delivered up to it with no counterweight, and which in its emptiness has no weight of its own. Thus, uncommitted people usually try to master sorrow, not by standing up to it (i.e., again by concentration), not by giving it meaning and overcoming it frontally, but by diversion, stupefaction, and closing the eyes, by the wishful thinking that in this way fear and the reality that causes it will go away of themselves. There is a dreadful — if unconscious — irony in the illusion that in this way one can treat the reality, for example, death, with contempt. This kind of contempt arises out of paying no heed, not wanting a thing to be so, and it is thus achieved with the help of an act of repression. But is it really contempt (*Ver*-achtung)? Does it not involve an immense if unconscious regard (*Be*-achtung) for the reality, even a fixation on it? (The repression that apparently banishes it from sight does not exclude this.)

The dissipation or scattering that ignores death and is thus latently an important existential interpretation of it can finally be characterized in various ways.

1. As a life-style, it expresses a failure to stand up to the things that cause anxiety, a diversion from them, and in that sense their repression.

2. That from which there is diversion is less the constellation of circumstances that give rise to fear, and more the fearful person himself in the manifestation of his inability to overcome fear, in his threatened bondage to fear and an anxious spirit.

3. The existential cause of dissipation is thus one's own emptiness or, more plainly, the fact that there is no counterpoise to its power, neither that of the spirit which can put the fear-evoking object in the light of some meaning, nor that of an ability to defy the shades.[24]

4. Hence the existential cause of dissipation is one's own emptiness in its flight from nothingness. In such circumstances we talk about a person being bored or, if there is more than one person, of their boring one another.

5. Hence dissipation is an expression, consequence, and fulfillment of nothingness or futility. It is an *expression* to the extent that it betrays anxiety at the obvious approach of nothingness. It is a *consequence* to the extent that in dissipation people can no longer be alone, that they have no self, that this lack terrifyingly reminds them that they ought to have, that they have lost the self and forfeited their identity.

Finally, it is a *fulfillment* to the extent that it impels one toward an increasingly complete loss of the self. People fall to nothingness as they foolishly allow the empty region of the I, the empty temple of God, to be occupied from outside (for there is no unoccupied zone). The more frenzied they get, the more wildly they plunge into frenzy. They seek liberation from the invading impressions that possess them by means of even stronger impressions, by the centrifugal tendency of a continually enhanced dissipation. Technology, especially in the form of the electronic media, provides ample opportunities for this. It fills the inner vacuum with ever new imports from outside. Even the impoverished imagination is replaced by imports of this kind.

It holds true of dissipation that from those who have not (and who for this very reason want forgetfulness and security in dissipation), even what they have shall be taken away. Dissipation may seem to be a search for happiness, but it is engendered by unhappiness. "If man were happy, he would be more so, and would know less dissipation, like the saints and God," Pascal can say.[25]

When dissipation is understood as the expression of an existentially conditioned life-style, in relation to death it is to be regarded primarily as an *indirect* diversion, that is, as a diversion from the lonely, impersonal I that cannot be represented in death and that hopes to rescue itself from death with the help of dissipation, of self-extinction by self-loss. (A typical symptom of both forms of diversion is that secular man needs to get drunk at two points in life that mirror his mortality most clearly, before battle and on New Year's Eve.)

6. Dissipation is thus a flight from futility and from the destruction that is still seen approaching. This twofold flight is intrinsically one. One may see this from the fact that futility, as a being for death, is a shadow of the destruction into which the existence that knows its own futility is plunged. Heidegger rightly connects fear of death with fear of being in the world,[26] for death determines this being in the world and is part of it. Fear of death, or, as we have put it, flight from it, is characterized by the knowledge that it is all up with us because soon it will all be over, and the approaching end in death is simply a confirmation that in a public yet secret way it is all up with us already. "All those who live securely are nothing" (Ps. 37). They live by repression. What the Bible calls a sense of security is to be understood as *repressed* anxiety.

In contrast *conquered* anxiety, the release that comes from God, is called peace. If Christ had not risen, if there were no real

27

overcoming of the power of death and liberation of the forfeited self, we should have to be called "of all men the most to be pitied" (I Cor. 15:14ff.). This would be because the security that encircles our lives, and of which we persuade ourselves by autosuggestion, would be no real peace but only blindness to the final reality that the self which secures itself in dissipation is unmasked as one that is forfeited to futility. In a dreadful enhancement of its futility — by dissipation and blinding — it has lost even what it had. Do we not see this written on people's faces today?[27]

Hence it comes about that repression of the last things, of the threatening horizon of life, in no way keeps futility and emptiness at their present level but makes them increasingly empty and accelerates the loss of substance as if by a mathematical law. Is not the flight into the impersonality against which dying has no hold (because death no longer finds a prey and its offering is evaporated into a collective), is not this flight itself a positing and producing of impersonality? Naturally this is in such a way that we cannot erase ourselves and must always keep enough personality to despair of the loss of the self and therefore to have to repress it and flee from the self (cf. Rom. 1:18ff.).

The last point makes one thing clear. The ideological repression of death with the help of the shifting of values to supraindividual forces, and its ignoring in one's life-style, can take place only in such a way that an underground awareness of the ineluctability of dying remains even though there are no longer any funeral processions on the streets to remind us that we shall die. The hurrying of people through these emptied streets, their glance that ignores everything eternal, expresses a supposed sense of security in face of the threat of futility and annihilation. But does not this glance, this hurrying on streets that have been freed from death, express at the same time a kind of spatial fear of the streets that are thus emptied but on which people still sense an obscure fate and have to flee from the attack of nightmares? Even here dying is the gruesome mask behind which the aestheticizing, repressing, and ignoring are still a dark sign of the fear of death: "... but undeciphered, eternal night was still the most solemn sign of a distant power."[28]

The only two options that are left open by this crisis of loss and impersonality are as follows. First, there is the option of the aristocratic ethos of the soldier of Pompeii to whom Spengler refers:

28

a brave endurance in destruction, the strength with which the pitiable people of 1 Corinthians 15 can look futility and annihilation in the eye. This is holding on without any hold. The second is flight into apparently tenable ideological systems, which we will discuss later with Marxism as an example.[29]

A shabby pseudo-Christian evasion of the confrontation with nothingness — I hardly dare mention it in this respectable setting but it would be unfair not to mind one's own business — is what Nietzsche called the misuse that Christianity has made of the hour of death. We may take as a macabre example Gellert's lines on the death of a freethinker:

> His end came, and he who had never trembled Was suddenly shaken by death. The terror of an eternity, A judge who cursed him as God, An abyss which sought to swallow him, Shattered the system of insolent security. And he who had dared oppose the whole world With all his empty teachings, Began to listen patiently to his maid, And by this pious maid, Whom he had a thousand times called a Christian animal, He let himself be refuted and converted. So strong are the teachings of a freethinker:

The Final Taboo

We live in an age of increasing taboos or, one might say, objectifications, materializations, and demystifications. From what we have already had to say about repression, we may almost assume that death will be no exception, at least to some extent.

For example, we have only just gone through the sex revolution, and the Victorian age of prudery has been abruptly and rudely terminated. What has been felt to be a liberation has simply been a changing of the mystery of sexuality into a more or less neutral hormone event or an impulsive mechanism whose planned use makes it possible to avoid a damming up of sex that might trigger aggressiveness. Psychoanalysis, whether along the lines of Freud or of Adler, enables us to escape Oedipus complexes or feelings of inferior worth, and to conduct uninhibited conversation free of taboos.

The same may be seen in literature, where authors exert themselves not to omit any details of the sex act. To assess the antithesis, one might consider the opposite of this mentality in Adalbert Stifter. In his stories there are no bad or even questionable people. To put it in architectural terms, his characters are like beautiful houses with symmetrical and well-proportioned facades. But there is no reason to suspect that these houses have no dark cellars full of spiders' webs where it may be "the wolves howl." That Stifter knew of the depths of humanity, of the "tiger" in people, may be seen not only from some of his observations in *Bunte Steine*, but also from its somber ending. But it is left to the readers to imagine that these human houses do not stand on smooth earth but sink into the ground and are thus built over cellars. Stifter does not explore the cellars as modern authors love to do; he does not stop to contemplate every wood louse in them.

I am not judging the modern preference but simply asking in passing whether sex is well served if we rob it of its mysteries and submit it to open observation, making it the subject of everyday chatter.

Even the most advanced sexual expertise cannot disguise the fact that before and after orgasm (for hours before and seconds after) there is perhaps nothing more to say, and there thus opens up the vacuum of a total loss of communication and personality.

But my main point here is to give some idea of the extent to which we have banished both restrictive and helpful taboos.

It is all the more astonishing, then, that we start back from the final taboo of death and hide from it. This is not contradicted by the fact that the reality guarded by this taboo may sometimes be very interesting to us, and that there are authors of both books and movies who enter its sphere and without breaking the seal enunciate the questions that it poses. I have in mind a basic book like Kübler-Ross's *Interviews with the Dying* or a film like that on a London hospice.

If people avoid any serious concern for the dying or any existential interest in the inner processes that accompany death, we must admit that here and there curiosity about death and dying exists, though not without attempts at transfiguration. These are often enough directed by mercantile propaganda techniques. Thus there is in America a whole industry devoted to death. The coffin becomes a casket, the undertaker a funeral director, and the hearse a coach, while interments become a spectacle and the corpse is given a semblance of life, all under the slogan of a beautiful life followed by a beautiful death. One school in Washington, D.C., even goes so far as to have mock funerals, but in view of the fact that some funeral homes provide background music and professional mourners or entertainers, the children's playing at funerals is perhaps little more than an empty show. Yet in all this one can say that no taboo is *broken*; rather, the taboo is *intensified*, being banished to an abyss above which a dancing and concealing film is developed.

Why is there this repression, this relic of a persistent tabooing? Perhaps one might say provisionally — we shall go into it more deeply later — something like this:

In death, when the circle of life closes and we can survey the seedtime and harvest of life, we are afraid to meet ourselves, not knowing, perhaps, who we are, or whether we really are at all. We perhaps confront ourselves as unknown people, as unreal shades, and this causes greater fear than the thought of an unknown hereafter or of the nothingness of the night of death. We fear the negative report of Mephistopheles. Not all of us have the bravery of Albert Camus to stand up to a Sisyphus existence in futility, although even he opens his pores wide to secret consolations. Perhaps we have rejected death-conquering words in life and dismissed them as illusory comfort for the weak. It is a serious question whether such consolations from beyond finitude are not in fact projections of our fear of both life and death.

But even if that be so — and it is not really true, but I will concede it for the moment — the question of what happens to me when I am transported from being to nonbeing is more than most of us can face. Hence the fog that burdens this riddle is made more dense by additional obfuscations, by silence, or by such euphemisms as "passing away" for "dying."

In the NT, if I may anticipate, death is put in the background in an astonishingly *different* way. Its reality is not overlooked or rendered innocuous. The Bible presents death in grim colors, finally at Golgotha itself, and even the risen Lord shows the marks of the nails. Yet death is not here an independent theme; it is volatilized as a shadow. But what represses it is not fear; on the contrary, a sense of victory is what breaks its power. Hymnic certainty bursts forth in the question: "O death, where is thy sting? O grave, where is thy victory?" (I Cor. 15:55).

We are finite beings; we bloom and wither like grass. Hence we know that it is fatal (that death will be brought from the last hour into our present) if like the rich farmer we rely on the things of this world, on what is around us, or, to use older terms, if we sow to the flesh.

It will also be fatal to become enslaved to a legalistic moralism, for we cannot change ourselves by our own efforts nor get across the boundary of our finitude. But as those who are summoned, we are no longer confined to this decaying aeon and therefore we do not go under with it. We have the promise of being new creatures who are united with him who has conquered death, and we will not be abandoned by him. Hence death can no longer be an entity that has any weight of its own. As Paul Gerhardt says in his Easter hymn, we are his constant companions as he bursts through death, the world, sin, need, and hell itself.

Death in its previous sense ("previous" because it has now taken on a new meaning) is only a symbol of our shattered existence, of frail and transitory attachments to what is corruptible, of stopping at what is penultimate and missing a final destiny.

To put it rather daringly, in face of what has now been overcome and left behind, one might ask: What is death? What can it do to us? It has now been given the lower status of a background extra on the stage of life.

This seems to be the reason why the NT puts death on the margin and does not make it an independent theme. Although it is still the "last enemy," its attacks do not affect the eternal life whose first installments we already enjoy in this life and whose fullness we await. Thus death ceases to be an end and takes on the quality of a new beginning.

With tongue in cheek, then, one might say that there is something like a "contempt" for death in the NT. But in content this is infinitely different qualitatively from a secularistic contempt for death. In a later chapter on Luther, in whom we find this thought, we shall have to go into this question more specifically.

Chapter 2

DEATH NATURAL
AND UNNATURAL

A. THE PROBLEM

In what follows we shall now take up and develop some of the more important insights of our preliminary survey. In particular, we need to consider more closely the tension between dying as a natural process and dying as a personal event. I will proceed by seeking the elements in natural death that transcend the natural process in such a way that this does not exhaust all that is meant by human dying. The biblical understanding of death and of victory over it will necessarily be alien and unintelligible to us so long as we are not clear about these transcendent elements. They also form a bridgehead in our subjectivity which the message of the resurrection can claim and by which it approaches us. Already at this stage in our reflections this message will also be the indirect source of light that enables us to see the personal dimension of human death.[1]

The remarkable saying of Paul that death is the wages of sin and that Christ's resurrection is thus the overcoming of sin and death (Rom. 6:23; 1 Cor. 15:42– 44, 55f., etc.) sets death in the light of the fall from creation rather than creation itself, and thus presents it as unnature and disorder rather than nature and order. As we shall see, this is already the decisive point in the debate with the concept of death held in world views for which it is usually a biological or metaphysical law and is thus understood as nature and order, a necessary constituent of life itself. On such a view death expresses our natural transitoriness.

This term expresses already the idea that death and destruction are an immanent part of reality as we can grasp it. In no sense does it point to death as an event that overtakes life; it suggests instead that death is a quality or state of life itself.

When the Bible in contrast relates death to sin and to the *fall* from order, this rules out at once the misunderstanding that death is a result of sin on its *biological* side. Instead, Scripture shows that

33

human dying is something that is indeed executed in the medium of biological death but still has to be differentiated from this medium. Human death is qualitatively different from the purely biological death of animals. The opposite of biological death is biological life. The opposite of human dying (executed in the medium of biological death) is life from God: "We live even though we die" (John 11:25ff.).

It is a mistake to think that natural science is the chief opponent of the biblical relating of sin and death. This view might appeal to the fact that human protests against this linkage usually make use of predominantly scientific arguments. These might take the form of the following rhetorical question: Does not death rule even outside the human sphere among plants and animals, where there is no good or evil, so that it is the phenomenon of an ethically neutral law? Could we not give this rhetorical question the naively subtle form that Adam and Eve did not just eat the forbidden fruit but probably ate animals as well?[2] And since one cannot eat living animals but has to slaughter them first, death darkened even the fields of paradise.

No matter what clever or comical answers one might make to this, one thing especially we must not fail to see. It is not natural science itself that speaks here, but people making use of arguments from it. Since one side of death is undoubtedly linked to certain biological laws that bring us into the sphere of scientific research, with the help of the methods of immanent investigation death can indeed be understood as an immanent phenomenon of the natural order. But this is to take a further sphere of existence out of the realm of exclusively religious or theological consideration and explain it in a purely immanent context. Hence the transcendent reference of death and sin drops away. Dying is biologically conditioned and what is biological is outside the sphere of good and evil.

The scientific argument here helps us primarily to understand humans in their self-resting finitude. Hence, although its content may be neutral and unprejudiced, its context has an unquestionable philosophical mark and concern. To that extent the means of argument must be carefully distinguished from its end — the human autonomy expressed and proclaimed in it.

When this is seen, it is immediately clear that the theological debate with a secular understanding of death cannot itself be scientific and apologetic in that sense — which usually gives rise to crude and dilettante nonsense — but must also begin with a philosophical concern which can then deck itself out in the robe of science or biological myth. The theological debate has to ask: How do humans understand themselves when they reply to arguments that sound so exact and religious but are so irrelevant? In other words, how far are they ready to face up to what we have called the transcendent elements in human dying?

B. DEFINING DEATH AS A NATURAL PROCESS

For laypeople, references to a biological definition of death must be confined to reporting some of the results of reading medical presentations. In these summaries I shall not be following the rules of research or attempting to prove the findings. Nor shall I be taking up any positions, but will be content simply to present the main options.[3]

1. It is the consensus of experts that human death is preprogrammed and that the length of human life rests on a genetic foreordination (apart, of course, from external influences). The American gerontologist Leonard Hayflick (Oakland Medical Center, California) was the first to show that human cells can divide and renew themselves only about fifty times. Even though the cells of an embryo can be frozen for several years after the twentieth division, they will still divide only another thirty times, the frozen period making no difference. At all stages of this process of division the cells loyally follow the information supplied in the DNS of the genes and chromosomes. They thus produce exact and effective copies of themselves until their power of renewal is exhausted. The inner clock has then run down. The organism has reached the boundary of death. After the thirty-fifth division or so the power of regeneration increasingly declines and the number of mutations mounts. After the forty-fifth the power to set aside harmful proteins decreases in such a way that the power of renewal is reduced to nil and organic death results.

It is not ruled out, thinks Hayflick, that in the near future, with chemical and surgical help, the span of human life may be extended by twenty or thirty percent. Yet the problem will not in this way be attacked at its root. The temporal determination of life will still be intact in principle. The question also arises whether a specific enhancement or at least a preservation of the quality of life will go hand in hand with an extension of its quantity. Since nothing seems to support this, actualization of the ancient human dream of an extension of the span of life might prove to be a nightmare. To conceive of human life and aging merely as a biological process would disregard the meaning and destiny of this life and finally lead to the production of a homunculus whose form it is left to our imagination to depict. Perhaps the preserved body would be only the vehicle for a senile or infantile spirit.

2. Discussion of the objective criteria of death or dying has become an urgent business among doctors, and also in the columns of the popular press, because of the transplanting of organs from the dead.[4] Sometimes there has been public scepticism about the possibility that a concern to get life-saving organs might in certain circles reduce the care that should be exercised to establish the death of the donor-organism.

This scepticism has made it necessary to offer a binding definition of the criteria for declaring a person dead. This is particularly urgent today for two reasons.

First, organs that can be used in transplants (kidneys, hearts, and soon perhaps lungs and livers) perish very quickly once circulation of the blood ceases. For this reason it might be demanded that organs should be taken from those who will certainly die and are already in an irreversible process of dying. But this demand triggers a question that transcends a purely biological approach to the issue and that is encountered again in the problem of euthanasia, namely, whether and how far an unconscious organism, whose breathing and circulation are being kept going only by artificial means, really comes under the taboo of a "human" quality, or whether it has in fact lost this quality, so that the surviving part of the organism has only the significance of a material object. To decide this question we need to differentiate between biological life and human life. The fact that medical conferences that discuss such issues seek the advice of scholars from other faculties —lawyers, philosophers, and theologians—shows in an impressively symbolical way that this side of the problem of death cannot be solved by a medicine that is scientifically oriented, but that a picture of humanity that is drawn from other sources must supply the needed criteria.

Second, it is clear that by reason of its very achievements modern medicine has raised problems in determining death that did not exist before. The classical criteria — cessation of the heart-beat, etc. — no longer apply today, or no longer do so in *every* case. For an arrested heart can sometimes be restarted nowadays by massage and resuscitation. Furthermore, even in those who have gone into an irreversible coma the cardio-respiratory functions can be sustained artificially, that is, by means of machines. Hence the organism can still enjoy a measure of life. Modern techniques enable even those who are in an irreversible and fatal coma to function in part for certain periods. The organs that are thus kept alive can then form a bank for intended transplants.

Here again the question of the quality of the remaining organism arises. Do we have here a real person who is to be protected as such, or do we simply have a living store of organisms that might bring help and rescue to others who are still genuinely alive? The question is again that of the break between the mere "bios" in which the partial organism shares and "human life" which no longer exists, perhaps, in this case.

All these considerations, including disagreements in the medical world, have led to a decision to allow organs to be used only after death has been plainly established. But the legal establishment of this decision demands a definition of the onset of death that takes into account the more difficult circumstances of the modern situation in medicine. (For this definition I am greatly indebted not merely to the literature but also to my medical colleagues, especially Prof. A. Gütgemann.)

Death takes place when the irreversible loss of all mental and intellectual functions of the human brain is definitively established, along with the loss of all involuntary mechanisms such as spontaneous breathing, blood pressure, body temperature, and the movement of the heart. In such a case the recording on the electroencephalogram will be nil.

This objectifiable death of the brain is to be clearly distinguished from two analogous conditions that do not denote death. First, there are conditions in which conscious mental activity ceases but the vegetative functions of the deeper centers of the brain continue to operate. Second, there are comalike conditions that might be induced by cold, narcotics, metabolic derangements, and the like. Those who are only apparently dead, for example, because the periphery of the brain is damaged, cannot be considered for transplants. To insure the objectivity of the determination in specific cases, the West German Republic allows only those doctors to establish death who do not take part in transplants and hence will not be swayed by wishful thinking or personal interest.

One might add that there is in Ernest Hemingway an interesting nuance on this objective biological description of death even though deeper aspects of anthropology are sometimes exposed (as in the point that the supreme point of the actualization of finite life occurs at the moment of death). His main interest is in the objectivity of the process. He displays a "clinical realism" (Haas) that considers dying from within. In his *Natural History of the Dead* he lists the various forms of death and corruption in a literary way. The way he links death and love *(eros)* reminds us of Freud. What fascinates him in both is the elemental force he finds in them. His objectification of the experience — Haas calls him the "Linné of the morbid" — reminds us of the complementary external side of a medical thanatology.

C. THE ELEMENT THAT TRANSCENDS A NATURAL PROCESS

To grasp the specifically human dimension of the reality of death, an objective definition of death and its onset is totally inadequate, valuable and even indispensable though it may be in other respects. Thus it is no help at all and has nothing to say when it is a matter of the break already mentioned between animal bios and human life.

As we discuss the elements that cannot be contained in a purely biological establishment of death but still belong to the essence of human dying, we shall take up some of the insights already reached in the first chapter.

1. In spite of its terminology, such as the use of the term "individual," the biological definition pays no attention to the fact that dying signifies the end of an *individuality*, of a "vast subjective world," as Hoche put it. In it we leave out of account for a moment the fact that individuality has the *personal* character that we have mentioned. Individuality here simply denotes a single entity whose elements are organically related and that comes to an end in death with the dissolution of these elements.

What is meant by the death of individuality in this sense may be seen from the contrast of the bacillus whose ostensible "immortality" is grounded in the fact that there is in it no organization of cells that can perish in death. Thus we learn of experiments in which for a period of seven years new microbes produced by division have been put in a culture and in this way have lived through 8400 generations. Since not the slightest diminution of the power of division was noticed after seven years, it may be assumed that under these conditions a kind of "eternal" life is attained. Theoretically the first cell must have lived the whole time.[5]

This (relative) immortality of the single-cell bacillus offers an instructive contrast to the death of individuality, because the idea of individuality is totally alien to it. If we still use the term "individual" — as biologists unavoidably do — it can have only the statistical significance of a single specimen, and has to be understood with a pinch of salt. Precisely because of the absence of a "profiled" individuality (that of an organic system), we connect the continuation of the microbe with its division.[6] If we force upon it the unsuitable concept of individuality, the division logically has the appearance of "individual" death. This is how Max Hartmann[7] understands it, claiming that it gives only the appearance of immortality but really means death. The parent organism ends its individual existence even though its organic substance lives on in the two cells that arise by division. The microbe dies, as it were, by division, but its organic substance does not become inorganic because it is taken up into two daughter cells prior to dissolution. If human reproduction were similar, we should undoubtedly describe the process as death. We need only think of an old person suddenly dissolving into two newly born babies.[8]

From this it may be seen that a filled-out concept of individuality arises only with an organic complex. In such a complex the debate as to death or immortality has no place; death is obvious. All that survives it is the legacy passed on through the cells to the next generation. Biologically, then, individuality as an organic complex is merely the interim vehicle of this immortal legacy; it can "go" when it has done its duty. One might logically say, then, that the genes construct the organism only to find temporary lodging in it and to use it as a springboard for other forms of life.[9]

If we try in this way to stay with a concept of individuality within the framework of biological considerations, it is plain that the end of the individual organism belongs also and primarily to the natural organic side of death. Only when this is established can and must we add that we are not overlooking the existence of a human individuality as well. In a wider sense we can speak here of the human "nature" of human dying, although in this usage the concept of nature goes beyond its purely biological content and carries with it the idea of "essence" — the essence of the human.[10] In what follows we have to ask how far death affects this nature of the human so that in *this* sense it is "unnatural." We are investigating the broader aspects whereby human dying transcends the definition already discussed.

2. The so-called objective physiological definition of death cannot in fact be anything more than a sign or pointer. One of the many factors that it leaves out of account is to be found in the circumstance that human death means a total loss of relationship.[11] The definition indicates this at best only in the sense that a loss of relationship occurs with the disintegration of the organic nexus. The organism is in itself a broad system of relations, an order of multiple connected relationships. This immanent system perishes in death. The organic "infrastructure" is destroyed.[12] But in humans there is also an "extrastructure" which in virtue of its individuality has the character of uniqueness.

As concerns the infrastructure, destruction and disintegration show that the system of relations is deprived of its organizing center, so that in death we speak of the separation of "soul and body," the loss of the sustaining connection.[13]

As regards the extrastructure, one may say that death breaks the fullness of connections in which we experience our humanity: our human encounters in love and hate, the "unrepeatable music of this world" that sounds in our senses (Gardavsky), our experience of history and nature, and of destiny in its many forms. We see ourselves abandoned to the amputation of this world of ours "with which we feel as identical as with our mostly hidden selves that have created it" (Gerhard Nebel). The breaking off of communication isolates the dying and makes the threshold of death a place of total solitariness. "We are all summoned to death and none can die for another but each must wrestle with death personally. . . . Each must be ready alone at the time of death; I will not be with you nor you with me" (Luther).[14]

The ending of the extrastructural relationships becomes a loss

40

of uniqueness only if we have discovered our ~~individuality and thus~~ arrived at a sense of particularity. Hence Isaiah can say (38:11f.): "I shall look upon man no more among the inhabitants of the world. My dwelling is plucked up and removed from me like a shepherd's tent."

Even the relation to God that exists for the living is put in question by death (we shall go into this more fully later); "I shall not see the Lord in the land of the living" (38:11).

This loss of uniqueness that is occasioned by death is not felt so long as there is no sense of individuality. In ancient Israel up to the end of the monarchy individuals were so fully integrated into the life of the people that they had no sense of being apart or on their own. In this early period there was no sharply etched individual guilt. As the fathers had sinned, there had developed a suprapersonal guilt that extended to the whole people, including future generations. "The fathers have eaten sour grapes, and the children's teeth are set on edge" is how Yahweh speaks through the prophet Jeremiah, although in opposition to this he now announces the coming of a new stage in the sense of guilt which presupposes individual guilt: "Every one shall die for his own sin; each man who eats sour grapes, his teeth shall be set on edge" (Jer. 31:29f.).

At one time, then, individual sins brought collective guilt and vice versa. Israel as a people was a totality not split by any individuation. Its indivisibility was manifested in the identification of individuals with the whole, the merging of the identity of the I into that of the We. Hence the significance of death as banishment into isolation, as the breaking off of relationships, could come to light only at a later stage.[15] Belief in the resurrection achieved relevance only as a sense of individuality emerged, a sense of apartness from the people; and this in turn posed the question whether the mortal end of individual life also meant a breaking off of one's history with God (exclusion from the people of God and its worship). As an example of the urgency of the resultant question I will simply refer again to the prayer of Hezekiah in Isaiah 38:18f.: "Sheol no longer confesses thee, and death? Does it still praise thee? Those who go down to the pit can no longer hope for thy faithfulness. Only the living, the living, praise thee, as I do this day."

If, as we shall see, the thought of death is found only in traces in Marxist-Leninism, and does not have the weight of an independent theme, this is again connected with the problem of individual consciousness. For here, in fidelity to the Hegelian origin of the system, individuality is submerged in suprapersonal, collective goals. The imposed or freely adopted "social organs" make individuals mere cogs in the social machine and bring them into conformity with it.

For this reason Gardavsky, in spite of his Marxist commitment, is a foreign body in this sphere. The Christian tradition that has influenced him keeps alive a sense of individuality, of the "infinite worth of the human soul," to use the phrase of Harnack. In him, therefore, death as the loss of all relations becomes a problem, for in virtue of individuality these have a uniqueness that cannot be transferred or merged into a trans-subjective entity like society.

Death, he says, is terrible because of this loss of relationships. Our inner being ceases to be their connecting point. Therefore, it is all the more unavoidable to have a present assurance as to our individual future.[16] This understanding of death leads him to some deviation from the Marxist view of life. He sees only two absolute certainties: first, that I am a social being, and second, that I must die. But there is a contradiction between the two, for death ends everything, myself included, while society lives on.[17] The Marxist thesis that society lives on is not, of course, contested. But Gardavsky cannot believe that dying individuality with all its relationships can be transferred to this society that lives on. That he is thus an ideological heretic is plainly shown by the fact that he illustrates his view of death with the passage from Luther already quoted, which hardly fits in with this system but speaks of the isolation of death: ". . . none can die for another. . . . I will not be with you nor you with me."

The younger Schleiermacher offers a Romantic variation on the same thought that the fullness of relationships connected to individuality is extinguished by death. The death of a friend means the breaking off of a sustaining note. A long echo remains and the music goes on, but with him the harmony breaks off for which I was the sustaining note and which was mine as this is his in me. My working in him has stopped, a part of life has been lost. Every loving creature perishes with death and we ourselves die with the death of many friends.[18]

3. The physiological definition of death also disregards what I have called the personal character of human dying. This personal

aspect is already brought out in *The Death of Ivan Ilych*. The process of human dying can be appropriately described only in the first person, that is, when one says "I die" and not in the more objective fashion, "people die." Because death is mine it is not just the objective result of sickness. Indeed, sickness itself cannot be understood as an objectifiable physical process, as a mere "case." It, too, belongs to me personally, so that we are offended when we hear someone referred to as "the appendix in room 33."

R. M. Rilke found some basic formulas for this extinguishing of authentic human death by anonymity. He calls dying of this kind a "little death" in contrast to "big" or "personal death" and describes collective death as an unreal thing. With the mass production of death, individual death does not fare too well; but this does not matter, for who wants a good death nowadays? The desire to have one's own death is becoming rarer. Soon it will be as rare as one's own life. People come, find life ready, and have only to put it on. People die when the time comes; they die the death that is part of sickness, for knowing all the illnesses, we also know that they — and not those who are ill — have a fatal outcome, so that there is, as it were, nothing for the sick to do.

Collectively we are forced into an impersonal death that is alien to us and characterized only by physical sickness. As Rilke laments, what makes dying alien and difficult is that it is not our own death, but one that finally snatches us away only because we do not mature; for this reason a storm comes to scatter us all. He thus asks for a personal death, the individual death that alone makes us human and distinguishes our dying from a purely animal end of life: O Lord, give each of us his own death, the dying that proceeds from his own life in which he had love and stress and meaning.

The shadow vision of an anonymous and alienated dying has increased today to an extent unknown to Rilke with the development of a most appropriate place where the physiological definition of death can find its full application, namely, the intensive care unit.[19]

One hesitates, of course, to bring basic objections against institutional measures that are taken in cases of extreme emergency, yet we cannot close our eyes to the threat of dehumanization that arises here. This threat is not merely against the human factor but even against the creaturely factor. We need only consider that day and night are obliterated under constantly blazing neon lighting, and thus disrupting the creaturely rhythm of the need for sleep. Patients — this is where the human sphere is attacked — are simply objects of manipulations whose impersonality harasses them not merely when they are mysteriously done through machines but even when they are done through persons, because there is practically no personal contact and everything focuses on purely somatic functions. The mark of the human, to be the agents of decision, to be theaters of personal conduct, to be consciously involved in what happens to us, is to a large extent erased here.

As Kautzky says in his *Dying in Hospital*, the little everyday measures are simply imposed on patients. Often it is not regarded as necessary even to explain their purpose to them and in this way to gain their consent. Hence the sick have no freedom of action. If they do not want further treatment, their resolve will not be respected.

The victims of this situation complain everywhere about the inhuman breaking off of all communication. As Kautzky says, doctors do not seem to be able to see the sick for the sickness and view them as they really are. Part of this would be speaking to the sick about their fears, but while doctors radiate professional optimism and bestow kindly attention, they do not enter into these fears but rather negate them.

Finally, it is part of this absence of communication that doctors and relatives usually deceive those who are fatally ill, so that they have no freedom to decide upon death, or an operation, or a final amour.

Undoubtedly this absence of communication is partly caused by a crisis that arises for doctors regarding such patients. This crisis arises not merely from their own failure to master the problem of the ineluctability of death, or their evasion of it, but also, and perhaps even more so, from the status that makes them advocates of life. The death of patients is thus felt to be a personal defeat. Doctors are like attorneys who lose cases and are thus forced to face up to the limit of their own powers. No wonder that they conceal their faces and turn aside! It is the more remarkable, then, that authors like Kübler-Ross address the human side of the process of dying and try to understand and do justice to its individual stages (resistance, depression, angry bitterness, efforts to prolong life, and finally a readiness to acquiesce). We also find comfort in reports that there are some hospices for the dying at work in

London which enjoy the services of honorary volunteers who with the doctor accompany the dying on the final stretch of their lives in love and with the truth, that is, in truly *human* fashion. Here an attempt is made to achieve the goal of winning back for dying its human dignity, and thus respecting that which transcends physiological processes and cannot be registered on machines.[20]

I have already discussed (Chap. 1) the other elements that cannot be contained in a medical definition of death because they rise above the physical process at a human level; but I will briefly recapitulate here — and supplement a little — for the sake of completeness.

4. In distinction from animals, as we have seen, humans know that their span of life is finite. They have an awareness of death even when they repress this awareness. They are the only beings, too, that bury their dead and set up memorials to them.

The self-awareness that includes a knowledge of the finitude of their existence is implanted at creation according to the two biblical creation stories in Genesis 1 and 2. Stars, plants, and animals are simply objects of the creative "Let there be," and have no sense of their creatureliness. But humans are addressed in the second person and given a task and destiny of which they are aware and to which they must take up some attitude or other, either accepting it or rejecting it. As the story of the fall shows, they have no possibility of refusing this subject-role and excusing themselves as mere objects of temptation (through Eve or the serpent) or of ineluctable processes (in the sense of environmental or other autonomous factors). They cannot confuse guilt and fate.

Along such lines Heidegger thinks human existence differs from every other form by reason of self-knowledge and self-acceptance. This self-consciousness is essentially an awareness of the future and therefore of death as the frontier of life. Humans anticipate their future in anxiety and hope.

One might say, then, that self-consciousness is what makes us human. This is what gives meaning to suffering. For with the gift of self-awareness are also bound up the task and possibility of reacting to suffering, of embracing it, of fighting or rejecting it — of suffering "ethically." (This is one of the essential reasons why one cannot put sufferers out of their misery.)

Self-awareness is also the decisive reason why death is not just something that "overtakes" us, but is something that we have to "fulfill," not being grasped as mere objects but still remaining subjects. This is what Rilke had in mind when he spoke about the "great" death. And this is what Heidegger was getting at (prodded decisively by Kierkegaard) when he defined death as a possibility of being that has to "take over" existence itself. To that extent what is at issue is that death should be my own, that it should be related to my uniqueness as an individual, so that it is more than a mere instance of perishing within a species, so that it is qualitatively different from this, so that it is not just the "ending" of life but real "dying."

5. The self-awareness indwelt by knowledge of the finitude of life also discloses to us the *totality* of our existence. We know that we have our time and that this time is irreversible. Only completed time will bring the totality of existence to light. Hence a biography ought to begin with death rather than birth, and a biography of the world — a universal history — could really be written only in the light of the end of the world, the consummated eschaton. Only when the whole is brought to light can the place and significance of individual events within the whole be perceived. Only eschatologically, then, can that which can only be "believed" as the meaning and higher thinking within the process of history become an object of "sight."

This applies to the temporality of individual existence, too. We have to leave the theater before the end of the performance. We cannot wait for the end. But if the end has not yet come and the outcome is not known, we cannot pass definitive judgment on the play (or on the meaning of the individual acts and actions).[21]

The fact of the totality of existence, even if it cannot be perceived in detail, weighs much more directly upon us than the totality of history. This is because the end of our time constantly accompanies us and is present with us, even if we repress it. Hence we do not have to wait for this end to be aware of the totality of our finite span. Life is indeed incomplete, but we know that the end is coming. This is why human existence is a "being unto death." To find our identity, to become what we should be, we have only a limited period of time at our disposal. Hence the "today" in which "we hear his voice" has unconditional weight.[22] This "today" is a station on the irreversible stretch of time and "now" can be an "acceptable time" that as *kairos* will not return.[23]

Even in the secular sphere we know that youth passes and that valuable time must be drained to the full.

That through this awareness of death life is an existential anticipation of total existence, that there is thus opened up to it the possibility of existence to the full, that self-commitment thus confronts it as the extreme possibility of existence[24] — this is the specifically human mark of the relationship to death. It cannot be contained in a purely physiological definition of death.

6. It is open to question where Freud's death-wish belongs, that is, whether it should be grouped with a natural or a personal understanding. This doubt is connected with the ambivalent features that mark all Freud's anthropology in this regard.[25] The most important source for his teaching on this subject is the work *Jenseits des Lustprinzips* (1920). Much of what he says there is also echoed in the later work *Das Ich und das Es* (1923).

Briefly, Freud distinguishes between two basic drives, first, that of eros, and then, discovered later, that of destruction (death). Eros embraces the tension of the instinct to preserve the self and the species, as also that of ego-love and object-love. It seeks to bind together, to set up and maintain greater unities. The instinct of destruction is an opponent of this. It was discovered mainly because Freud's earlier attempts to explain phenomena like the lust to destroy in terms of sexuality (sadism, aggressiveness, etc.) were obviously inadequate. He thus had to give this drive an instinctual form of its own. He linked the idea of a death-wish with the very speculative thought that we have here a drive that is oriented to regression, to restoration to a prior state, its final goal being the attainment, by all kinds of detours, of the starting-point that the living organism has left.[26] The instinct is thus to go back to an inorganic state, to death.

In this light one can see why it is doubtful that Freud's death-wish rests on a natural or a personal understanding of death. In fact, a similar doubt rests over his whole anthropology. This has personal features inasmuch as the ego finds itself in conflict with itself, and especially with the id and the super-ego. Yet in the analysis of the ego there emerges the analogy of a physically determined, instinctual mechanism. A. Görres finds the main thrust in Freud's anthropology precisely at this point, and in his interpretation he goes so far as to regard Freudian man (and woman) as an instinctual being directed by hormones. Freud himself refers significantly to a mechanism of the soul governed by regulatory mechanisms. The human spirit is not here the "shepherd of being," as Heidegger put it, but the shepherd of a psycho-physical metabolism.[27]

Freud could not easily harmonize the two dimensions of his anthropology, but constantly allowed the instinctual side to screen the human aspects. This is betrayed in a letter in which he says that the moment we ask for meaning (i.e., put the specifically human question of destiny and self-discovery: Author), we are sick.[28]

The death-wish has always had elemental significance. This supports Freud's factual conclusions even though we may reject his speculative explanations and find them limited by the framework of his conception. By way of example I might quote from the apocryphal book of Wisdom (c. 150 B.C.), which describes this wish as ungodly: "The ungodly try to induce death by hands and words; regarding it as a friend, they pine after it and make a covenant with it" (1:16). In modern terms we should talk about nihilistic longings: "We have come into being by chance, and we shall be as though we had never been" (2:2).

Finally, we might take note of a biting remark by the French President Clemenceau, the "Tiger" of World War I (and a German-hater!), who shortly before his death said to his private secretary that it is natural for people to love life, but Germans do not know this. Instead there is in the German soul a sick and satanic love of death. Germans shiver ecstatically before the deity of death. Why? Clemenceau did not know, but observed that Germans love war out of self-love, and because they expect it to lead to a bloodbath. War is a contract with death, and Germans go to meet it as though it were their best friend (cf. K. Barth, *Die Deutschen und wir*, 2nd ed., 1945, 12).

D. RESISTANCE TO THE TRUTH OF THE INELUCTABILITY OF DEATH
What Does It Mean to be "Truthful" with the Dying?

1. The Conflict between Truth and Love

As we have maintained, humans are beings that are aware of death in their self-consciousness. Hence they have to have some attitude toward it. They cannot be overtaken by death as mere objects; they have to fulfill their "own" death. If this is so, there is no escaping the difficult question whether we do not owe the truth to the mortally sick. Patients who are deliberately deceived by doctors, nurses, and relatives with every possible method of concealment are prevented from fulfilling their deaths in this way. They are "blindly" delivered up to death as offerings and objects. I have already pointed out how widespread this concealment is; indeed, it is the usual practice with the dying.

There are many different reasons for this. Not by a long way can it be explained merely by the law of inertia (because silence is the easiest solution). It offers deeper insights into the understanding of humanity and the self that is found among those who do the deceiving. I should like to suggest three normative motives.

1. The most common is the desire to spare the sick. The conflict between truth and love that arises here is decided in favor of love. A realistic disclosure of the truth regarding the death of patients may come as a shock that not only causes pain and anguish but also hampers any efforts at healing on their part and thus hastens the end. C. W. Hufeland (the doctor of Goethe, Schiller, and Herder) had this in mind when he wrote in his *Macrobiotics*[29] that to announce death is to deal it. And its influence may be seen in the verse in Goethe's *Der Westöstliche Divan* that praises Allah for separating pain and knowledge on the ground that patients would despair if they knew their complaints as doctors know them. Possibly the Japanese doctor Senji Umehara has the same point in view when he argues against F. Hoff[30] that there are lies that express profound human love, and he quotes in support a saying of Buddha to the effect that lying is a way of teaching the truth. K. Jaspers, in a discussion of the question of truth, once suggested that even if the seriously ill press doctors to tell them the truth about their condition, all they will hear is that things are *not* so bad with them, so that we do not say what they really want if we yield to their insistence upon certainty.

2. In place of this sparing and therapeutically meant withholding of the truth, another motive may be at work, especially among doctors. I have in mind (and have already mentioned) the reluctance of doctors to declare their capitulation as advocates of life. This motive may be strengthened by the failure of doctors to come to terms with the truth that they have to die themselves, by the

restriction of their thinking to the more obvious physiological aspects. There are some truths that disclose themselves only when they strike home to us — I shall come back to this later — and that can thus be imparted to others only when they have done so. When this existential dimension is absent, a helplessness results that can only mask itself and choose the way of deception.

3. A much deeper reason for silence, which may again be related to the love that wants to spare people, is to be found in the desire not to rob the dying of their last potential of hope. This desire may be based upon a prereflexive (and more instinctive) awareness that we are beings that in principle are oriented to hope. Ernst Bloch's *Principle of Hope* is an ontology of the "not yet"; for Bloch, to be human is to be on the way to something different. When asked to put his philosophy in a sentence, he said: "S is not yet P." To take away a reference to the future by means of hopelessness is to rob people of a decisive existential element, at any rate when they have no — e.g., Christian — hope beyond death;[31] and even then the elixir of life (T. Wilder) that an elemental earthly hope provides should not be underrated.

For this reason the saying of an experienced doctor like Ferdinand Hoff is worth pondering when he observes that although people — self-evidently — know that one day they will die, usually they are not ready to confront death in the immediate future. Nature itself, he thinks, spares us this shock, for the dying normally deceive themselves regarding their condition. Hence it is nothing but arrogance for doctors, with the disrespect of omniscience, crudely to upset the benevolent natural order.[32]

Stories that hope stirred up in this way has helped to sustain or prolong life are legion. Ignorance of the real or supposed hopelessness of a situation can help people to get across a crisis in productive blindness. Maintaining hope can thus be a therapeutic factor that activates the powers of life and healing through euphoria. This prop of hope that the doctor gives may also seem to be justified by the fact that it imitates nature's own approach. Nature usually conceals the last stages by the veil — often colorful and beautiful — of semiconsciousness. This concealment obviously corresponds to the wisdom about life and death that Ulrich von Hutten found on a sundial in the monastery garden when he was a student: Death is certain, but the hour of death is uncertain.

Dostoevski in his novel *The Idiot*, alluding to the occasion when he was pardoned from execution at the last minute, depicts the dreadful nature of complete hopelessness. To be executed is far worse than being murdered. If we are attacked by robbers, there is hope of rescue up to the last moment. But this alleviating hope is taken away by an irrevocable sentence. There is no escape, and this is the terrible thing about the pangs of death in this case. There is no greater torment on earth. Even when you fire at a soldier in battle, he still has hope — but if you were to read an irrevocable death sentence to the same soldier, he would go out of his mind and break down in tears.

Obviously, then, we are faced by a difficult and even perhaps insoluble conflict between two opposing thrusts.

The first is that of a duty to the *truth* that alone can make us free (John 8:32), that is, that can open up the freedom to fulfill death as one's own, so that it may be what Rilke calls a "great" death.

The other is that of the duty of *love*, which imposes on us the task of dealing gently with the potential of hope that even the dying still enjoy. This readiness to spare rests on an awareness that the truth of irrevocability, when abruptly disclosed, may have a fatal effect, "dealing" death, as Hufeland put it.

2. Different Forms of the Truth

To speak about the abrupt disclosure of the truth is to use a phrase that opens up a deeper understanding of the truth, which is at issue here. For it suggests that there are different forms of the truth according to its timeliness and therefore according to the specific situation in which it is disclosed. This does not apply, of course, to mathematical truth. In the multiplicity, then, there is manifest a certain band of forms of truth that prevents us from comparing truth with truth without distinction. Mathematical truth may be appealed to at any time. Its timelessness means that it can be spoken directly in complete independence of time or situation.

But this is not true at all of truths that concern people existentially. A poor teacher who tells a child before the whole class that his or her father came home drunk the previous day may be saying something that is quite correct, but it is not at all identical with the truth, for it shames an innocent child, undermines respect for the family, and does not do justice to the truth of childlike existence. A sadistic and destructive emotion, perhaps incited by resentment, is making use of something that is correct but that is fundamentally opposed to the truth and hurts it. With the help of such sham truths it is possible to express hatred, envy, jealousy, malice, or anger in relation to others and thereby to do no less than attack the truth of humanity itself while trying to hide behind a wall of formal correctness and make oneself impregnable by means of some ostensible or alleged truth. Thus the correctness of the statement that the poor teacher made, being the truth at the wrong time and in a wrong context, was nothing but falsehood and slander. If the facts had been told to a colleague in the teachers' common room with the purpose of helping the child or the family, then they might have taken on the quality of truth.

In his *Buch der Freunde* (p. 21), Hugo von Hofmannsthal offers a quotation from Pascal which is to the same effect. It is not enough, Pascal tells us, to say things that are true; it is also necessary not to say all the things that are true — one should reveal only what it is good to know and not what can only do harm without doing any good. The first rule, then, is to speak the truth, and the second to speak with discretion.

The similarity between this situation and that at the sick-bed is obvious. It lies in the relationship of truth to time, place, and occasion, to what might be called its *kairos*.

Along these lines an abrupt disclosure to the dying might not have the quality of truth because it would be truth at the wrong time. It would be truth that is blurted out and does not mature like fruit in Rilke's sense. The appropriate form here is truth that grows with life and into which we grow, that is, it is developing truth that always contains a bit of futurity and with which we are never *wholly* contemporaneous.

I shall again try to give a simple example. If a teenager writes in a school essay that "Goethe is the greatest German poet," one can hardly contest the correctness of the statement. Yet one might not be happy about it because it ought *not* to come from these inexperienced lips. It is more a fraud than the truth, being simply repetitive. To take on the quality of truth, its correctness would have to be brought to light in a process of personal experience. Only if the student has a wide range of literary knowledge does he or she have the criteria by which Goethe can be given the palm in comparison with other authors. Without this background of a process of growth, we have here truth at the wrong time, which is consequently no truth at all.

Similarly, with the dying there is needed a long and careful "process" of introduction to the truth of their condition, an introduction that enables them to go along with, and thus grow into a relative contemporaneity with, this truth. Above all it seems to be important that the hopes the dying still have should not be dashed at a stroke, that these hopes should be allowed to stand and help the dying gradually to achieve clarity about their condition. What is needed is a kind of Socratic form of "releasing" the truth to those concerned. It should not be hurled at them but found by them. Only when it is found by them can they become "synchronous" with it and learn to master it.

This form of retarded approach to the truth can bring great relief to the sick. The dying usually know much more about their condition than they tell others or even admit to themselves. Repressed knowledge is still knowledge. It may be on the threshold of consciousness or below it, but at the same level of consciousness there is a gnawing doubt about the optimistic assurances of others that seek to banish all anxiety with a smile. A point usually comes when the sick find the resultant contradiction between these assurances and their secret doubt more of a burden than the truth about their condition.

Regarding premature disclosure of the truth at the sick-bed, someone — I think it was Hoche — once made the fine statement that we should certainly tell the dying that the train (of death) will leave, but we should not leave them too long on the platform with this certainty.

We have seen that in the sphere of human relationships the truth is conditional upon doing justice to the truth of others, or, more precisely, to the truth of their existence and situation. In this sphere, then, it has a *communicative* side. As existential truth it is also the truth of a human relationship. Here, then, we have not just to *speak* the truth; we have to *be* in the truth (John 18:37), whether or not we bear in mind the Christian background of this formula. Being in the truth always expresses a relation which in the NT is the twofold relation to God and neighbor. Even if this twofold relation expresses the fact that it is primarily determined by the relationship to God and that others take on meaning as "neighbors" only in this light, it is still true for non-Christians that their being in the truth — here in *human* truth — always includes a relationship to fellow humans.

In relation to the dying this comes to expression in the fact that we can *tell* them the truth only if our *relationship* with them is in the truth. But it is in the truth only if it is determined by participation with them in their destiny, by loving address and solidarity.

Those who have experience in such situations will be able to confirm that we gain courage for truthful disclosures to the dying only by this truly sympathetic address and not by keeping at an objective distance. Involved address alone can do what is humanly possible to lessen the terror of approaching death, the final loneliness. At the risk of sentimental misunderstanding, I might say in all simplicity that in experiencing the truth of my imminent death I should like to feel the hand of a loving person in mine right up to the end. The lips that speak the truth and the hand that holds me constitute the truth together. This would be true *love* — and not the deception that ostensibly spares me.

If we cannot achieve this solidarity within which the truth of the ineluctability of death can be free, we are not up to the truth and therefore we can hardly do the work of comforting in the truth. Our only option, then, is to seek refuge in the sham love of silence and deception.

The existential character of the truth in this situation points us to the decisive question with which the task of telling the truth to the dying confronts us. Far more important than the question of how we are to tell others, possibly close relatives, that there is no way back from the threshold of death, is the self-critical question that I have to put to myself, namely, who am I that I can tell them this? Do I exist in the truth of the solidarity that alone enables me to tell them the truth?

As regards the spiritual word of truth at the death-bed, the saying that links love of God and love of neighbor has already shown that for Christians the universally human and, in a deeper sense, "natural" solidarity of sympathetic address is grounded in God's address to us and in our imitating of this in love for our neighbors. A special feature of the comfort that Christians offer the dying is thus the elucidating of the background of sharing in their suffering and the triggering of the power for good that is concealed in this. For this reason a looking to the cross of Christ should always accompany the last hours of life.

It is, of course, the message of the resurrection — the sustaining note of the whole of the New Testament — that gives meaning to Christ's suffering on the cross. For this shows that he who came from God and has been raised up to him again trod in love the way into the depths of solidarity with us, despising the glory of the heavenly radiance and in loving condescension choosing the way of lowliness in order to share with his brethren their human plight (Phil. 2:5ff.). In his death, therefore, we have something other and greater than the disaster of a martyrdom.

Although the true depths of the mystery of this death would be hidden were it not for the message of the resurrection, this message as a direct promise of our own resurrection with him can have intelligible and consoling significance only for those who already in faith have lived this life in the light of this message. Only to them does it make sense that in a life of resurrection they will "see" what they have "believed" and that they will come face to face with what they have so far perceived only in a mirror and as an enigma (1 Cor. 13:12). For this reason the message of the resurrection cannot serve as a truth that might be disclosed at the last moment when it has escaped the notice and faith of the dying during their lifetime. This is one of those truths that can only grow and mature. Even among the first disciples it had to develop in this way. It did not come first, but last. When the risen Lord met the two on the road to Emmaus (Luke 24:13ff.) they had not the least inkling of what had happened after the death of their *Kyrios* even though they could say later that their hearts had burned within them during the encounter and a spark had leaped across to them from his transfigured life. Until one of the disciples could say: "My Lord and my God" (John 20:28), the seed of a first inkling had to swell and ripen into fruit.

Hence the message of the resurrection is not a truth that can be let loose at the last minute. It is not a timeless truth that can be evoked at any moment, but one that has to mature. As deathbed comfort, then, it is only for disciples. For the dying who are far from faith it would make too big a demand and would only trouble them. It would be regarded as a dogma that is beyond their understanding (especially in their condition), and consequently could only bring disquiet instead of peace.

This gives rise to a difficult pastoral problem for Christians in their ministry to the dying. Their faith demands that they should approach the sick in both love and truth and enter sympathetically into their death. About this there can be no question. But the truth that they have to represent carries with it here demands that cause distress. This truth, as we have seen, cannot be told merely out of a sense of duty or in a routine way by blurting out to the sick — I am now caricaturing — that they are going to die, and then dishing out to them Christian truths and heavily accented platitudes. Poor counselors of this kind — and there are some — are like the poor teacher of my earlier illustration.

If, however, Christians have to represent a truth that is not timeless but is concerned about time and situation and communication, this involves the task of differentiating between Christians and non-Christians in those whom they address. They have to bear the spiritual situation in mind as well. What may be comfort and help for dying servants of God might be a stone of stumbling for others, and make their death intolerably more burdensome.[33]

These considerations present counselors with the driving problem of what their obligation to dying non-Christians really is when they are summoned to their side or go on their own initiative. Perhaps these sick people merely want a brotherly or sisterly hand that will prevent them from plunging into final isolation. Certainly it is part of the truth that is to be represented that it demands this address if the sick desire it. But is a readiness for this solidarity all that is needed? Does Christian witness consist only of this sympathetic being there for others, or does it also owe the *word* of truth? But if so, *what* word ought that to be? Is there indeed a word if this obviously cannot be — at any rate at first — the word of the resurrection?

The word at issue here is that of the cross — even if the fullness of its content can hardly be brought out explicitly on such occasions. A love that is unto death can touch the dying even if no faith can be presupposed. Though the message of the resurrection may not be included — or at any rate with the same emphasis or reflectively — this, too, will be implied in proclamation of the crucifixion, for as the risen Lord bears the marks of the cross, the marks of the cross proclaim the resurrection even though it may not come to direct theological expression in extreme situations. Under the pressure of the last moments of life the point of the death and passion of the crucified Jesus will not be that others have suffered in the same way and perhaps even worse than those who are now preparing for the last. Experience shows us that references to the sufferings of others carry little comfort. No, the reference to the crucifixion of Christ will always be connected with the affirmation that Christ took death upon himself because he gave himself up to the final solidarity with us that does not leave out dying, so that this dying one goes with us in our dying and does not leave us alone in it. This is the point of the verse of Paul Gerhardt in Bach's *St. Matthew's Passion* when he asks Christ never to leave him but to be with him in death and to relieve him of its pangs by his own suffering.

The crucified Christ who accepts the experience of death "for me" will thus go with me through the valley of the shadow of death, and will not forsake me. Since he took over my dying there can be no more loneliness in death. The words of those who repeat that verse to the dying will grow silent and become inaudible before and at the final threshold, but the promise of companionship, of never leaving or forsaking, will go with them over that threshold and still be in force on the other side.

Even the dying can understand and accept this promise, though they may not comprehend the mystery, having refused the faith that carries with it what the Heidelberg Catechism calls "our only comfort in life and in death." For in receiving the very human comfort of this companionship they have at least touched the hem of his garment like the woman in the NT. In that story of the woman with the hemorrhage (Matt. 9:20ff.), it is enough that she establishes contact with the Redeemer. The woman is not put to shame even though she makes no confession of Christ and may have been the victim of superstition. Jesus turns his face toward her and accepts her simple desire for contact as valid faith. He stands high above all Pharisees and clergy who make the acceptance of dogma a criterion of belonging or being outside.

The garment that is touched in this way, however, is the garment of him who has conquered death. And the human — perhaps all too human — comfort of the thought that in virtue of *his* death he can share in *ours* and will not leave us is finally that of a thought that has its root in the mystery of the resurrection. For how can one who died once go with us now, how can he be more than a parallel sufferer, unless he is the living one who has power both in this world and in the next?

Reflection on this may be ruled out at the last hour, but the reference to the cross and to Gerhardt's verse carries with it the implicit assurance that there is a <u>living one who relieves me of the pangs of death by his own suffering. The truth bursts forth here, which is a match</u> for the time and situation — the truth of solidarity, the truth of love, the truth of unbreakable fellowship.

E. THE UNNATURAL AND INCONCEIVABLE CHARACTER OF DEATH
Poetic Illustrations from Homer, Shakespeare, and Others

After the preceding excursus on truth at the death-bed, we now return to our thesis that human dying transcends the medical and biological definition and makes the impression of being not just "natural" but very "unnatural." The transcendent personal elements that are not included in that definition cannot be objectified; and to that extent they confront us with something that is inconceivable and even absurd. We have collected some experiences that will enable us to explore more deeply this impression of absurdity to which we made a brief reference in the first chapter.

It is probably the Christian understanding of the person, of which we still have to speak, that specifically causes us to take note of this experience of inconceivability and absurdity. But it would be wrong to regard the Christian view of humanity as its only stimulus. Even apart from this there may be analogous experiences of death. One need only think of the Greek concept of the mode of existence of the dead to realize this. From the wealth of material I will take just a few examples that bring the analogy to light.

As I see it, the inconceivability of death comes to expression in Homeric religion predominantly in the fact that the dead exist in a finally incomprehensible twilight between existence and non-existence. Communication, which is an essential part of human life for the Greeks as well, is broken off between the living and the dead.[34] The dead are not deprived of being; they exist in another mode of being in which continuity with the present mode is severed and which can be depicted only mythologically. They have a shadowy existence in the world of Hades, the Zeus of the underworld, the god of another world that is separated from ours.[35] Hades takes the psyche of the dying as it hastens away from this beautiful earth and puts it in the house of his underworld where it still lives on as an unconscious and perhaps dreaming shade. The absolute end of earthly life finds expression in the fact that there is no more growth in this world of shades, that there is no more future, and that another decisive mark of human existence — along with communication — is thereby lost.

Death, then, means entry into another world that is alien and inaccessible to the living. The dead exist — not in being, but in mere *having been*. They lose their temporality. This loss is experienced as an expulsion into nothingness.

Thus the soul of Achilles tells Odysseus, when he comes down into Hades, not to extol death, for he would rather live as a farmer tilling the fields than rule over the whole host of the dead. Heinrich Heine, who feared nothingness more than he did the judgment, constantly quoted this verse because he recognized his own anxieties in it.

These losses — the loss of the I-Thou relation and the loss of temporality — deprive us of specific human elements, so that we see here the personal marks of humanity and their cessation. But this understanding of the personal differs fundamentally from that of a Christian anthropology. For in Homer, everything that constitutes life relates to the body, and it is with the destruction of the body that all the energies of life, all the possibilities of life, and the relationship to time come to an end.[36]

Even if people survive death, they are robbed of the power of life and are no longer centers of action. What does this mean for their *identity*? The shade in Hades has at best a broken identity; to bring out the contrast with Christianity, it is not called by name nor does it stand under the patronage of a faithfulness in virtue of which its identity is preserved. The I that vegetates in a mere "having been" has only a private existence that is more a vegetating than a real existence. But plainly this shadowy mode of existence makes death inconceivable and absurd.[37]

The torchbearers that are found on many of the bases and inscriptions of antiquity, symbolizing sleep when the torch is lifted up and death when it is lowered, and thus showing that the distinction between sleep and death is merely one of nuance, undoubtedly express only one side of the Greek understanding of death, the side that is not touched by fear of its inconceivability.[38] But is it not really touched by this fear? I should like to pursue this question for a moment.

If we leave out of account the profound *mythologoumenon* of

Hades with its suggestion of the absurd, the image of the torch seems to suggest that a certain form of nonbeing might be conceivable, namely, death as a dreamless sleep. Epicurus alludes to this, and so does Socrates in his *Apology*. Death seems here to be an indescribable relief, if it can be thought of as an unconscious state untroubled by dreams. Shakespeare takes up this experimental idea of Socrates in Hamlet's great monologue in Act III, Scene 1, and follows it to its logical conclusion. But at the end the polish of the idea of dreamless nothingness is suddenly rubbed off and the ghosts return. For although I can think abstractly of nonbeing, it seems that I cannot really conceive of it. It is still tormentingly inconceivable.

"To die, to sleep — No more," and in this way, says Hamlet, "we end/The heart-ache and the thousand natural shocks. . . ." But sinking into the Nirvanah of complete nothingness in which "this mortal coil" is shuffled off is something we cannot really imagine. Something of earthly life, however reduced, still enters the picture. There thus arises the idea of dreams in which this life reproduces itself and thereby fills up again the vacuum of dreamless nothingless. "To die, — to sleep, — To sleep, perchance to dream; ay, there's the rub." One cannot conceive of remaining alive if the stresses of life might be exchanged for nothingness by the mere thrust of a bodkin:

> For who would bear the whips and scorns of time,
> Th' oppressor's wrong, the proud man's contumely,
> The pangs of despis'd love, the law's delay,
> The insolence of office, and the spurns
> That patient merit of th' unworthy takes,
> When he himself might his quietus make
> With a bare bodkin. . . ?

In place of an inconceivable nothingness there then comes a vision of what might constitute this condition after death: "the undiscover'd country, from whose bourn/No traveller returns. . . . "Death threatens to be a continuation of life with other means. At once, then, the liberating, narcotic idea of a sinking into Nirvanah changes into fear. Since we do not know what threats this "undiscover'd country" might hold, would we not "rather bear those ills we have, Than fly to others that we know not of?" Once we use our minds and imaginations to go more deeply into the mystery of death, "conscience does make cowards of us all," and "sicklied o'er with the pale cast of thought," we lose the courage to leap into a state that is certainly unknown to us but is still a different mode of being rather than nonbeing.

I ask myself whether the thing that makes death and the transition to that "undiscover'd country" so inconceivable is not again the individuality of which Hamlet was conscious. That the I should cease to be a center of action, that it should be snuffed out as the center of perspective of a world that goes on without it — this produces the experience of absurdity that we found in Hoche. We cannot accept pure absurdity because it means the negation of the familiar and given. Hence defensive forces rise up against it, which like pioneers build an emergency bridge over the abyss of nothingness even though we can conceive only of the fact of this hereafter and not of its nature. Fear of a vacuum shifts from nothingness to the unknown. Améry has tried to explain the resultant problem for thought with his concept of the logic of life — a logic that relates only to this living world.

To give a richer picture of this inconceivability of death, I will give a few examples of the encounter with it.

1. Hermann Hesse in his *Narziss und Goldmund* describes Goldmund's thoughts before his execution. Life is a being in the world, and to this it is a terrifyingly alien idea that we shall be snatched away and the world will go on without us. Goldmund had to say farewell to the hills and the sun, the trees and the woods, to his own hands, to food and drink, to love, to playing the lute, to sleeping and waking, to everything. The next morning a bird flew through the air and he no longer saw it. Everything went on without him. It was no longer his. He had been snatched away from everything.

2. In his story *Der Landvogt von Greifensee*, Gottfried Keller narrates the death of a child for whom eternal rest holds no terrors, so that we seem at first to have an exception here. The ten-year-old boy did not want to die, but when Landolt, quietly puffing his pipe, sat on his bed and told him very simply that his situation was hopeless but that death would be a blessed release and bring him to a state of unchanging rest, and when he went on to assure him of the love and sympathy that he had for him, the boy changed his attitude and bore his suffering with cheerful patience until the end came. But a deeper analysis will confirm our view that death is terrifyingly alien. We can be content with the idea of dreamless sleep and unchanging rest only when we have not yet awakened to individuality, and the I has not yet seen itself as the center of

a particular section of life and the world. The child had not yet reached this stage. Hence what is a help and comfort here, as I know from other experiences, is terrifyingly alien when individuality has awakened.

3. Encounter with the alien nature of death — as in Camus and his friend, the molecular biologist Jacques Monod[39] — may change into an experience of the alien nature of *life*. We live today in a universe that has been suddenly stripped of illusions, says Camus, and we feel alien in it. Once we realize that life is not intrinsic to the universe, nor humanity to the biosphere, but our number simply came up by chance, then our value systems crumble. When the full significance of this sinks in, we awaken from our thousand-year-old dream and recognize our total solitude and radical freedom. We know that we are like gypsies on the edge of a universe that is deaf to our music and indifferent to our hopes and sufferings and crimes (Monod). The more death is seen as a boundary that robs life of meaning, questions all values, and makes impossible any transcendent fulfillment, the more, then, it becomes a determinative factor in life, the more radical becomes the impression of the absurdity of life itself, and the more we are forced to choose between capitulation and a freedom of unconditional self-assertion in the midst of the absurdity of existence.

4. Finally, the inconceivability of death can arise with the idea of an endless continuation of life after it — a kind of pseudo-eternity. The problem here is not so much that of an infinite extension of time as that of the continuation of a futile and burned-out existence. Christopher Marlowe expressed the horror of such a state in his *Faust*. After twenty-four years of his pact with the devil, Faust is afraid of immortality. He begs the hills to fall on him, the earth to swallow him up, the universe to dissolve in him. His request, one might say, is for de-individualization because his I belongs to the devil and is lost. If his futile wish were granted, this would be a liberation. To have to carry this nullified I around with him to all eternity, to have to be immortal under the ban of evil and apart from saving grace, is a dreadful thing. To have to go on when the eternal foundation has been lost and nothingness encircles us, is hell. Here, too, endless continuation in a meaningless and accursed existence is only a mythical reflection of life that has itself become absurd, of a life that has been cut off from its original source and is lived even now in a shadowy Hades.

Chapter 3

THE CONNECTION BETWEEN THE VIEW OF HUMANITY AND THE UNDERSTANDING OF DEATH IN THE PHILOSOPHIES

A. OUR DIVISION INTO AN AUTHENTIC AND INAUTHENTIC PART

1. Clarification of Plato's View of Immortality

The attempt of the philosophies to overpower — and perhaps to "repress" — the reality of death utilizes tools that are primarily anthropological. In other words, the understanding of death rests on a total view of human existence. Or, conversely, this understanding of existence is decisively characterized by the understanding of death as its limit. Only when we see these two things together and thus get a picture of the total structure in which humanity lives and hides can we appreciate the radical nature of the attack that is made by the biblical message of the relationship between judgment and death on this supposed life without death, on *athanasia*.

The philosophical attempt to overpower death constantly utilizes, on the anthropological side, the same device of dividing us into an authentic part that as an immortal substance survives death, and an inauthentic part that is an unimportant vessel for that substance which can and should perish.

I believe that in this way I am formulating a basic principle of all "natural" anthropology. What this means may perhaps be seen most clearly from the Platonic idea of immortality, which gave classical expression to our division into an immortal part, the soul that is liberated by death, and the body that holds us captive.

In contrast, the principle of division is hardest to find in Nietzsche — for reasons we shall present later. In spite of their differences, I am thus associating Plato and Nietzsche closely in a single chapter. The very different ideas of death in the two will bring out all the more clearly the similarity of the law of division and offer the most important criteria for our later philosophical analyses.[1]

First, death means — according to Plato's *Phaedo* — the separation of the *psyche* (soul) from the *soma* (body). The soul, which can be detached from the body and is actually detached from it in death, has its own existence. Linked with this is the boldly accepted conviction of its preexistence and postexistence.[2]

Birth and death, then, are not creation and destruction, but are new relations to bodily matter, that is, the seeking of a body at birth and detachment from an existing combination with it at death.[3]

In Plato birth and death involve a rhythm of becoming and passing that is identical with that of the union, separation, and reunion of soul and body. Hence the soul itself does not come into being and perish. As an identical substance it underlies the unions that are contracted with the body and then dissolved, that is, changed. The body as a sensory phenomenon represents the fleetingness of such phenomena; in contrast, the soul epitomizes continuity.

Obviously the acts of union and separation are never restricted to the moments of time when they take place. They are not confined to the fixed chronology of birth and death. They determine the life that is lived between these. Nor do they determine it only quantitatively, by beginning and ending it. They also determine it qualitatively, constituting its *content*.

This is clear from what might be called the philosophical content of life, which depends entirely on the attitude that one takes toward death or that one attains in the course of life. In other words, the degree to which life presses on to knowledge, and thereby achieves an essential relation to the ground of being, depends on one's attitude toward death.

One might elucidate this as follows: In Platonic thought the immortality of the soul is closely connected with the relation of the soul to *ousia*, the essentiality of things. This relation might be expressed by saying that the soul is ordered to the *ousia* of things but the body as an adequate counterpoise is ordered to the sensory phenomena of this *ousia*, the multiplicity of the world of sense.

Body and soul are both referred, then, to the spheres from which they derive. The *psyche* belongs to the eternal sphere that is immune from corruptibility. It is the citadel that death cannot take by storm. The body, however, belongs to the sphere of the transitory that is presented to our senses.

One may thus conclude — and here the Platonic Socrates reduces the childish[4] fear of death to absurdity — that the soul is as little exposed to dissolution or destruction as the sphere to which it belongs (*ousia*, ideas, concepts), or, even more sharply, as the sphere of essences from which it comes. For these metaphysical essences (e.g., the ideas of the globe or cylinder) never dissolve but always remain the same even when their concrete manifestations perish. The invisible always stays the same; only the visible changes.

With this is linked the further thought that the soul, which is as such invisible and essential, cannot perish. For the soul is conceived of as the principle of life, as its invisible *ousia*.[5] By nature and definition, then, it cannot die. Things that do not have the quality of being even we call uneven; what does not have the quality of death we call nondead (*athanatos*). "As snow cannot be warm or fire cold, so the soul that dispenses life cannot be dead."[6]

When, therefore, the soul, being nondead, survives its separation from the mortal body, it achieves its material fulfillment; it goes to its like. Yet a distinction has to be made here: there are two types of souls. The soul that has already detached itself from the body and the senses hastens to the blessed life appropriate to it. The soul that has been in bondage to the body and the senses (a kind of nonsoul) must wander around until it is again united with a body, which according to its previous disposition may be that of an ass, hawk, wolf, bee, or ant.

The myth of the feathered soul in the *Phaedrus*[7] develops this distinction in the quality and destiny of souls. The soul has an eternal destiny only because it existed in an original association with the gods when it roamed on high across the world. Its sinking into mortality was a fall by which it lost its feathers. Burdened with offenses, the horse that pulls the chariot of the soul, unless it be fed by the driver, sags and falls to the earth. Already in their original state souls constitute a hierarchy. Some stay closer to true being, others see it only with difficulty and fall when their forces fail. Some souls remain companions of the gods, but others lose their feathers in finitude. They are then associated first with humans as the core of their lives, but again in ranks, from philosophers who seek the truth all the way down to sophists, sycophants, and tyrants. Finally, souls come to be located in the animal kingdom. At every earthly stage they longingly remember what they were originally. This is especially true in the case of philosophers, who reach up to essential being, to the ideas — and whose spirits are justifiably feathered again.

All this shows how death as a determinant of life is integrated into it as an existential feature. As the union of body and soul shapes the soul on the one side and thus brings a measure of satisfaction, so it is a liability and burden for the soul on the other side. It interposes between the soul and its true sphere (the *ousia* of things) the disruptive and confusing medium of the senses. Death signifies the reawakening of the soul to what is essential to it. In it the disruptive factor of the body with its alienating function falls away again.

What is the attitude of philosophers to death? If it is the life's aim of genuine philosophers to draw close to the *ousia* of things even now, and thus to pierce through the world of shadows with its purely external appearance, then their concern might be characterized as a seeking of death or dissolution. In fact, Plato speaks of the *thanatan* of philosophers (their desire for death) in his *Phaedo*. The philosophical life is an exercise in dying, a being for death.[8]

Death simply means the separation of the soul from a body that obscures its true orientation. It also means the loss of a world whose disappearance we are not to bewail because something incomparably more perfect replaces it. But it is not the moment of death that first makes possible this transition to nobler things; we can know it during life itself by means of philosophy. Philosophy enables us already here and now — before death — to see through the illusion of the senses and thus to enter the future world of *eidos*; it enables reason, which is above the world, to achieve freedom even during one's lifetime. This act of intellectual liberation is anticipated death. When death itself finally comes, the souls of philosophers, being ready, float easily upward to the gods, while other souls cannot break completely free from the bodily chains and have thus to wander about in their graves in ghostly fashion.

In regarding philosophy as a concern for death, or even as a particular form of being for death, Plato does not view death as annihilation (as existentialist philosophers and other analysts of anxiety should remember), but is thinking exclusively of the future state to which dying leads. He has in mind the attainment of the goal to which death can lead only as an "adventitious" transition.

Death, then, may be defined both negatively and positively. Negatively, it means destruction of the peripheral and nonessential sphere of existence, the body. Positively, it means the resultant awakening of existence to true life. The negative side is a dialectical transition. It is the shuffling off of what hampers the positive aspect of being.

We see clearly here the anthropological principle of division to which we have referred, and it involves not merely the momentary act of dying but also the determination of life. We are "nondead," immortal, because only something "of" us, that is, the body, is mortal, timebound, and corruptible.

But what is the nature of this immortality of the soul? Is it the preserving of personal identity, or perhaps the achievement of it?

This question raises a problem that I shall not presume to clarify here but that is very significant for the correlation of death and individuality discussed earlier. For this reason we must at least indicate the problem.

Plato in his *Phaedrus*, in Socrates' third speech, says something about the nature of the soul. Socrates is distinguishing between living bodies and dead ones. A body is dead when it cannot move itself but can only be moved. It lives when it can move itself. That it can do this, and is thus alive, is because it has a soul. Soul is an entity that moves itself and other things. Hence life and soul are identical. In Book 10 of the *Nomoi* Plato refers to the cyclical character of this movement that obtains throughout the cosmos. It is like the spinning of a disc whose center remains still while the speed increases the further a being is from the center and the closer it is to the periphery. On the outer margin is the sphere of the stars moving across the cosmos.

The psyche takes part in this cyclical movement. It moves in constant repetition of a triple measure from embodiment by way of disembodiment in death to reembodiment.

In the *Phaedo* one gets the impression that Socrates is not just advocating the survival of the soul after death (i.e., *athanasia*), but also its return from death in a new body. Transmigration of souls stands in the background. This makes it possible that the opposite of death is not the mere immortality of the soul but is its reincarnation. This forms the true heart of the conviction that robs death of its finality.

A question arises here whether the psyche that survives death and enters a new body possesses individual contours during the waiting period, or whether it is just a cosmic principle of life — to use a non-Platonic modern term.

In the myth of the figure of Er, the son of Armenios,[9] Socrates gives an unequivocal answer to this question. It seems at first as if the soul has no individual contours, as though it were individualized only when incarnated in a bodily creature, whether human or animal.[10] But this is not quite true, for Socrates speaks of souls being able to choose their bodily form even though fate narrows the choice. Nevertheless, at the moment of choice souls do not have any pronounced specificity. This is linked to the concreteness of the form of life, the historical situation, and a habitus that is possible only in bodily existence and therefore lacking to the soul that floats inessentially in the hereafter. On the other hand, one cannot view souls in this state merely as blank slates on which nothing individual is written. If they were, individual choice would be impossible. There could only be blind grasping by chance or the choice of the same thing by all. Ajax and Agamemnon choose their new bodily forms very definitely and "individually." Their choice plainly carries with it recollection of their earlier (individual) lives. Both have suffered at human hands, and for their reincarnation choose an animal rather than a human existence.

In the intermediate state, therefore, the soul remains in an indistinct twilight between individuality and nonindividuality. Perhaps one might say that the cyclical view of time that lies behind transmigration is against the development of constant individuality. The idea of uniqueness that is related to a pregnant concept like individuality obviously needs a linear and oriented understanding of time. It is no accident, then, that the unconditional stress that biblical thought lays on individuality (at any rate in the later OT and especially in the NT) occurs in the framework of a linear view of time in which our time, our *kairos*, is as unique as we ourselves (2 Cor. 6:2). At any rate, when one considers the indistinctness of the individuality of souls in Plato, it would be overly bold to say that the psyche retains its identity in the hereafter. Again the biblical contrast is the "name" by which we are called; this represents our identity before God that cannot be erased by death.[11]

2. Nietzsche's Nontranscendental View of Death

The most recent attempt at a nontranscendental view of death, and the one that is closest to modern biologism, is that of Nietzsche. It differs sharply from Plato's understanding of death.

We shall give a brief sketch of this anthropology because it presses the observed law of division to the limit. We shall also need to be particularly attentive to discern this law, for the consistent immanentism of Nietzsche does not allow us to assume too easily that there is an immortal core of the I that survives the present world.[12]

Nietzsche's message on death is directed polemically against the Christian "distortion" of its reality. If he can call fear of death the "European sickness,"[13] the cause of this sickness is Christian concern for the hereafter, the "pitiable and terrible comedy that Christianity has made of the hour of death,"[14] the fear of what might happen to this life in and after death in view of what lies beyond it.

In opposition, Nietzsche wants to view death as part of life and therefore — along the lines of the concept of corruptibility — as an end that comes from within and not from without. "Let us be careful not to say that death is opposed to life."[15] It cannot be so, for Nietzsche's view of life is emphatically nontranscendental. Life and its limit in death can be understood only from within themselves and not in terms of something beyond. But if death is part of life, it is in our own hands in the same way as life is. It is in the same sense something to which we ourselves can give shape and meaning.

But if life does not happen to us but is something that we live, something to which we give shape and meaning as subjects, then we are subjects or Promethean lords of existence in relation to death, too. Death that overtakes us, death in contemptible conditions, unfree death, death at the wrong time, is a coward's death. Out of love of life we should will death freely and consciously, not let it come upon us by chance.[16] To do away with oneself is to do the noblest thing there is. It almost makes one worthy to live.[17] Freedom to live is identical with freedom to die when I choose, so that death does not just happen to me, thus bringing life into bondage to it. I commend my death as a free death that comes when *I* choose.[18] I am free *for* death and *in* death.[19] Those who bring about their own deaths die victoriously, surrounded by the hope and praise of others. Hated equally by those who fight and those who conquer is the grinning death that creeps up like a thief. In death your spirit and virtue should glow like a red sunset around the earth or your death is a poor one.[20] The brute physiological fact (i.e., death as a biological happening) must be changed into a moral necessity.[21]

If we have thus to shape our own deaths and grasp them in freedom, the question arises: When is the right moment? or, more deeply, What is the norm by which I can measure my time? Nietzsche's answer is that we should stop eating when our taste is best, that is, when the peak and limit of a value-filled life is reached. We must speak a holy No when the time for Yes is past. This shows understanding of both life and death.[22]

If there is a time like this when we should voluntarily put an end to life because our human potential is exhausted, Nietzsche is necessarily engaging in a basic division of humanity.

There is on the one side the evaluative side of us that can engage in critical assessment and at a certain moment condemn itself to death. There is also the side that is judged, whose time has run out in terms of value, so that from the next moment its life will not be worthwhile.

Not by chance, then, Nietzsche can make anthropological statements that almost have a Platonic ring, distinguishing between the kernel and the pitiable substance of the husk.[23] In natural death the body is the hampering, frequently sick, and stupid prison-guard, the master that decides the point when his distinguished prisoner must die. Natural death is the suicide of nature, that is, the destruction of rational being by irrational.[24]

Life, then, decides when it is no longer worth living, and is thus its own judge. It rises up for a moment above itself and enters into an assumed transcendence in order to judge and condemn. Yet this transcendence, this higher judicial zone of the I, is not a genuine transcendence that survives this present life, but is something that itself sinks into the nothingness of death.

Similarly, the norm by which the end is measured is not a norm that really survives this life. Nietzsche's norms are immanent to life in basis, goal, and meaning. Only what enhances life is good and true. Life itself, one might say epigrammatically, is always the normative norm (*norma normans*), and all other norms are derived and secondary (*normae normatae*). Hence these norms are subject to life and not authoritatively superior to it.

Thus the norm that for a moment transcends and measures and ends life is really life itself. This is both arrow and target, both wave and ocean. It controls itself in such a way that it controls death, too.

We have thus distilled out the decisive element in this attempt to master death. Death is robbed of its power, not because it is assumed that there is an immortal part of the I in relation to which the body is a mere bauble, but because death ceases to be a power *over* us and becomes an *instrument* of our own power, namely, the power of noble folk to decide that they have become worthless and no longer measure up to what they should be.

Yet even in this view of things that banishes all immortality and transcendence there necessarily arises the basic division of the I that I have tried to show to be intrinsic to every natural attempt to master death. The only point is that it is here carried to its extreme limit, a limit at which it threatens to make the concept meaningless.

For the assumed transcendence in terms of which the I judges itself is diametrically opposed to the nontranscendent nothingness into which it sinks at death. (This is why all Nietzsche's statements about death have something unstable and contradictory about them.) What comes to expression is the unrestricted overemphasis on human life — its deification. The I has charge of itself in both life and death. Death is simply an instrument, a symbolic means by which to show how it posits and ends itself, how it creates and destroys itself, how it is always in control of itself.

This life is not a creaturely one that is given and accepted. It is not under the authority of a divine norm. It does not find its limit in God. It is its own creator and the author of its own norms. It is lawgiver, judge, and angel of death all in one. Every path leads from it and by it and to it.

We have here the wildest, the most vital, and therefore — on the very edge of meaninglessness — the most consistent attack on death that was ever mounted. We ourselves are God — O death, where is thy sting? Hybris and nihilism, self-deification and delusion are closely linked here.[25]

EXCURSUS I ON NIETZSCHE: AMÉRY'S THESIS ON THE RIGHT TO TAKE ONE'S OWN LIFE.[26]

I shall now try to follow through to its most recent manifestation the Promethean thought that occurs in Nietzsche. This may be found in Jean Améry's apology for suicide.[27] Under the impact of escalating secularism Nietzsche's *homo creator* is here given a final twist. This also produces a type of reflection that is saturated with the dark experiences of our century in terror, liquidation, and torture.

Nietzsche himself — and this is strange — figures only on the margin in Améry. But there is hardly a thought here that he did not originate and that Améry has not simply developed and sharpened.

Natural death for Nietzsche, we recall, is a contemptible coward's death at the wrong time. Out of love of life we ought to choose death freely and consciously and not let it overtake us by chance. Améry, whose thinking is along the same lines, does not contest the fact that planned and intentional suicide is a flight. But it is a flight of a particular kind. If, when life has become unbearable, we escape from it in death, we can no longer answer the question of where we are taking refuge. Where? Nowhere. The goal of this flight can be described only negatively as nonbeing, or being no longer. But this is an absurdity that, as Améry cleverly explains, defies all scholarly elucidation. Because there is no bridge from being to nonbeing, we are helpless when we think about death. Our logic is tied to the horizon of life. Necessarily, as we have seen, it is the logic of life.

Hence death, whether natural or self-inflicted, is inconceivable in principle. This alone is reason enough why the question of the whither of our flight must remain absurdly open. Yet we cannot let this question alone, thinks Améry, and it is not good enough to say, as Ludwig Wittgenstein does, that if we cannot state an answer we cannot state the question. This may be true academically, but it loses its force when we are existentially confronted by our nonbeing in death.

Now we can expose ourselves actively to this nonbeing; we can desire it. We can go on strike against our will to live. We can escape from the distaste for our existence, for the emptiness and unworthiness of a life that has become helpless and meaningless, by laying hands upon ourselves. Suicide, then, is presented as an ethical act, a human privilege that distinguishes us from animals. This freedom to die, it is argued, is an inalienable human right. It belongs to the original core of what is human, so that one can not only distinguish it from the animal instinct to preserve the self and the species, but one can also isolate it from purely social considerations.

Améry is right, of course, when he describes suicide in this way as a specifically human possibility. My only objection is to his attempt to find it sanctioned by the fact that it is this human possibility. Cannibalism — the urge to feed upon one's fellows — is an almost exclusively human possibility, and so is war or crime. Humans, to quote a saying of Faust, can use their reason to become more beastly than the beasts — another human privilege! All the horrors of history, which do not occur in the animal kingdom, are the result of human privileges and form their reverse side.

Animals (e.g., in relation to killing their own) have restrictive mechanisms that humans, being released from instinct, lack. There would no longer be any ravens or wolves, says Konrad Lorenz, if there had not been such restrictions. Doves, hares, and chimpanzees cannot kill members of their own species by a stroke or a bite. Moreover, animals that are not especially well protected can flee, and this is enough to enable them to escape beasts of prey.

Everything is radically different among humans. Lacking instinct, these have to use the sphere of freedom that has opened up to them to bring their understanding into play as a substitute. They have thus to subject themselves to self-selected norms that will replace the lost directives of instinct.

This opportunity for cultural development also leads to the invention of weapons. And this invention, which is possible only for them, disturbs (according to Lorenz) the previous balance between the ability to kill and the instinctive restriction of killing. With modern long-range weapons we are also protected to a large extent against the remaining situations that might release restrictions and evoke pity. Thus good, brave, and worthy fathers of families lay carpets of bombs.[28] The terrible deaths and burnings and torments that take place at a safe distance cannot trigger any restrictive mechanisms that might still exist.

I myself can never forget how, during the war, a Stuka pilot told me how he and his copilot went down on their knees with enthusiasm when they had blown up a column of vehicles on a bridge. Yet he was a very correct young man who would never have gone through a door before a lady.

All these possibilities of killing our fellow human beings are the products of human privileges that offer the opportunity for advance, but also for every kind of destruction. This should make us careful when we come up against attempts to glorify these privileges and in so doing to glorify all the mischief that humanity has done, and still does, with their help.

The biblical story of the fall is salutary and sobering medicine here. Humans, not whales, trees, or stars, revolted against the Creator. This revolt, too, was a human privilege exploited in negative fashion. I fail to see, therefore, why saying that suicide is exclusively a human possibility provides any justification for it.

The human privilege that Améry has in mind consists essentially of the freedom of self-determination. But in the radical form championed by the author this can be valid only on *one* presupposition, namely, that we belong to ourselves, that we have complete control of ourselves, that we do not owe an account to anyone else.

On this view we are our own creators. If we create ourselves and have full control of ourselves, then we have the right, as Nietzsche says, to do away with ourselves. But the transcendence we are here assigning to ourselves is one that is usurped.

What depths open up here! The illusion that might seize us in face of this self-mastery certainly should not give rise to the mistake that all that is at issue is ungoverned caprice. Améry obviously does not mean this. Even if there is no Thou of a Creator to whom I owe an account, I am accountable to myself, to the human essence, the *psyche* of Platonic thought.

To this extent Améry recognizes criteria that offer or deny me the possibility of suicide. The decisive criterion is human dignity — not the inferior, external, social dignity accepted or denied, for example, in a military officer's code of honor, but the dignity that my human self has within itself.

I ask, however, whether this recognition of dignity might not itself be a capricious act, whether the illusion of self-ownership that is axiomatic in Améry does not reach a peak here and decree absolutely what dignity is and what is appropriate to it in the conditions of life.

What this kind of underlying caprice might mean is clear when we listen to the Christian partner in Améry's dialogue. The author concedes with respect and understanding that Christians will have to dispute this thesis that we control our own lives and cannot, therefore, regard it as justifiable arbitrarily to anticipate God's decree concerning our death. It would have been better, however, if this Christian rejection of suicide had not been presented as a purely dogmatic counterthesis that is not itself to be critically investigated. This counterthesis has a significance that goes far beyond suicide. I can only hint at this here, but I want to do so in the form of a question to Améry.

What results can one expect if humans emancipate themselves from the Creator along the lines Améry proposes, and if they make their own idea of dignity a universal criterion for wanting either to live on or not to do so? Will not others inevitably begin to pass the death sentence on us when we do not achieve the required dignity? Perhaps in our desolate condition we are no longer able to see ourselves critically, to note our lack of dignity, and consequently to put an end to ourselves. Perhaps the decisive sign of sinking below the human level will be the loss of the power of self-criticism and the resultant possibility of resolving upon suicide.

If we accept Améry's presupposition of self-ownership, it seems to me that there is nothing to stop the conclusion that others, such as doctors, relatives, and politicians, will act representatively when self-direction has been lost or is no longer present, and will decide upon death on the basis of the established lack of dignity. They will be able to regard themselves as attorneys and executives for lives that have no dignity, or embryos that are not expected to have it, and to act accordingly.

Does not our supposed self-ownership lead in fact to the thesis of a nonworthwhile life and all that this entails? What prospects open up here for euthanasia! Does not Améry in fact share some of the basic anthropological ideas of the Nazis even though he personally detests the racial concept of a master race and its brutal implications?

The serious question that Améry puts in this connection is as follows: If Christians reject human self-ownership in a way that commands respect, do they have a right to regard this as valid for non-Christians as well and to denounce ending one's own life as suicide? (Améry complains that the believing philosopher Paul Ludwig Landsberg claims such a right.)

If one is convinced — as I am — that the Christian belief that we do not belong to ourselves carries with it a proclamation of worth or dignity that sets human life under a taboo and protects it against horrifying inferences, one can hardly do other than decide in favor of this belief. Christian humanism carries with it an insight into humanity that has to be championed and applied even when its theological presuppositions are no longer shared or have been forgotten.[29]

One cannot say this, of course, without adding at once that if the motive power of Western humanism — the divine Yes to us that is heard in faith — is no longer a living element in our consciousness, the wheels will increasingly slow down and we shall find ourselves on the fatal slope — we have mentioned it already — that leads from divinity (relationship to God) by way of emancipated humanity to bestiality.

That there may be legitimate suicide in marginal cases (e.g., to escape torture and betraying friends)[30] may be conceded to Améry. But this does not alter in any way our fundamental and definite opposition to his thesis of self-ownership.

If the Christian churches have come to deal more kindly with suicides, and have done away with the defamatory burial patches for them, the reasons for this are not as Améry supposes. Christianity has simply learned from empirical pastoral study that by far the majority of suicides are due to pathological compulsion — the result of overwhelming depression or despair — and that we have no right to judge in such cases. Améry, however, has in view planned acts of self-destruction undertaken in freedom. The Christian objection to this Promethean program has never ceased, and will not do so in the future.

The principle of division that we have sought to demonstrate in the various anthropological conceptions as they relate to the understanding of death may thus be seen in Améry, too, in exact analogy to what we found in Nietzsche. For Améry, inasmuch as we bear the essence of humanity, we are very different from the human garbage and waste that we see ourselves to be once we can no longer achieve the happiness, fulfillment, and accomplishments in life that we should. It is thus our privilege to do away with ourselves when this comes about.

This is a freedom not merely to do away with ourselves, however, but also to fix criteria by which to judge ourselves. What constitutes happiness or fulfillment or destiny is not received and ordained but decided independently by us. It lies in the sphere of our own autonomy. The usurping of Promethean transcendence (or sham transcendence) reaches a provisional climax here.

EXCURSUS II ON NIETZSCHE: THE PROBLEM OF EUTHANASIA

In discussing the problem of suicide in Nietzsche and Améry, the problem of euthanasia necessarily arises, as I have already indicated.

If we create ourselves, we not only have the right to do away with ourselves, but as doctors or relatives we have a similar representative right in relation to others. As we have said, these others may be unconscious, weak, and helpless, so that they cannot act on their own behalf. In terms of Améry's thinking this might be a sign that life is superfluous for them and that the dignity of full humanity compels us to take the initiative and end what has become an undignified state or hopeless and meaningless torment.

Thus the thesis that we may decide on our own death and not just be passively delivered up to it involves the problem of euthanasia. I shall take this opportunity to deal with this problem in the form of an excursus.

Probably the Dutch sentence on a doctor who ended the life of her 78-year-old mother, who was incurably ill and in great pain, by giving her an overdose of morphine has not yet been forgotten. It attracted great attention and has in fact paradigmatic significance for our problem. The judges imposed only a "token sentence," which betrayed their helplessness. A minimal tribute had to be paid to the letter of the law that forbids killing on request. This definite minimum, however, makes it clear that no punishment could be hazarded because the "killer," tormented by severe inner conflicts, was no criminal, but had acted out of a motive of helpful love. Could one expect more of the guardians of law and order? Did not such a case of conflict lie outside their legal code?

As we saw on television, the sentence led to all kinds of demonstrations. But on none of the placards did I see any protest against the bending of the law, although some of them claimed that the Christian faith had been violated and the commandment against killing broken. If the law had to hide its face in silence, or speak only in a whisper, should it not be possible to resolve the conflict on the Christian side and make a valid confession *against* this helping on of death?

In the interests of clarity, we should first free ourselves from the shock effect of the term "euthanasia." This word was compromised by the massacring of the unfit during the Third Reich. What happened then (and what the psychiatrists Hoche and Binding mean by the term) is worlds apart from what the Dutch doctor did.

This doctor certainly did not want to end a nonworthwhile life for ideological reasons. On the contrary, she found it impossible to look on while the very precious and worthwhile life of her mother was being consumed in senseless torment. The Nazis acted with ideological and economic calculation. This doctor took the extreme step out of sympathy and love.

Yet is an act justified by mere purity of motivation? Ought not my subjective impulses to be subject to binding criteria? Do we not have enough examples of wrong things, which later avenge themselves, being done with the best of intentions? This is the question, and it leads on at once to the further problem of whether there is any binding suprapersonal court that allows us to take measures of this kind.

The much quoted Hippocratic oath that serves as a criterion for doctors does not give us the desired information. The relevant passage is to the effect that doctors will not give any deadly medicine to anyone if asked, nor suggest any such counsel, nor give to a woman an instrument to produce abortion. The motive for medical procedures is also given: "I will follow that method of treatment which, according to my ability and judgment, I consider for the benefit of my patients, and abstain from whatever is deleterious and mischievous."

But do not these two extracts plunge us into the conflict — no more! — in which we now find ourselves? For the issue is what is really deleterious and what is beneficial for the patient. Determining this is itself the problem.

The question is a particularly urgent one in modern medicine. If medicine is meant to preserve human life and health, it may be doing too much today as concerns the preservation of life. By artificial respiration and other measures it is possible to keep life going and to prolong the torture of death or to maintain an unconscious plantlike life with the help of absurd medical devices (intentionally I abstain from speaking here of the medical "art").

Do we not have to think through the ancient problems of euthanasia afresh in face of our new technical abilities? Does not the question unavoidably arise — as with atomic and genetic advances — whether we ought to do all the things that we can? Is it not perhaps an easier and less risky course for doctors to keep to the letter of their ethical code and prevent the flicker of life from being extinguished? In other words, when do doctors incur the greater guilt, when they do this or when they cease to take heroic measures and close down the machines? These are difficult and frightening issues.

The following basic matters need to be considered. First, we have a right to death as well as to life. The supposed service of keeping us alive unconditionally may produce a reign of terror for humanity if death is increasingly broken down into installments. When our hour has struck, the clock should not be set going again. Otherwise the medical aiding of life may become a hybrid claim over death.

The ancient saying that no one can be required to do the impossible is no longer adequate today when the limit of the possible has not yet been reached. Modern medicine is not to be required to do all that it can.

Second, although there are clear laws against taking life in all our traditions — Hippocrates as well as the Bible — there is nowhere any command to prolong a failing life at all costs. Whose conscience says that if a person who is in severe pain with an inoperable cancer is dying of a circulatory problem he must be put on a machine so as to live an hour longer? Who will call a doctor who does not take this course a murderer? (R. Kautzky).

Third, insistence on prolonging life at all costs can in practice lead to ridiculous situations whose absurdity testifies against it. If all the dying were put on machines, they would take up almost all the time of the attendants and the real work of medicine would be neglected.

Fourth, a distinction has to be made between biological life and human life. If we are talking about the duty of doctors to sustain life, we have to mean human life and not just biological life. But to describe human life we need criteria other than those indicated on electrocardiograms and encephalograms. At least a trace of self-awareness is part of human life. Only on this basis can we suffer ethically, that is, make something out of our suffering. This is the only reason why biological life should not be prolonged indefinitely when self-awareness and the possibility of suffering ethically have been irretrievably lost and only a vegetable type of life remains.

In all these cases, then, to refuse to take heroic measures is not to violate human dignity. On the contrary, precisely when we respect this dignity and see Christians as standing under the patronage of God—the saying about our divine likeness is relevant here—we shall accept the pronouncement of the Lord of life and death that the last hour has struck for someone. We shall not cause what we are doing in the name of this Lord—namely, serving human life—to become a self-willed rejection of this pronouncement. Orthothanasia—"right dying"—is a term that I like better than euthanasia.

Reflection on the Dutch sentence has forced us into the general problem of euthanasia and led to a new formulation of it. Only against this broader background can we discuss the special case of actually hastening death.

It is immediately obvious that giving an overdose of morphine can hardly be listed among the cases considered thus far. This is not just allowing to die, but is administering death on demand. There is much in me that resists passing judgment at a distance, and with the help of normal rules, on a desperate act that was motivated by the doctor's love for her mother. I am only too well aware of all the people and patients who knew and cherished her and expressed their joy at her de facto pardon. I also understand the burdensome imperative expressed in the saying: "Do not put me to death or you are my murderer." Can we indeed refuse to be murderers when we see people in torment, even though their illness is irreversible? The hour is about to strike but does not do so. The finger seems to creep on ever more slowly. It cannot stop, however—and why should we not push it on, bridging the short distance to twelve?

Only when we feel the terrible weight of this question and accept some solidarity with the pain and compassion of that doctor have we any right to question her action.

On this presupposition I should like to say this: There is profound wisdom in the statement of Pius XII to a congress of anaesthetists that if the dispensing of narcotics leads of itself to two results, first, the lessening of pain, and second, the shortening of life, it is permissible. Negatively, putting to death is rejected here, but positively, death is allowed even though it is a by-product of drugs that reduce suffering.

Naturally, the question arises whether differentiating between putting to death and allowing death is not sophisticated hair-splitting, or, even worse, a way of saving the doctor's face morally by permitting a death sentence to be passed and executed without any legal responsibility. I find it impossible to deny that the distinction can be abused. There is no set of norms that can rule out such abuse in principle.

Nevertheless, the distinction between allowing to die and putting to death on demand is a fundamental one. Apart from any ethical theory, the development of which would take us too far afield, the distinction is shown to be valid if one brings out the consequences of not observing it.

If the patient's wish to die were normative, where could the boundary of a readiness to hasten death be fixed? K. Binding, the great legal advocate of full-scale euthanasia, said once that it is quite unnecessary that the desire for death should be triggered by intolerable pain. Hopelessness even when there is no pain deserves the same compassion.[31] In opposition, F. Walter rightly pointed out that sometimes it is the doctor who is hopeless, sometimes the patient, and sometimes the illness.... What is to decide.[32] This is what makes the problem so extremely complicated.

We seem to enter a slippery slope of decision making if we take as a criterion for the right to death on demand not just the objectively measurable pain of the patient but the subjective condition of hopelessness as well. Who among the severely ill has never had the openly expressed or silent wish that this hopeless condition should be terminated and wrestling with pain should not get worse?

Where will it lead, then, if we set foot on that slippery slope? Does not respect for our human inviolability, for our divine likeness, provide protection against the frightful blunders of an unrestrained rationality that passes arrogant sentence on what it takes to be worthwhile life or not? Are we not brought back here again to the claiming of pseudo-transcendence that we discussed earlier?

The final conclusion of wisdom as I take it from our Christian tradition seems, then, to be this: We are forbidden to hamper the

Lord of life and death by medical gadgetry that can also lead to madness. We are also forbidden to try to be more divine than God and to disturb the hourglass that he has set for us as the measure of our time.

After this excursus on euthanasia I will resume the interrupted chapter on the division of humanity that we observed especially in Plato's anthropology. The point here, as we saw, was to master death with the thought that only the bodily part of us dies while our true substance, the soul, is *athanatos* ("deathless").

I shall now turn to another form of this division.

B. OUR DIVISION INTO INDIVIDUALS AND REPRESENTATIVES OF SUPRAINDIVIDUAL POWERS

1. Clarification of Germanic Religion

If Grönbech is right,[33] our ancestors had not the least fear of death. The reason adduced for this is that the reality of life was felt so strongly that death did not count. But this makes no sense to me. The reverse seems more plausible, namely, that a strong sense of the menace of death corresponds to an intense feeling for life. For death terminates vitality, and daily experience and a glance at its normal structure show that precisely those who live vitally are threatened by fear of life's end.

Walter F. Otto rightly points out that in Greek religion, experience of the divine as the fullness of life meant that death was not regarded as a normal or natural phenomenon, but as something alien and unnatural. The living find death most alien and cannot believe that it is part of the meaning and plan of life itself.[34] It is a mistake to think that in Homeric religion the spirit is so fervently directed to light and life, and that it is as it were blinded and cannot see death but views it as absolute and inconceivable nothingness.[35] The idea of Hades as a new and shadowy mode of existence opposed to life is a clear sign that death is not a negation but a perversion. The gods of life are powerless and have to yield to deadly Moira,[36] which opposes a greater and ultimately victorious contradiction even to them and to their divine life.

Hölderlin, too — precisely, as one might say, in the name of the brightness of the Greek belief in life — proclaims the inconceivability of personal death as the antithesis of life: "I have no concept of corruption (when our heart, the best in us, the only thing worth listening to, pleads to go on even with all its sorrows)—may the God to whom I prayed as a child forgive me—I do not understand death in his world."[37]

This survey of Greek religion, which at this point stands in some analogy to the Germanic belief in life, supports, I think, my thesis against Grönbech that with intensity of life and belief in it the alien and unnatural character of death is felt more strongly.[38]

If our Germanic ancestors still had no fear of death in the modern sense, there seem to be other reasons for this. The ancient Germans hardly regarded themselves as individuals, but rather lived, with an exclusiveness which we find hard to understand, as members of their tribe, being totally bound up with its welfare, peace, and honor. Thus, individual death could play no decisive role for them. Heroes lived on as mythical realities—and not just in the sense of an immortality of name or memory—in the glory and well-being of the clan.

Thus in the *Vatsdoelasaga*, the young hero Thorolf, having been mortally wounded, asks his brother to perpetuate his name. He has carried it such a short time that it will soon be forgotten. But his brother will enhance the tribe and bring a great deliverance. He would like him, then, to call his son Thorolf, and he will give him all his own qualities. Then, he believes, his name will live so long as the world is inhabited. When Thorstein, his brother, replies that he will gladly do this, for it will be to the honor of the tribe and good fortune will attend this name, he clearly does not have in view the handing on of the name in our modern secularized sense; the name is merely a symbol of continued life in the clan.[39]

The heroes, then, are quite content to find new life in other members of their tribes, and the question of individual identity simply cannot penetrate the mass of ancient presuppositions regarding supraindividual clan membership. What constitutes their true humanity is not individual existence, but life, or continued life, in the welfare and honor of the tribe by which they are represented.

There is a Greek parallel to this to the extent that *kleos* and *doxa* (glory) are analogous in the overcoming of death to the welfare and honor of the tribe among the Germans. Acquiring fame offers the possibility of integrating the act of death into life.[40] To use our modern concepts, death loses its character as an absolute end. Since glory is usually acquired in fighting for the *polis*, and this plays a big part in the winning of immortality, the parallel to the Germanic reality of the well-being and honor of the tribe is all the more pregnant.[41]

At any rate, this is the Germanic idea of immortality. Individual members of the tribe fade out in death and the tribe — the bearer of well-being and glory — confers these sacred powers on others. So long as life is so inseparably linked to a unity (namely, that of the clan) that the individual cannot exist as such, there is nothing to trigger the concept of personal identity (Grönbech).

Here is obviously the reason why death is regarded as unimportant. It can slay only what is inessential, the individual bearer of the tribal powers, not the powers themselves. As the ideas of individual incarnation and immortality are impossible on these presuppositions, so is that of individual death. The individual is not even there. Since today the individual is so much emphasized, the problem of death is greater. The various phenomena of the repression of the thought of death, the refusal to speak about it, the placing of a taboo on it, which are all to be seen nowadays, are certainly connected with the modern sense of individuality and the psychological, social, and political proclamation of individual rights.

2. The Contrasting Biblical View of the Totality of the I

Before we continue our discussion of Germanic religion and what corresponds to it (in a broken sense) today (Hegel/Marx), we must first clarify a decisive factor. That is, from a Christian standpoint we are unique as persons or individuals in a way that is not seen in the Germanic idea of existing in the tribe, and this uniqueness first dawns in our consciousness when we have to see ourselves as being in an individual relationship with God.

The difference reaches back into the anthropological presuppositions. On the Christian view, death destroys individuals like lightning and the tribe cannot act as a lightning conductor. But this makes sense only if one assumes that we are individuals that cannot be represented by others or transferred to them. We cannot be represented by anything. Our wealth cannot represent us. Jesus tells the rich young ruler to sell all that he has (Mark 10:21). The rich farmer has to leave in death the packed barns in which he has found security for the continuation of his life (Luke 12:20). Nor can the tribe represent us or perpetuate our life. God tells Abraham (Gen. 12:1) to leave his father's house and his kin. Jesus tells his disciples that they must be ready to hate their fathers and mothers for his sake (Luke 14:26). When Adam is summoned before God, he suddenly finds that he cannot transfer his guilt to the wife that God has given him (Gen. 3:12). Nor can Eve transfer her guilt to the serpent that has deceived her.

Before God we have our own identities. There is a region of the I in which no one and nothing can represent us. We are completely alone. This is the sphere where God calls us by name, where we are called "Adam."[42]

In *this* region we have to die. And in *this* region death is an insoluble problem. For here it means real destruction and not just transformation.

The problem of the seriousness of death is the problem of the seriousness of the I. It arises when I cannot be represented but am held to my own identity and cannot take "the wings of the morning" (Ps. 139:9) to abandon myself and become someone or something else (tribe or idea).

Individual existence in its uniqueness is totally different from the stage of pupation from which I emerge to a butterfly state of supraindividual values. We shall see how the Bible teaches the seriousness of death indirectly by stressing in the law and the gospel the seriousness of possessing before God an I that cannot be represented.

Is not the fear of death that remains in spite of every explanation or consolation an anonymous sign that fundamentally we have some knowledge of this destruction, that we know that the I perishes and at best only an It remains in the sense of our name or achievements or the society around us? The mystery of death is none other than the mystery of this I.

The people of the Bible experienced death as an enemy because they had to say "I" under the binding claim of God's Word: "Wretched man that I am" (Rom. 7:24). They knew that I alone am meant when God proclaims judgment and asks for decision, and that at this moment everything else drops away: Jewish or Greek descent, family, friends, money. At the moment of the divine address these things can only be means to lose the self, to seek security, to try to escape the threat. They can only be like the trees in which Adam hid from God (Gen. 3:8). Similarly, as we shall see, the positive assurance: "I have called you by name; you are mine" (Isa. 43:1; 45:3f.), is directed in NT thinking to the individual and individual identity.

We thus miss the decisive point if we find the Christian view of the fear of death only in the isolation that it entails when we have to leave everything and go out of the world as naked and empty as we came into it (1 Tim. 6:7). This negative fact is not the real point of the biblical statement. The stress falls instead on the fact that leaving possessions behind throws the spotlight on the self that confronts death and can no longer hide in possessions but has to give itself up to death while the It with which it was linked goes on. Retirement with its frequent crises can illustrate this because as we grow older we are asked whether the I has merged into its functions and what self or identity remains if the functions are discontinued and the trees in which we hide are burned down.

Only when the human self-hood or individuality before God (Kierkegaard) that cannot be represented becomes plain does death become an infliction. This is concealed so long as we do not see ourselves as persons, like the ancient Germans. And the anthropological form of this impersonality that we have tried to pinpoint here is the division of humanity into an individual part and a supraindividual or impersonal part which is imperishable and in which individuality is dissolved.

3. Hegel's Understanding of Death

If it is natural to speak next about Hegel's distinction between the personal and the suprapersonal, I must presuppose some acquaintance with his basic conception. Without it we shall find it hard to understand Marxism, whose understanding of death we shall have to go on to discuss.

Briefly recalling the basic thoughts in Hegel's system, I might mention that the true subject of all that happens in nature and history is for Hegel the (suprapersonal) world spirit. This actualizes itself in the infinite plenitude of forms. Traces of universal reason may be found already in inorganic nature (as the laws of nature show). But *history* is first truly rational. It is not, therefore, an accumulation of blind accidents. Emanations of the world spirit are actualized in it much more directly than in nature. The infinite spirit uses the finite spirit, for example, the human brain, to achieve awareness of itself.

Strictly speaking, then, a person cannot say, "I think," but rather, "The world spirit thinks through me." I am simply its instrument. I place my finite consciousness at its disposal to be the organ of its achievement of consciousness.

This is particularly clear in significant people in world history, in such outstanding characters as great statesmen and revolutionaries. In them one might suppose that, seeming to make history, they are autonomous subjects of their own plans and intentions. But this is not so. They are in a privileged sense instruments of the world spirit that works through them and simply uses them. They work out great ideas for shaping and changing the world without realizing that they themselves are simply part of the concept of the world spirit.

Napoleon had definite ideas for the reshaping of Europe and pandered to his subjective will for power. As he satisfied both, the world spirit used his ingenuity and dynamism to carry through its own program with his help. It used him as a piece in its own game of chess. He did not realize what his function was in the game as a whole. In this context Hegel refers to the cunning of reason, to the supercunning of the world spirit, which allows individuals, especially the great figures of world history, to cherish the illusion that they are pursuing their own goals. They develop their full historical power and passion for the sake of this illusion. They will do so only when they think that they are doing it for themselves. There is no greater passion than that of self-realization. But in fact individuals are only puppets dancing on the strings of the world spirit.

In its conceptual shaping of history the world spirit always has the large-scale and the universal in view. It uses the individual only as a little stone in the total mosaic, as a transitory means that quickly becomes superfluous.

History as the self-realization of the spirit has a place for individuals only as inauthentic agents or interim steps. As particular specimens individuals are subsidiary to the species that represents what is general and is thus closer to the idea. One might almost say that as the species develops generally in the flow of generations it constantly makes individuals transitional, and thus destroys them. The mating of individuals is the first step to their absorption or annihilation. The species maintains itself only by the destruction of individuals who fulfill their destiny in the process of reproduction and hence have no higher destiny than to perish.[43] It may even be said that the original incommensurability of the individual with universality is the original sickness and the native seed of death.[44]

Death, then, does not relate to the sphere of the idea as that which is truly authentic in life, but only to individuality as an inauthentic transitional stage. And even here one cannot say that death is destruction. On the contrary, it is the creative self-liberation of the species, that is, the idea, from individual attachment and self-alienation.

In keeping with this view of death immortality is not the prolongation of the life of the individual nature. Rather, it consists of what is actualized through and in spite of this natural basis, namely, the thought of a self-existent general entity. To this thought belongs as its subject the spirit which breathes into the natural individual, which uses it as a means, and in which the individual transcends itself. In this thought no less takes place than that the absolute spirit thinks itself in the individual spirit. The destiny of death is thus grounded in the ontological presupposition that the idea, the universal, does not exist in an appropriate form during this transitional stage but is subject to alien individuation and must constantly overcome this to actualize itself.

Therefore, the dying of individuals is not a radical death — if one may put it thus — since individuality is not radical or lasting uniqueness but merely a transition. The dying of individuals is the triumph of the species as it escapes the individual bond. It is thus the triumph of the spirit, the true self-actualization of the idea.

Death, then, is not a radical fact and hence is not frightening. For while it means cessation and nonbeing, it does so only in relation to the part of the I that has no real being, only an alien one, even from the very first, so that its being cannot in the strict sense be ended or put to death. This part of the I is individuality. The true part of us, the spirit, cannot be affected by death. On the contrary, it comes to itself through death. Death does not contradict our destiny, but rather makes it possible. It is a meaningful law. As corruptibility, it is what makes immortality possible.

In debate with Hegelian idealism, it is obvious that the real problem of death is simply a modified form of the anthropological problem. The real question is whether we can be split up into peripheral and central zones of the I, that is, into nature and spirit. Can we lose our specific selves, become other than ourselves, raise ourselves up above ourselves (Hegel), and be absorbed by the species? Can we bring it about that the bullet of death hits our individual covering only when we have left it and changed into some other form, so that we can see it hit us from outside without feeling affected by it anymore?

The thought of the eternal presence of the species that allows the individual to perish and sink into the past is perhaps nowhere treated in so profound and visionary a way as in Schopenhauer's treatise *On Death and Its Relation to the Immortality of our Life in Itself*.[45] Everything, he says, lasts only for a moment and hastens toward death. Plants and insects die at the end of the summer, animals and humans after a few years. Death cuts down tirelessly. Yet everything is still there as though this were not so, as though everything were imperishable. Plants bloom, insects fly about, animals and humans are indestructibly young, and we enjoy thousands of cherries every summer. The nations are still there as immortal individuals even though they change their names at times, and their acts and aspirations and sufferings are always the same even if history has other things to tell, for it is a kind of kaleidoscope that produces something new at every turn, though the same thing is always before us.

Inevitably, then, the thought surfaces that the rise and fall of things is not their true essence, which is unaffected by it and is imperishable, so that everything and all things that will to be are there continuously and without end.

At a given point of time all animal species from gnats to elephants are present together. They have renewed themselves several thousand times and are still the same. They know nothing of their predecessors or successors. The species is what lives on, and the individuals are present and cheerful in the sense of its immortality and their identity with it.

The will to live manifests itself in the unending present, for this is the form of the life of the species that never ages but is always young.

For this, death is what sleep is for the individual or winking for the eye, by whose absence the Indians recognized their gods when they came in human form. As the world disappears with the onset of night, but never ceases to exist for a moment, humans and animals seem to disappear with death, but their true being persists indestructibly.

4. The Influence of Hegel's Understanding on Marxism

Marx, as he himself said, put Hegel's philosophy back on its feet. It was standing on its head when it rested on the idea of the world spirit. Marx, with his dialectically materialistic view of history, regarded certain material realities (social, economic, and industrial) as the true determinants of all historical processes. Essential dimensions of the spirit such as art, morality, and religion, though not these alone, are functionally dependent on these basic material factors.[46] Yet in spite of this reversal of Hegel's system, certain structures of the historical process, especially its dialectical nature, remain intact in Marx's antithetical system.

What Marx takes over from Hegel is especially the decided and almost exclusive focus upon the universal or supraindividual element and upon society, and the corresponding lack of interest in individuals.

On this basis we can almost calculate what will be the view of death in this system. And we can guess that it will be much the same as in Hegel. Concentration on the supraindividual aspect will rob the individual event of personal death of any particular significance.

I said that we *can* guess this. But if we go on to check this view, we run into some difficulty. Consulting the pertinent lexicons of Marxist Leninism, I found a lacuna at this point, and I thus asked whether my guess as to the irrelevance of death on the Marxist view was unsubstantiated because of this, or whether the very lacuna substantiated it. Does it not speak volumes that practically nothing is said about it?

Naturally, I did not give up looking. So far as I can tell, there is only one place in which Marx speaks basically about death,[47] namely, in an essay on "National Economy and Philosophy," where he describes death as a harsh victory of the species over the individual. This may seem to contradict the unity of the species, but the individual is only one of the species — and mortal as such.[48]

In death, therefore, individuals merge into the species. They have their true being in this as a supraindividual collective. In death, they achieve their true life. They shuffle off the alien garb of their individuality and surrender that which always involves the hindrance of the special case. As in Hegel, then, the individual is simply transitional.

We thus seem to have once again the division of the I that we constantly find in the non-Christian sphere and that occurs also (with a different thrust but the same structure) in doctrines of immortality.

The supraindividual dimension may at times take a cross materialistic form rather than the much sublimer form of dialectical materialism. Thus Friedrich Engels can relate death to an understanding of *bios* whereby life, even human life, is by nature a matter of constant natural metabolism. Engels can thus say that no physiology is scientific that does not regard death as an essential element of life. As life's negation it is part of life itself, so that to think of life is to think also of its outcome, which is contained like a seed within it, namely, death. Once this is understood, there is no place for any talk about the immortality of the soul. Death is either the dissolution of the organic body, which leaves only its chemical constituents behind, or it leaves behind a life-principle, more or less a soul, which survives all living organisms and not just humans. At any rate, living means dying.[49]

Individuality, then, is not essential. It transforms itself into the sphere of true reality. It either goes back to the material world, to the protein from which it emerged for a brief moment and to which it returns in death, or it changes into the universal life-principle of all organisms in which its transitory individuality is lost.

If to the sublimer view of Marx or the crasser one of Engels we react by saying that human death is again repressed, we can do so only if we first establish the premise that it is primarily the individual that is repressed, that the individual is completely overlooked in the name of society. Only when the real individual in empirical life and individual work and relationships has become a member of the species, only when we do not separate ourselves from our true social force, is human emancipation achieved.[50]

Hence we come to ourselves and find our identity when already in this life (and not just in death) we accomplish the transformation into the species and do not hold aloof as individuals. This is most plainly elucidated in Marx's doctrine of the social organs that ought to develop in us and lead to a new spontaneity of collective (and not just individual) reactions.[51]

The question arises here whether this anthropological construction will not founder simply because reality and its enclosed truth will break through such dictatorial schemes, or, more simply, because life will maintain itself against such constructions and shatter the ideological Procrustes' bed.

For in spite of every denial, individuals finally remain such, their world is extinguished in death, and they cannot evade Rilke's question of the big or little death, whether it be put naively or more reflectively. It may well be, L. Kolakovski thinks, that the question of the meaning of life, and therefore of death too, is a luxury of nature. But once it arises we cannot suppress it again.[52] Hence human death can no longer be reduced to a mere mortality of the species. It shatters our universal personal nature and our individual personality.[53] It dissolves the personal bonds of love and friendship. It snuffs out that which constitutes individuality. It separates life's meaning from membership in society and the functional goals this sets for individuals. These qualities cannot survive those who have them, no matter how painfully achieved. In this regard Adam Schaff says that each individual is a specific microcosm whose end is the end of a particular world.[54]

Marxism can hardly feel any constraint to consider the idea that individuality is a microcosmic world, or the way in which individuality reflects the world. Reflecting means nothing to it; it is irrelevant to its thinking. For Marxism, everything depends on individuals being at the disposal of the whole, of serving it as instruments, of being integrated into it in virtue of their social organs. Only in this way can it change the world. And this, according to the famous slogan of the Communist Manifesto, is the goal of Marxist philosophy.[55]

Precisely for this reason we have to realize how remarkably helpless — and therefore evasive — Marxist doctrine is when it has to confront the phenomenon of death. Death as a passive event is the end of all activity and therefore of the relation to the world which alone for this philosophy can have thematic rank. Hence death cannot be brought under intellectual control except as the great abstraction that denies all specificity to perishing individuality and represents the triumph of the species over the individual.

K. Mehnert perhaps has this in view when he suggests in *Der*

Sowjetmensch[56] that this ideology can offer no help when faced with the ineluctability of death. The death of individuals does not fit into a forced optimistic view of the world. As little is said about it as possible. (There is thus little prospect, as I said at the outset, of finding explicit statements about death in official Soviet literature.) At most, Mehnert thinks, the death of heroes may be discussed because here the form of death represents a kind of action — and also, we might add, actively effects the triumph of the species or the ideological system that represents it.

Typical of the need to avoid death are the statements of a meeting of Soviet and Italian poets (according to the account given by H. F. Steiner).[57] Here the following dialogue could take place. Italian: Soviet literature in its optimism overlooks the problem of death. Answer: Yes, we do not think about death very much — and this is a philosophical position. (The meaning is that philosophy can only use the argument that death is not a valid subject for reflection and therefore has to be passed over.) We have learned to ignore death completely because we think about life. In the name of the active we dismiss the passive from our consciousness.

On the margins of the Marxist scene, among critics or dissidents, one sometimes finds uneasiness about this process of repression. The indelible character of individuality is asserted here, and this raises again the problem of death, which is eliminated with the denial of individuality. A typical example of the way in which the problem can emerge again may be seen in L. Kolakovski and his lifelong struggle with Marxism.

In his work *Der Mensch ohne Alternative. Von der Möglichkeit und Unmöglichkeit, ein Marxist zu sein* (1960) there may be seen a gaping conflict that involves unreconciled and irreconcilable contradictions for his understanding of death. What we seem to have is a gradual realization of the antinomies that usually arise between ideological constructions and the elemental power of life to assert itself.

Kolakovski differentiates first between fear of "concrete" death and anxiety in face of "abstract" death. The former is in the full sense natural. It is a system of instinctive orientation, found also in the animal world, which serves to protect against danger.[58] It is not peculiar to the human race. What is peculiar to the human race is anxiety in face of abstract death. For this is a revolt against the unavoidable that is unknown elsewhere in nature. When he

93

asks how this revolt can come about, Kolakovski hits only on the fact of individuality. Anxiety in face of abstract death is our fear as individuals of losing awareness of ourselves. This awareness — he appeals to Bergson here — is identical with the sum of recollections of all previous experiences as these are preserved in the memory as a conscious past. Thus, fear of death is fear of the loss of the past. More precisely, it is fear of losing continuity with all one's previous life, of being completely destroyed. What is at issue is spiritual death, the loss of the sense of personality.[59]

Here fear of unavoidable death is openly linked with the loss of individual personality and therefore with something that is a negligible quantity in Marxist doctrine. But hardly has Kolakovski granted this quantity a place in his thinking, and impressively portrayed it for a moment, than he tries to dismiss again this guest that has made so forceful an entry. Anxiety in face of abstract death, he thinks, has its root in a sense of meaninglessness.[60] But the sense of meaning or meaninglessness is not connected with the relation of individuality to its final ground of being — as in religious or metaphysical anthropology — but to a broken relation between individuals and the world of society around them. The experience of meaninglessness that triggers this anxiety in face of abstract death (but is not triggered by it) is "a product of the alienation of the individual from the historical reality of humanity, the consequence of discomfort with the external world." Hence the feeling of meaninglessness is the individual's sense of alienation from external or social existence. By not paying heed to their continuity with society individuals are forced to seek the meaning of life in their constricted individual existence and to regard themselves, we might add, as self-enclosed monads or entelechies. But awareness of death makes this retreat into I-immanence impossible, for an infinite continuation of self-restricted and self-oriented individual consciousness cannot confer any sense of meaning. Such an experience is possible for mortal beings only when they are in active coexistence with the world that really determines this consciousness independently of the will of individuals.

In this second train of thought Kolakovski erases the picture of individuality and falls back into a Marxist anthropology in which individuals have meaning in life and death only as they are integrated into an ideologically conceived nexus of history and society, and actively cooperate in the humanizing of this nexus. According to Kolakovski, one can hardly imagine a more comprehensive or important task than that of creating conditions for a social life that offers other people real meaning in life free from all self-deception. An understanding of death according to which death results in the triumph of the species over the individual again threatens to establish itself here.

Nevertheless, in Kolakovski's intellectual pilgrimage there is still an unresolved conflict between the individual and the supraindividual determination of the meaning of human death. In a later interview with François Bondy,[61] Kolakovski says that he could not be content with the Marxist principle that death is the triumph of the species over the individual; he detected in it the frivolous idea that there really is no death. Hence he found himself thrown back again upon the hard fact of the individual existence which includes youth, maturity, and age, the sexes, and the phenomena of death and love. These phenomena are given factors that influence history but cannot be derived from it. They thus belong to the specificity of nondeducible individuality.

In an even later interview[62] Kolakovski further criticizes his Marxist period. He finds in the Marxist thesis that human self-realization can come through the shaping of historical structures, that the victory of the species over the individual is in some sense justified thereby, and that this gives meaning to life and death, a Promethean hybris that rejects all the limits that are set to human perfectibility. Everything is humanly made, everything develops historically, nothing is already given. This illusion is grounded in a lack of awareness of original sin, of the human liability that radically calls in question human perfectibility. On subsequent reflection, then, he finds particularly dangerous in Marxism the very thing that he previously found particularly attractive. Marxism is a program of self-redemption that results inevitably in the radical destruction of meaning in either life or death. At this point Christianity has preserved something decisive with its contradiction of all self-redemption (though new powers of self-destruction are at work within it with the deemphasizing of evil).

Perhaps in conclusion, following up these deliberations, we might observe that Marxist philosophy with its absorbing of the individual in the species, offers no comfort to the dying. In illustration I might offer a personal experience, though not with an "edifying" purpose. I was visiting a dying man who had spent his last years in an intensive love-hate dialogue with Marxist thinking. One day shortly before the end he said to me, "How far behind me all that is now that I myself am going to die. The bridges are down. That voice no longer reaches me."

C. OUR DIVISION INTO PERSONALITY AND THE REFLECTION OF COSMIC LIFE (GOETHE'S *FAUST*)

1. Presuppositions: Activity and Journeying as the Fulfillment of Life

Whereas the division of the I is easy to see in Plato, Hegel, and Marx — to cite only a few of the models offered — we have to look more closely to find it in Goethe. The particular difficulty here is that for Goethe the concept of activity, the active life, stands at the center. To be active is our first determination, we are told in *Wilhelm Meisters Lehrjahre*. There is less interest, then, in a core of the I that survives activity, that ceases to press on. Such interest can be only speculative. Hence it is no longer active but sterile. This is clear in Goethe, especially in the concept of the entelechy — in the context of which the problem of immortality arises. Here, too, the scope of every thought is the activity in which life comes to expression from within its organizing center, in which it streams out and manifests itself. For this reason life should not be wasted in idle, inactive speculation about a future life — unless the state after death, the return to the aether, be regarded as one of continued activity on the part of our entelechy.[63] Any other preoccupation with ideas of immortality is only for the upper classes and women who have nothing to do.[64]

To turn to Goethe's thinking, we shall first analyze the death of Faust, where through direct contact with the active life there is the least ballast of speculation and pure proclamation. By way of interpretation we shall use Goethe's concept of the entelechy and the monad.

In no form of being does the seeking Faust find the actualization of the unconditioned or the absolute that he wants: neither in theology, medicine, any other science, or anything else. No specific form offers the final thing that holds the world inwardly together. Faust is no specialist who regards his own restricted field as the totality. The book of magic shows him symbolically that everything is woven into a whole, that one thing works and lives in the other, that heavenly forces mount and fall, and golden buckets are extended. But this is only a spectacle and he grows tired of it. He finds the ultimate thing that gives meaning only as he hurries from form to form, none of which in isolation, not pointing to the fullness of all the others, can give any lasting satisfaction or guarantee eternity. Moving on, he finds torment and happiness but is never content. The peace of satisfaction does not lie in reaching a goal and therewith in a state but in the act of seeking, in dynamic movement toward a goal.

Guilt necessarily arises on this journey when one of the infinitely many forms that Faust has to rush up against and experience and leave again (finding the center of life in each) is a unique living person, that is, when Gretchen crosses his path.

Here he has to leave again a living person that believes in him, because even this person is not the bearer and incarnation of the underlying meaning of life, so that he has to resolve to journey on. But he must go also because this person is only an example of the eternal feminine that attracts him as an idea, not in virtue of its individual manifestation in Gretchen. Hence even here his path must lead on from form to form on an infinite road. Eros cannot come to fulfillment in a single encounter or partner. On the way to self-fulfillment, to the development of his own entelechy, human relationships can be only transitional stages and can have only instrumental significance (like the studies that he had to pursue). The path is the goal, and all that might go with him on it can serve only as means and hence can accompany him only for a limited period.

More drastically than in Goethe, though much less notoriously, the same sublime egoism that uses the other as the means to an end may be seen in Wilhelm von Humboldt. Here everything from one's profession to all communication with others has the significance only of an instrument of self-realization. Nothing is done for the sake of the outside work, but everything for the sake of the inner energy.[65] We should live to ourselves, impertinent though others may find this. Let them all begin to live to themselves, too![66] For Humboldt, then, even one's partner in life — the Gretchen problem — has no independent significance but simply serves to release one's own entelechy. Love is not a matter of making happy.

Love means that the wife is totally absorbed in her husband, having no wishes or thoughts but what he demands, no experience except in subjection to him, leaving him completely free and self-active, and being regarded by him simply as a part of himself that is appointed to live for him and in him.[67] The point is that Faust does not find the meaning of life, the unveiling of that innermost bond, in a single figure, whether in a philosophical truth that gives him peace or in any other finite entity. Individual figures are simply similitudes of the totality that can reveal the bond only in an infinite number of encounters.[68]

If the meaning of the whole cannot be reached by making an individual figure absolute, this is not to discredit the present order. Faust does not live in a sphere beyond this life, dedivinizing life itself and making it only a dusty march to a goal that lies beyond it. Even the aging Faust, who has desired and achieved and wanted, who has stormed through the first stretch of his life, and who now closes it with the wise circumspection of old age, does not accept any emergency exit to the next world or any disparagement of the present life. We are not to look in that direction. It is folly to do so. It simply thickens the clouds around us.

With all the ardor of his early day, which once made heaven-storming demands on life but now draws experienced conclusions from it, he confesses the torment and happiness of moving on, of moving on as an act and not as the reaching of a goal. He is totally committed to this life in which he can press on and which involves the many figures by which his way of conflict leads.

But with this immanent teleology of life, which corresponds wholly to the macrocosmic law that is Goethe's entelechy for the microcosm, the question of death arises.

2. Death as the End of the Journey and Its Overcoming in the Mirroring of Life

Self-resting finitude points to the disclosure of meaning within itself. It does so in a centripetal direction as an organism that organizes itself from its own center. Death, one might suspect, brings about a crisis for this centripetal direction and meaning by putting an end at least to individual participation in meaningful life. It thus seems to remind us that the phenomenon of life is not merely determined by the timelessness of the eternally centripetal movement, but is also related to a specific stretch of time that will come to an end. Faust's earthly day has this dimension. It comes to an end. It is subject to death.

What does death look like when it means the cessation of a journeying that would like to be eternal as such, a constant aspiring, but is no longer available to us when its hour has struck? Has Faust a place to which he can then go and which will give him more life? No, we are not to look in that direction. Time is master, the old man lies in the sand, the clock stops. It is as silent as midnight. The finger falls. This is how Mephistopheles sees the break that is caused by death.

What sense does it make, however, if suddenly in the midst of the circular movement the linear stretch of time reaches its end? The finger of the clock moves around its face in a circle. This circular movement is potentially infinite. But the clock itself is on a linear stretch of time. Its movement will come to an end. For it, too, there is the immobility of midnight.

But does it not mean that Faust's wandering and seeking are doomed if this final point is not taken into account (whether as a disruption, an alien body, or an end), if it is not at least admitted to discussion? Has not Faust ignored the request of the psalmist that God will teach him to remember that life has an end (the request so familiar to us from Brahms' *Requiem*)? Without this awareness is not Faust on a journey to nowhere? Is he not a mere wanderer who has no goal and will never reach one, like someone who is seeking God without really wanting to find him, finding satisfaction in the act of seeking and perhaps toying with the idea of himself as a seeker? Is he not less of a wanderer than an adventurer roaming about without any commitments?

At any rate, Faust is in fact visited by the thought that death will end things and that the *mene tekel* of a stretch of time that leads to death will appear on the final wall of life. But this *mene tekel* does not have the light of a truth that necessarily blinds and overpowers him. It has instead a pallid and ghostly appearance and its sound is that of an unreal, nightmarish whisper. For all the arguments are put on the lips of four spectral old women: Want, Care, Guilt, and Need — dreamlike figures in which the dark forces entangle him. Or they are put on the lips of Mephistopheles, who is at least a reality, though at the end his hold on Faust is broken. Death as the end is the thesis of the shades and the message of the devil. This, they say, is where it all leads.

Recollection of the end, of the stretch of time that comes to a brutal close, may thus be heard in the circular movement of this self-resting life. The clouds gather, the stars disappear, and brother death comes from afar. But this vision fades before the triumph of the dying Faust. He can tell this last moment to tarry because it is so beautiful. For him the end-point becomes an eternal present, a present in which the whole round of the way on which he has battled, and of all future ways, rests in the depths of a mirror: Everything real is purified, dissolving in symbols.[69] This end-point, this hour of death, is also for Faust the moment when, as a reflection of life and action, the dam that he has built against the threatening sea comes before him, the dam that will force the dwellers on the coast daily to achieve life and freedom in their conflict with the hostile element, the dam that is also the renewed realization of the battling way of life that Faust must now leave. In relation to this course that he has finished he can thus sing in triumph that the trace of his earthly days will never perish throughout the aeons.

Why will it not? Why can he triumph in this way over death? Faust is not saying that he himself will live on after death, but only that this trace will. How?

I have already indicated the decisive point when I referred to the dam and the new land that Faust's genius won from the sea. Faust lives on, in a special way that has still to be described more fully, in his work. He is not immortal in himself, but rather in his deeds that bear witness to him. *He* does not live on, but an *It* that owes its existence to him does.

But this alone is not enough to explain Faust's triumph over death. It has a deeper meaning. One might bring against the work that praises him the same objection that it, too, has a stretch of time and will finally reach a definitive end-point. For it, too, time is master. The day will come when holy Ilion falls. The dam — at least in the form in which it came from Faust's hands — will perish, perhaps soon, and have to be rebuilt.

This brings us closer to the decisive element in Faust's idea of immortality. The very fact that the dam is destructible and the protected land will have to be won back again is precisely what insures Faust of immortality. For the dam becomes a symbol of corruptible life that has to be constantly won back in conflict. Corruptibility and immortality are paradoxically related as the constitutive beats of life's rhythm. Thus the dynamic act of acquiring the land — not the little plot of land itself as the result of the act — is the true representation of immortality. For this reason the winning of the land, as a static result, is no more an end in itself than philosophy or Gretchen. The act of winning it is the true goal. Only those deserve freedom and life who have to win them daily.

At this point in our analysis it is plain how Faust masters death. The trace of him cannot perish for two reasons. First, his life as battling, seeking, and wandering is a likeness of life itself as it goes on continually. Second, his work as something that has to be constantly achieved afresh is also a reflection of life and may not be regarded as a sediment that can be separated and isolated from his personality. It is simply a new mirroring of his personality as this was simply a mirroring of life. All these things are just variations on the same basic phenomenon in which they exist, of which they are a likeness, and in which the individual manifestation is both dissolved and elevated (Hegel's *"aufgehoben"*). Wherever this phenomenon seeks manifestation, wherever life is lived as battle, search, constant aspiration, and action, Faust the eternal wanderer will live and be reincarnated in it. Life itself is the immortal monument to this life of Faust that was lived as a paradigm and reflection of all life. In all life he will live on and retain his life. He will be "aufgehoben" in the many senses of the term.

And if the blessed spirits finally carry away the immortal part of Faust, this does not mean that the gate is opened to some transcendence (there is no such thing for Goethe), but that a symbolical gesture is made by which the validity of Faust's life experiences its being "aufgehoben," its transcendent confirmation.

It is perhaps an impressive indication of this immanent conclusion of the Faust drama that while later editions speak of the angels bearing off the immortal part of Faust, the original reference was to his entelechy being borne away. But his entelechy[70] is simply the immanent teleology of life itself, which has the immortality of the organism that lives by its immanence and perpetually reproduces itself. The entelechy of Faust is simply a microcosmic reflection of macrocosmic life, not in the sense of timeless parallelism, but in that of a magically real participation, as the *Orphische Urworte* show when they relate the concluded teleology of the individual life, which cannot run away, to the macrocosmic regularity of the courses of the stars and the planets. As we were when we came into the world, we shall continue to be according to the law of our beginning. We cannot run away from ourselves, and no time or force can chip away the living, self-developing form. We are integrated into the universe with the sun and moon and stars. We mirror the world at large and symbolize its law.

The mythical confirmation by the choir of angels represents, then, the inner meaning of the forgiveness sought and not the pardoning reception of Faust into a hereafter that would derive from dualism and contain only an antithetical eschatological "good." As the angels in the upper atmosphere confess that this noble member of the spirit-world is saved from evil, in context this can mean only that evil could not hold Faust, that Mephistopheles had only a teleological meaning in his life, that he was being simply an instrument of the eros that pressed on to fulfillment.[71] The more transcendent the play sounds at the end in virtue of the scenery and the transfigured forms, the more this-sided it really is, and the more striking is its confession of the inner teleology of the life that rounds itself out and repeats itself in ever new circles. According to the song of the "holy boys," the final transformation granted to Faust is simply a liberation from the state of pupation. It is a last development of the entelechy that shows him to be "great and beautiful with holy life."

3. The Manifestation of the Law of Division

Faust's immortality, then, is that he lives on in the universal life whose likeness he is in person and work. Only for this reason is death the supreme moment in which the meaning of his life is compressed, being both fulfillment and transition. Faust's outward husk falls away, but in this he was only in transition, just as one generation is only a transition in the endless chain of generations that lives by it and by its individual members.

Here again we see the device of the division of the I upon which everything depends. There is an inauthentic part of the I that is at issue when we think of Faust the individual, and another part that is at issue when we think of his immortal part, his entelechy, that is, when Faust comes into view as a representative of life itself. Only because individuality is simply a symbolical husk for Faust is his immortality possible. In his particularity, the isolation of his I, he is not important enough for his dissolution to mean anything.

All that matters is his representing of the event of life. For Faust the cyclical time of eternal recurrence rules, the time of life that develops in dying and becoming and that does not know death in any definitive sense.

Taken seriously, however, human personhood does know this death; its time is the oriented and limited span that is marked by the boundary stones of guilt. One cannot go back along this span to wipe out the guilt, for once it is lived life cannot be repeated and the past stands perpetually before God's eyes as an eternal present.

For Faust, then, there is no eternity in which God can investigate this once-for-all Faust with the once-for-all liabilities of the span that he has lived through and cannot repeat. This once-for-all Faust does not exist; nor is there any once-for-all guilt that is fixed forever. His guilt is a beat in the rhythm of life that he represents. It belongs ontologically, not to Faust, but to this rhythm. There is no eternity against whose shore the span of time of the once-for-all Faust will break. Eternity is simply the fluctuating time in which there is infinite striving. Hence the forgiveness of eternity is not the gracious Nevertheless of God to our guilt-laden span. It lies in the atoning achievement that is the confirmation of the infinite striving, as the chorus of penitents puts it.

At this point, in spite of the biblical imagery, there is an obvious difference from what the Bible calls eternity. Eternity in the Bible does not mean continuation; it means conclusion (the conclusion of our span), and this eternity comes *to* us. It comes upon us as the judgment in which God finds the self, for he has called us by name and in eternity he can no longer lose us nor can we lose or hide ourselves.

From this standpoint Faust is the representative of a monstrous concealment. He hides his self by dissolving it in the rhythm of life, by destroying in a cycle the dangerous eternity that comes to him and engulfs him. Eternity becomes the immanent infinitude[72] of the periphery — the eternal returning of life to itself in dying and becoming, in enjoying and languishing with desire, in pressing on to the fields of higher surmise and being bound to the wasteland of earth, in being in league with Mephistopheles but maturing even thereby. Faust wins immortality only as his self is borne away or, in other words, transformed into a microcosmic reflection of the law of life, so that death leads to unity with the reality that has previously been reflected.

Faust becomes immortal by ceasing to be personal. His authenticity does not really lie in his personhood — whose dying does not signify any decisive break — but in his participation in the macrocosmic mystery of the law of life as a struggle, which his life, his individual entelechy, had reflected.

The division of the I that is manifested here is carried out so consistently that one can clearly discern the different concepts of time. On the one hand there is the inauthentic and finally invalid concept that relates to the individual span and that is swallowed up by the cyclical view; on the other hand there is the authentic concept that relates to the cycle that as the epitome of Goethe's eternity (infinitude) closes the play.

The division of the I is not so easy to see as in Plato's anthropology where we have a higher and a lower I (soul and body). For Goethe, the individual is an indivisible whole, an entelechy. The division comes to light only when one sees that this total being is seen from two standpoints, first as an individual point of transition with a destructible and inauthentic uniqueness, and then as a bearer of the macrocosmic law of life — but always as the same individual. Similarly, death and immortality are different standpoints from which this individual is considered.

4. Mephistopheles' Knowledge of Death

In Goethe only the devil rather dreadfully grasps the thought that Faust is mortal and will perish. Here as elsewhere in the relation between Faust and Mephistopheles the same reality is reflected in both; but the mirror is different, the one being convex, the other concave. Thus we find in Mephistopheles the same two concepts of time — that of the cycle and that of the limited span — but they are given a different ranking and significance.

First, Faust's death is for Mephistopheles an unconditional end. It terminates an oriented and irreversible stretch of life. Time is master. Yet the devil, too, raises the question, or a caricature of the question, whether this end might not be merged into an ongoing law of life that Faust's existence has microcosmically embodied. Mephistopheles is capable of this thought. But for him such a merging is not the way to immortality. It is a cynical parody of immortality, a plunge into eternal emptiness, into the eternal spinning of nothingness.

For what meaning can eternal striving have — this is the tenor of the devil's question — if it remains a mere act, if the goals reached can be no more than transitions to new phases of the struggle? The fight as an end in itself is meaningless; it is a cycle of eternal futility. He thus taunts the dying Faust with the thought that he has struggled and achieved in vain. All is over and is as good as though it had never been. Cyclical time that moves in a circle is not eternity, but rather, is nothingness. The supposed journey is simply a trip on a merry-go-round. Something lasting arises only if something eternal is achieved within the span of time. But the finger falls and it is all over.

This is the other side of human reality, the Mephistophelian side, which accompanies Faust on his way to the very end. Mephistopheles is the great question-mark that Goethe puts on the margin of his view of life and to which he provides no answer. We can and must see human reality in the forms either of death as an end or of the deep, deep eternity that overcomes death, taking either the view of Faust or that of Mephistopheles.

Only after the conclusion, after the fall of the finger in the death scene, does the liberation from Mephistopheles begin and the redeeming song of the heavenly choirs strike up in praise of Faust's fulfillment.

This is Goethe's own position. It transcends the dualism that cannot be resolved here below. It has the form of a *deus ex machina*, which poets invoke in order to venture a decision that existence this side of death does not provide, at least on the basis of any knowledge that we can have. This is why Mephistopheles is a constant temptation for Faust. Even for those who hear the final elucidation, the question arises of who has the profounder sense of eternity: Faust, who thinks he sees it in the cyclical immortality of the suprapersonal, or Mephistopheles, who at least recognizes the shadow of eternity when he sees the finger fall and confronts the nothingness of the finite endlessly returning to itself. (Being the devil, he cannot see the reason why it does so, and therefore even here — at the moment of his supreme grasp of truth — he is still necessarily the spirit of negation.)

In his dreadful experience, then, there may be seen a spark of the biblical view of eternity. For in this view, eternity, as I have already said, is not endless continuation but something that comes to us with the end of time. It means judgment. It is judgment on time, which pitilessly and irreversibly comes to an end even as macrocosmic time, even as the container of suprapersonal powers to which I think I may go when I die. For even the sun and moon will cease to shine, and the stars will fall from heaven, and the end of the world will be its tomb in which it will come to an end as the world (Matt. 24).

The only light that shines here is that of the resurrection, the light from beyond the tomb, the light of the other side of that end. The devil Mephistopheles knows about this break in human existence — and trembles (cf. Jas. 2:19).

EXCURSUS: GOETHE'S CONCEPT OF ENTELECHY

To fill out Goethe's idea of immortality, a brief survey of his teaching on entelechy is needed. I have already given some hint of this when mentioning that in the final scene his immortal part was originally called his entelechy. To be sure, we are to treat with great caution the few references to the linking of entelechy and immortality. What we have here is not a dogma of immortality but a series of incidental tentative and speculative observations. Furthermore, they are restricted almost exclusively to the argumentative form of the "negative way," as when Goethe said to Chancellor von Müller on October 19, 1823 that it is impossible for a thinking being to conceive of a nonbeing or cessation of thought and life. But in the very same statement he warns that we must not try to prove this certainty dogmatically or to dress it out in Philistine fashion. Similarly, in his conversations with Eckermann he made the cynical remark already quoted that preoccupation with ideas of immortality is for the upper classes and women who have nothing else to do, whereas others have their hands full dealing with the affairs of this life.

What is the link between Goethe's cautious idea of immortality and his concept of entelechy? First (on the basis of his classical talk with Falk on January 25, the day of Wieland's funeral), a hierarchy of the constituent parts of the personality is assumed, the innermost of which contains the monadic core of the I and is thus analogous to Goethe's "basic phenomenon." This core of the I has the character of teleological completeness like Aristotle's entelechy, and is the indestructible part of the I. The following points about this immortal monad are worth noting with reference to the anthropology developed in *Faust*.

1. The immortal monad forms a part of the I that Goethe comes up against in virtue of the division of the I that we have found underlying all doctrines of immortality: the division into a personal core, the entelechy, which is immortal, and inessential peripheral parts, which perish.

This is plain when in relation to Wieland's death Goethe expressly asks: "How much or how little of this personality deserves to live on is a question and a point that we must leave to God."[73] Within the personality there are steps of different value.

2. The immortal part of the I, the monad or entelechy, is in its teleological structure a microcosmic copy of the totality of life. This reminds us of the way in which Faust's life is shown to reflect the basic laws of struggle in suprapersonal life as a whole. The entelechy is the cosmic part of the I whose immortality is identical with that of the constant, self-renewing cosmos. In this sense Goethe says in the same conversation that the becoming of creation is entrusted to the monads. Bidden or unbidden, they come on every path, from every hill, from every sea, from every star; who can stop them? The same analogy between entelechy and cosmos may be found in Wilhelm Meister when under the starry heaven Wilhelm asks what his attitude to infinity must be when he gathers together in his innermost depths all the spiritual forces that are drawn from many sides. Is he not at the heart of this eternal order inasmuch as something that is constantly moved comes forth in him to circle around a pure center?[74]

It is along the lines of this eternal participation in the comos, this eternal self-identity, that we are to understand the thought of eternal recurrence with which Goethe closes the conversation with Falk, saying that he has confidence he has been here a thousand times before, and will be here a thousand times again, as Falk now sees him. This idea occurs earlier in a note on the Italian journey[75] and lies behind the statement to Eckermann[76] that every entelechy is a part of eternity and the few years of its association with the earthly body do not age it.

What dies, then, is only the individual container of the cosmic content, the entelechy. This is eternal even though it is engaged in eternal change. Sometimes this thought can be expressed in a way that echoes the Platonic conception, as in the *Bekenntnisse einer schönen Seele*:[77] "The body is torn off like a garment, but I, the well-known I, I am."

3. It will be apparent already that what we have here is not personal survival or the preservation of the person in its individual, contingent uniqueness.[78]

This impersonality follows from what has been said and also from the pictures of change that Goethe occasionally draws, as when he seriously considers the possibility that after many millennia he might meet this Wieland as a star of the first magnitude and see how he enlivens and cheers with his kindly light everything that comes near him.[79] Similar ideas, based on Leibniz and Spinoza, may be found in Lessing.[80] The statement also expresses the character of the entelechy as our cosmic constituent.

At any rate, one sees no connection between immortality and the concept of the moral person. Goethe's "activity," which can only be thought of as unlimited and stretching beyond death,[81] and is thus an essential root of his concept of immortality, is not activity in the sense of moral effort, or is so at most only inasmuch as the moral can be one of the possible forms of this activity. The activity itself is metaethical. It is a primal expression of life itself, which Goethe describes most pregnantly as the rotating of the monad around itself without either pause or rest.[82]

Along the same lines the love that is granted to Faust from above, and that gives him a share in perfection, is a part of the teleological eros of the entelechy that Eryximachos, the physician in Plato's *Symposium*, describes as the basic force in the cosmos that inwardly holds the world together (in Goethe's sense).

In this light the impersonality of continued existence (from the biblical standpoint) is plain, for this existence does not have the particularity and inexchangeability, the self-identity, which is present in the judgment of God as this applies to "me," isolating me from everybody and everything on whom or on which I might lay my guilt and with whom or with which I might confuse myself, but which is present, too, under the grace of God as this also applies to "me" and gives me a name by which it calls me. The lofty power of the soul in Goethe's sense, the entelechy, is a suprapersonal part of the cosmos that changes its forms, being carried off by the angels, as in Faust's case, to receive a new form in which to reflect the mystery of struggling, striving, and rotating life in new ways that are always the same.

Our true authenticity here is not the self in its contingent particularity, but is the transparence of the self for struggling life, just as the true authenticity of the plant is its transparence for the primal plant.[83]

Chapter 4

THE BIBLICAL UNDERSTANDING OF DEATH

A. THE PERSONAL CHARACTER OF HUMAN DYING

Our deliberations thus far have finally circled in different ways around a single problem, namely, how human dying differs from the purely animal or biological cessation of life. That which in human dying goes beyond the dimension of nature or *bios* is that which transcends this dimension in every sphere of human existence. We have described this transcendent factor as personality, the element in existence in virtue of which we do not merely confront the processes of nature as objects but have to grasp them as subjects and actualize them in our own necessary being, no matter how this may be understood.

In this way we have prepared the ground in general anthropology for the biblical — and especially the NT — understanding of human death to the degree that this, as we shall see, moves very definitely in the dimension of the personal. In anticipation of what I shall have to say about the biblical view, I may mention already two paradigms in which the personal character of human death finds illustration.

First, the Pauline statement that death is the wages of sin (Rom. 6:23) and that judgment is executed in it points to a factor that transcends natural processes at the ending of human life, that involves guilt and punishment — no matter how we interpret it — and therefore an I that is taken personally.

Second, the OT already introduces the personal nature of death at least as a problem when it sees death not merely as the end of the functions of life but also (even in the earlier strata) as something that comes between God and us. Thus Psalm 90 speaks about the wrath of God under which our days vanish: "For we are consumed by thy anger; by thy wrath we are overwhelmed" (90:7). Death sets the seal on our separation from God in life; it confirms it.

This is radicalized by the ancient idea of sheol because the realm of the dead means separation not merely from life but from God: "In death there is no remembrance of thee" (Ps. 6:5); "I am . . . like one forsaken among the dead . . . like those whom thou dost remember no more, for they are cut off from thy hand" (Ps. 88:5). To be cut off from the remembrance of God is a definitive handing over to the nothingness to which I already give myself in life when I do not remember God.

As human life is thus understood not just as *bios* but as life with God — so that there is a dying away from God — the personal element in the understanding of dying is intimated. We then have variations on this right on into the NT. The first stage of development, one might perhaps say, is that identity is lost in death with the ruling out of life with God. The last stage, disclosed in the new covenant, is that identity is preserved beyond death with the preservation of the name by which I am called in the resurrection life. I remain in the fellowship of those who are raised again.

As we have seen already, the division of the I is not made in Platonic fashion as a division between the corruptible body and the incorruptible soul. Paul uses these terms, but unlike Plato does not relate them to divisions of the I in such a way that the flesh (*sarx*) is an inferior part and the soul (*psyche*) is a superior part. The terms "flesh," "body," and "soul" all denote the whole person, but from different angles.[1] In the NT as distinct from Plato, soul does not denote the immortal side of the I but is simply used for the living quality of the person in the physical sense.

Nevertheless — in spite of the threat of possible Platonic misunderstanding — the soul can also be understood as more than this. It can stand for that in us which death cannot seize, or which can be put in a position where death cannot seize it. Thus Luther can speak of the incorruptible soul.[2] The distinction from Plato is that "soul" can be used in this sense — and is theologically nonnegotiable — even when one has to speak of bodily death and can say that the history that God has begun with us does not break off in death. In this sense "soul" is not the term for a substance that has a constitutive quality of immortality; it describes our partnership in the history with God. It is used for the I in its fellowship with the Thou of God and is thus relatively defined. What survives death is not some substantial part of us, but rather, God's faithfulness in his partnership with us. When soul is understood in this way we are on a radically different level from that of Plato.[3]

B. DEATH AND THE OVERCOMING OF DEATH IN THE UNDERSTANDING OF THE OLD TESTAMENT[4]

Those who in the old, pre-Christian covenant live out their lives and the number of their days, die old and full of years. Thus Abraham is said to die "in a good old age, an old man and full of years" (Gen. 25:8). Isaac, David, and Job die similarly.[5] Death here seems to be less a judgment and more a gift and fulfillment.[6] It is a natural law of life that does not yet evoke questions and problems. That we have to end our days, or may do so, is taken to be a natural order in the same sense as sexual union. Both can even be described by the same phrase as going the way of all the earth.[7]

Sociological reasons have been found for the fact that death raises no problems at this early stage in Israel's history. It is suggested that nomadic peoples did not develop any religious relation to death because they were always at some distance from their burial grounds and thus had no symbols by which to keep death in mind.[8] Yet we do find elaborate ceremonial mourning.[9] It is more likely, then, that death is not felt to be a problem but, along with birth, is seen as a law of life, because prior to the monarchy the life of individuals had not been emancipated from that of the nation. Before a sense of individuality awakened, the goad was lacking that would make the end of the person a terrible question and enigma. We have here a kind of security in the thought of the tribe, a kind of mnemosynic immortality. When the woman of Tekoah refuses to hand over to the clan her son, who has murdered his brother, her argument is typical; she answers those who want him handed over: "So they would destroy the heir also and quench the coal that is left, and leave my husband neither name nor remnant upon the face of the earth."[10]

Dying becomes a real problem only later, especially in the Wisdom writings, which deal more with the questions of individual life and thus presuppose a certain emancipation of the individual. Death here sets an imperious term to the relationships of life that

God himself has established.[11] In Job it is called "the king of terrors" (18:14). These terrors may be reserved for old age, as when Jacob fears that his gray hairs will be brought down with sorrow to sheol (Gen. 42:38). Here, then, there can be the resignation that compares dying to water that is spilled out on the earth and cannot be gathered again (2 Sam. 14:14; Job 14:10ff.). Though this image is taken from nature, it points to something that goes beyond nature and constitutes the true terror for the awakened individual, namely, that a unique life cannot be brought back.[12]

The domain of death,[13] however, is not restricted to life's end; it penetrates deeply into life itself. Sickness, weakness, imprisonment, oppression by enemies — all these are an anticipation of death, a state of relative death. Many statements in the Psalms, von Rad thinks, are to be construed along these lines when the psalmists say that they have already been in death, in sheol, but Yahweh has brought them out again.

The darkest form of the irreversible ending of life may be found in the idea of sheol, especially in earlier statements that say nothing about Yahweh's power in it. L. Köhler thinks sheol bears only a limited similarity to the Greek Hades, in which the individual is at least retained in shadowy profile and may be recognized. Sheol, in contrast, is a nonland, a sphere that does not exist, and it is to this that the dead come.[14] Here the nonbeing of the dead is not just a substantial cessation of life — though that is naturally included — but it is the breaking off of the relationship to God. For this is what constituted the life of the living; it was a life in relation. This is why "in death there is no remembrance of thee; in sheol who can give thee praise?" (Ps. 6:5; cf. Isa. 28:18f.; Ps. 115:17, etc.).

The most dreadful thing here is not that the dead cease to remember Yahweh, but the very opposite, namely, that God does not remember them when they are thrust into this nonland: "like those whom thou dost remember no more" (Ps. 88:5). Since life in the OT is life for, with, and under God, since it is life in relation, the nothingness of death means a total loss of relation.[15] It is exclusion from the service of God and the history in which God bears witness to himself by his guidance. Those who overlook this total end and trust that things will go on forever are fools in their security. Hence the psalmist prays: "teach us to number our days that we may get a heart of wisdom" (Ps. 90:12; cf. Ps. 39:4–6).

With this understanding of death the OT concept of God is plunged into a theological battle that cannot be left unresolved.

On the one hand it is held that death as the true, the "last" enemy (1 Cor. 15:26), means an absolute break in the assurance of God and closeness to him. On this view we are alone in nature in our very individuality (we might add): "For there is hope for a tree, if it be cut down, that it will sprout again, and that its shoots will not cease ... but man dies, and is laid low; man breathes his last, and where is he?" (Job 14:7– 10).

The extinguishing of human existence in the nonland of death is thus irreversible. The sphere of God's power seems to end at the frontier of sheol. There is no way back into his hand.

On the other hand — and this is what causes the conflict — the OT leaves no room for a dualism that grants autonomous power to death and thus makes it a kind of demonic antithesis to Yahweh.[16] This being so, a conflict seems to arise within God himself. Since, however, God cannot be at odds with himself, the only way out — which Job takes — is that the conflict must be between our idea of God and God as he really is. In fact, Job wins through to the certainty that behind what seems (but only *seems*) to be in God a hostile will, injustice, and the power of consigning to death, there has to stand a different God, the God who forgives sin (7:10f.), the God who cannot turn aside from what he has created (10:8f.), the God who was and is a witness in heaven, an advocate on high, a pledge for those who are scorned (16:19; 17:3); in short, a God to whom Job can turn when his spirit is broken, his days are extinct, and the grave is ready for him (17:1).

Hence Job and the psalmists (e.g., Ps. 36:8– 10; 88:2, 13f.) turn to God as the source of life, to the God who can liberate from the remote prison of sheol and restore lost fellowship with himself. The dominant theme of Job is the question: Who has the last word? The God who withdraws from the nonland of death, or the God whose rule obtains there, too, and of whom the vision in Amos says that "though they dig into sheol, from there shall my hand take them" (9:2)? Which God is the true God, he who in wrath destroys the work of his hands and plunges it into nothingness, or he who overcomes his wrath with the omnipotence of his love? This is the crucial question. It grows out of Job's wrestling with God in prayer.

Thus Job hopes and prays first only that God will keep and

hide him in the realm of the dead, that he will take him into protective custody (Weiser) until his wrath is past, until he remembers him again (14:13), until he comes forth as his advocate (16:18– 17:9). But then Job comes increasingly to the certainty that his redeemer lives and will at the last stand on the earth (19:25). Here we find some first traces of a resurrection hope (cf. Dan. 12:2), though it should not be overlooked that these foreshadowings are qualitatively different from the resurrection faith of the NT with its very different basis. The thisworldliness that reigns in the OT is always very reserved about belief in another world. The thought of an overcoming of death is limited to two certainties.

First, it is limited to the conviction that Yahweh is unique as God and does not share his power dualistically with rival gods or powers, including those of the realm of the dead. But this implies that his kingdom does not end at the gates of death but has power over them. This sway of God does not extend only to those who try to find refuge from his face in sheol (Ps. 139:8; Amos 9:2), but applies to his own people, too, for "Yahweh kills and brings to life; he brings down to sheol and raises up" (1 Sam. 2:6).

Second, if Yahweh is powerful in the realm of the dead and keeps his people in his own hand there, then the certainty arises that the history that God has begun with the human I continues in death, and that the fellowship that he has established is unbreakable — whether it be that the dead are under his protection (or judgment) in sheol, or that God will take them out of sheol as in early intimations of resurrection. The human person is still an I before God whose identity is upheld by fellowship with God.

The decisive break with the older idea of survival in the memory of one's descendants may thus be characterized as follows: Over against the scepticism of wisdom about life and death, and in face of the radical nothingness of the life that is banished to the nonland of sheol, the thought of living on in the memory of later generations could no longer bring any comfort. The awakened sense of individuality could find here only final and irreversible extinction. But continuation of the name as a symbol of the individual person could be thought of only if this name were entrusted to the memory of God. Only then did the prospect of life after death truly open up, for the faithfulness of God could be trusted and there could be confidence that as the only God he was mighty in the realm of the dead, too: "My flesh and my heart may fail, but God is . . . my portion for ever" (Ps. 73:26).

What survives death, then, is not a substantial quality of the soul but rather the gift of fellowship with God. This is what has an indelible or indestructible character. The dialogue that God has begun with us will not be broken off. (We shall continually run up against this theologically basic thought in the NT and later reflection.)

In this sense it is permissible to relate indestructibility to the human person, that is, so long as one clings to the concept that this person is not an entelechy or monad but a "relation." Here again, then, we come up against the idea of alien dignity. We find survival not in what we are, but in God's turning to us.[17] Here is the connection between survival after death and the NT belief in resurrection.

We see, then, that the Bible does not bring a single message concerning death and the overcoming of death. We find instead a chorus of many voices, some of which accept the finality of death with resignation while others sing triumphantly of Yahweh's rule over sheol, and thus give intimations of the belief in resurrection which will be fully presented in the NT.

The comparison with a chorus is not very exact, for the voices are successive rather than simultaneous. We have here a historical process in which the message of the overcoming of death begins to unfold, with the NT as the culmination.

Yet it is essential that we do not describe this unfolding as an "evolution" under the impulsion of immanent forces. We get the point of the process only if we realize that this history is a history with and under God, a dialogical history. Israel learns only gradually what it means to be a partner in covenant with Yahweh, and that what it calls Yahweh's faithfulness to the covenant knows no temporal limits and therefore cannot come to an end when we are called away from this temporal scene.

The growing certainty that death will be overcome is not, then, an autonomous development, but is the increasing discovery of a mystery that is posited from the outset in partnership with the covenant God. This certainty is merely freed, as it were, from its incubation stage and becomes increasingly virulent.

The essential thing is to note *how* this development takes place. It does not take place through a process that works for greater cognitive clarity and thus brings out the hidden implications of faith in the overcoming of death. No, what finally kindles faith in the resurrection of the dead is a radically new thing, a fact that is not just cognitive but is ontic, and that does not just arise but is newly posited by God as an act. This fact is the awakening of him who is "the firstfruits of those who have fallen asleep" (1 Cor. 15:20). It is the resurrection on the third day. This third day is not the logical outcome of the saving event of the old covenant; if it were, there could be no difference between Judaism and Christianity. Instead, it is itself a new and decisive act in that whole event. One might put it as follows: This act is more than the opening of eyes that were previously closed;[18] it is also the offering to such eyes of a new fact that surpasses all that God had done before.

C. NEW TESTAMENT AND GENERAL BIBLICAL LINES IN THE UNDERSTANDING OF DEATH

1. The Biblical Petition for an Open Awareness of Death

We shall now try to discover some persistent lines in the biblical understanding of human finitude and subjection to death. In so doing we shall first ask what the psalmists mean when they pray for a knowledge of death, and what significance, or new significance, the NT attaches to this petition.

By way of example we may be content to adduce two passages that might easily be multiplied. In Psalm 90:12 the psalmist asks that God will grant this awareness of death. He wants God to prevent him from repressing this awareness, as we might put it nowadays. "Please, Yahweh, tell me my end, the number of my days, that we may bring wisdom (into our hearts)." Psalm 39:4–6 is to the same effect: "Tell me, Yahweh, my end, the measure of my days, that I may realize how fleeting life is. Man goes about like a shadow; he makes much turmoil for a mere breath. He heaps up [treasures] and does not know who will gather them."

This open awareness of death is important to the psalmists for many reasons. First, at issue is the relationship to the *world* that is intimated in death; the futility of the things of this world. If I know the finitude of my life, I can no longer live solely for things. I can no longer commit myself to them with confidence. For as death ends all relationships, it ends in a particularly flagrant way the relationship to things, even though I find this hard to grasp, and derive no comfort from it, and thus try to get past it with a good deal of noise and intensive self-delusion.

Naturally the chief of these things is mammon as the representative of those powers with whose help I try to find security and to buy time. Such security is so empty that the righteous with their eternal commitment can look its loss in the eye in a relaxed and confident way. They will no longer be distressed if their ungodly opponent seems to be rich and at ease, for "when he dies he will carry nothing away; his glory will not go down after him" (Ps. 49:17; cf. Luke 12:16ff.). We brought nothing into this world, and we can carry nothing out (1 Tim. 6:7). We do not "consist" of these attributes, these artificial and secondary fulfillments of life. For these things do not last; they leave us at death. We consist rather of a self that exists beyond these things and in detachment from them. Believers are the subjects of an achievement in them of godliness (*eusebeia*) and contentment (*autarkeia*) (1 Tim. 6:6). It is in this dimension that they are in touch with what abides. But in this regard the self is the object of a history into which God has entered with us and which he does not allow to be broken off in death.[19]

It is not as though *we* were not broken off in death — we are! it is not as though *we* were immortal — we have to die! It is not as though we had anything more than that "house not made with hands, eternal in the heavens" (2 Cor. 5:1). Nevertheless, God holds this "heavenly dwelling" in readiness for us. He holds it in readiness in spite of the death that in all reality encompasses us.

As noted already, Paul does not say that God has given us an immortal substance that victoriously overcomes death. There is no way past death (cf. John 12:24). But God has given us the Spirit as a pledge of the hope that on the other side of the great break God is still Lord, that he will not let his history with us be broken off, that he is for us a God of life and resurrection, that he is still a Creator out of nothing (2 Cor. 5:5). This Spirit, again, is not an immortal human spirit or a divine spark that will not cease to shine, but the Spirit of God himself who is still in control and in relation to whom we are always petitioners and worshipers at a distance, so that we cannot pay homage to ourselves in that Spirit.

In relation to him we must always continue to pray: Come, Creator Spirit.

Second, the issue is the relationship to *God* that is intimated in death. The biblical affirmation that in death we have to leave everything we have trusted in here below is not made, then, in the name of scepticism or a negation of all life's values. This would be so only if we stopped at the negative side: "It is all up." But the goal of the admonition is positive, namely, not to annul all values, but to rank them properly before God. This is plain in Jesus' debates with the wealthy adherents of mammon. We have already quoted in illustration the story of the rich farmer (Luke 12:16ff.).[20] This man was abandoned in death because he had trusted in his full barns, found his wealth in things, and forgotten the riches in God that would have been faithful to him in death and could not be eaten away by moth or rust (Matt. 6:19f.).

When we ignore these riches in God, we lose in death not merely our treasures but above all the self that is invested in them and that perishes with them. Thus the rich farmer put the wrong value on himself according to a true ranking of values and forgot to include himself in the history with God into which an offer of acceptance came. Being rich in God means nothing other than being rich in hope of that "commonwealth in heaven (*politeuma*) in which we have the privilege of citizenship" (Phil. 3:20). It means being already united to the Lord who will not let death have its prey because he is the Lord of *life*. Only insofar as we have a part in this history of God do we have a self which, while it does not "survive" death, is a member of the head which, as the head of the risen Lord, stands out above the night of death and does not abandon its members.

It is particularly clear here how qualitatively different is this view of the overcoming of death from the Platonic dualism of body and soul. (*Psyche* in this story can hardly be translated "soul" but rather denotes the physical life from which the rich farmer will be summoned this coming night — this brings out the difference.) It seems, however, that theology cannot dispense with the word "soul." Even Luther, who had a firmly anti-Platonic view of the victory over death, as we shall see shortly, can still speak of the incorruptible soul (*anima*) in his *Commentary on Romans* and his *Table Talk*, and this undoubtedly means something different from the body.[21] Yet in using the term "incorruptible" we must always keep firmly in mind the "ec-centric" aspect that derives from abiding fellowship with God. And who among us, I might ask, would like to omit Martin Schalling's concluding chorale from Bach's *St. John's Passion* in which he asks God to let his dear angel carry off his soul at death to Abraham's bosom? "Soul," as the term is used by Luther and in this chorale, is undoubtedly to be understood as the essential part of us as those who are called by God's Word into an unbreakable fellowship with God and find shelter there. Perhaps I might state it thus: The term "soul" cannot in fact be dropped when we have to speak about bodily death but have still to express the truth that the history that God has begun with us does not break off. "Soul" is a cipher denoting our partnership in this history.[22]

That the rich farmer does not first lose his "self" — or his "person" according to our earlier terminology — when he dies, but has already lost it in life even though he has well-filled barns; that he has already become an impersonal shadow wandering about with no true existence and already under judgment (John 3:19), is all too evident even though it may be concealed from human eyes. For human eyes look at appearances and not at the true person (Matt. 22:16; John 7:24; Rom. 2:11; Gal. 2:6; 1 Pet. 1:17).

The real issue for the rich farmer, then, is not just the next life, to which death is a transition; rather, it is the impersonal and hollow life here and now for which death is the end. Death simply brings to light the destiny of a life that is dead even though it lives.

This makes it plain that the message of death is not part of a sceptical, relativizing, and negative world view, but of a transvaluation of all values in accordance with their supereme or, as we might say, their true criterion.

It is thus wrong, or at least imprecise, merely to say that death is the end of our riches, our possessions, the content of our lives. This is not the real concern of Scripture. Riches as such have no interest. They have material value and in some sense stand for the order (the economic order) from which none of us need withdraw but in which we may still stand even if only within the limits of having as though we had not (1 Cor. 7:29). Death is not important in the Bible as the end of material values but as the end of the idols that we have made of these, substituting their treasures for riches in God. These treasures are not relevant as such in connection with the reality of death. What matters is the rank they have achieved, the throne they have usurped as other gods besides him. The loss of treasures as material values is undoubtedly a *psycho-*

logical problem, as Hoche so well formulated it. But the *theological* problem arises only when we experience the end of treasures as idols, as illegal rivals of God. Treasures become idols when we have as though we had forever.

The decisive thing is that when we are separated from our treasures in death we should not fix our gaze upon them — they are important only for moth and rust, and not for God or us. Or rather, the decisive thing is that we should keep in mind our relation to these treasures; or, in terms of our present problem, that we should consider the personal relation in which they set us, either the personal relation to themselves as idols or the personal relation to our real Lord in whose eyes we have them as though we had not.

This is why the Bible never speaks about riches as such but always about rich people, about those who are characterized by riches because they live for them and are possessed by them, because riches have become their god. If Luther says that God is God for us, not in himself, but only in relation to us, the same may be said of riches. Theologically they are not relevant as material values but only in their relation to us. They set us in a personal relation. And this is what triggers the question of whether we belong to God or mammon. (Values may, of course, be intellectual as well as material. These, too, can be given a false rank. These, too, can be absolutized and make us impersonal in life and death. We need only consider such values as "spirit" or "class" or "health" to see what is involved.)

To ward off all sceptical or negative misunderstanding, we thus affirm that the boundary of death is important as the boundary of the false kingdom of our idols. It also refers us to the Lord who waits for us at this boundary and for whom we must be prepared. The boundary of death, therefore, marks our personal existence.

But how does it stand with the Lord who waits for us at the boundary of death? We must consider this relation more closely after speaking about the false gods for whom death is the end.

Psalm 90 teaches us to ask for a clear realization of death so that we may get hearts of wisdom. According to verses 7f., this wisdom consists of knowing that we perish by reason of God's wrath,[23] and therefore seeing that we are in the relation to God in which we do in fact stand, so that we can be sure of not overestimating ourselves and be proof against dreams of an eternal life that we carry substantially in ourselves. To know this is wisdom, for it means stripping away all illusions and false security and giving us the necessary and urgently needed realism of counting on the "only" value and measuring all else by it.

It is important to realize that this "only" value is not a timeless quantity, a summum bonum, even God in himself, as though he had no bearing on us. Instead, this only value consists of a very concrete relation to this God, of a personal act, an event. This event is the self-disclosure of God in judgment and grace by which he declares himself to be *my* Lord. An event, then, is the true measure of value. (We are thus dealing with personal, nonmaterial matters here.) Hence the term "value" is not quite right, for in common parlance it is far too freighted with timelessness. We have used it provisionally by way of introduction. We shall now drop it.

This personal event that is intimated in death and that throws a shadow over every sphere of life is described by the psalmist as judgment, God's wrath. In the language of the Bible the wrath of God signifies the reaction of the divine holiness to human aberration or "sin." Death is the place where this wrath is most clearly experienced. It means that human life cannot stand before God. Human life is not God's eternal life.

That we have to die means that we are emphatically dust. We came from dust and we shall return to dust. For the world of thought of the Psalms (103:14; 104:29, etc.), "dust" is not just a symbol of the destructibility to which flowers and grass are also subject. For this perishing, like becoming, is seen only in relation to God. "When thou sendest forth thy Spirit, they are created," but "when thou takest away their breath, they die and return to their dust" (104:29f.).

Flowers and grass and nonhuman creatures never have any self-resting finitude that would give them self-sufficient life. Their becoming and perishing, their death, is also due to God. But flowers and grass and whales and hills have no knowledge of their relation to God. Only humans know this, rising up in lonely death above the rest of the creaturely world and thus having a more intense form, as it were, of corruptibility. Only humans have to ask in what sense God is at work in their dying.

The fact that they ask this question, that they have to ask it, makes it plain that the return of humans to dust is qualitatively different from that of purely physical creatures. Something obviously happens to them here in face of which they have to ask for a reason, since it is no longer a matter of some self-evident law that cannot be questioned. Clearly a decision is taken against them with which they have to wrestle.

What is this decision, this element, that transcends the physical law? This brings us back from another direction to the problem that was raised already in the phenomenological section, namely, why human dying is not just a matter of biological law.

2. The Wrath of God as the Mystery of the Relationship to God Intimated in Death
Death as the wages of sin (Rom. 6:23)

We shall first let the great thought of Psalm 90 speak for itself. From the human standpoint the fate of death meted out to us is grounded in our guilt. From the divine standpoint the decision of death that is made against us signifies wrath. These two things, guilt and wrath, have to be seen together. The theological question here is how and why they come to expression in human death.

Orthodoxy both ancient and modern gives us adequate warning that we should avoid the shortsighted and oversimplistic conclusion that death is just a punishment, with the addition, perhaps, that it falls particularly severely on us; children are born with pain and the field brings forth its fruits only with sweat and tears. With such teaching, which breaks off at the decisive point and might rightly be called doctrinaire, we should be relapsing into a false and much attacked causal thinking that is much better and much more credibly taken from natural science.

The cardinal question, then, to which we have now come from every angle, is why guilt and wrath come to expression precisely in dying. We can grasp the mystery only if first we wonder at it. As we read in the opening verses of Psalm 90: "Lord, thou hast been our refuge in all generations. Before the mountains were brought forth, or ever thou hadst formed the earth and the world, from everlasting to everlasting thou art God. Thou turnest man back to the dust, and sayest, 'Turn back, O children of men!' For a thousand years in thy sight are but as yesterday when it is past, or as a watch in the night. Thou dost sweep men away; they are like a dream, like grass which is renewed in the morning: in the morning it flourishes and is renewed; in the evening it fades and withers." If we take these powerful introductory verses alone, we already gain some inkling of death and corruption — but more in the sense that the sea of time breaks eternally on the shore, that it surges against that for which a thousand years are like a single day. One has the feeling that the sea of time is hemmed in on every side by the shore of eternity and its billows are small within it.[24] If human death is seen only in the light of these opening verses in false isolation, it seems to be explicable in terms of the economic-dynamic relation between time and eternity. Death simply represents human finitude in contrast to divine infinity.

Clearly, however, there is more to it than this quantitative distinction between God and us. A qualitative category is introduced, namely, that of guilt and wrath: "For we are consumed by thy anger." What is finally at issue is not just the quantitative difference between two entities but the qualitative break between two persons. Hence what is expressed is not a different ranking but a judgment. Death does not manifest distance; rather, it manifests judgment. It is to be found where fellowship between God and us is broken. We have to be clear about this if we are to try to understand it.

Naturally, death does represent quantitative finitude. It is important to see, however, that this finitude and its economic-dynamic inadequacy in relation to God's eternity are permeated and colored by the distance that separates sinners from God's holiness, by the awareness of judgment. To put it negatively, we are not just aware of falling quantitatively short of an ideal so that we can postulate quantitatively infinite progress toward overcoming the limit of death.[25] We are aware of being sinners, and as such separated from God's person, so that the sense of quantitative distance has only secondary and derived significance. The phenomenon is a wholly personal one.

Typical here is Peter's confession at the miraculous catch of fish: "Depart from me, for I am a sinful man, O Lord" (Luke 5:8). This confession is the more eloquent because the miracle seems to be outside the range of personal relations. As a dynamic demonstration of Christ's power, it seems to play off the divine omnipotence and omniscience against the naive helplessness and impotence of human limitation. Yet we should note how Peter immediately gives a personal turn to this economic-dynamic difference and thus transposes it into another key. Peter is not a mere chit in face of such omnipotence nor a mere atom in face of the divine world-governance, as he would have to be on the purely dynamic level. If he is a chit or an atom on this level, it is due to the shadow that is cast by his true reality, by the fact that he is a sinner. The shadow is that of the personal break that is manifested here. The two things are related as a body is to its shadow. On God's side, then, the miracle and the forgiveness of sins are also inwardly related (Mark 2:1ff.). The miraculous act of power is simply a normative expression of the event of forgiveness, that is, the restoration of a broken personal relationship.

We find the same phenomenon in the closing verse of Psalm 104, which is much contested philologically but undoubtedly authentic materially. This psalm seems to be one long hymn to God's dynamic supremacy over the world and to the quantitative distinction between Creator and creature. Yet in the light of this distinction, in what seems to be an unmediated way, but only for those who regard the dynamic aspect as an end in itself and not as the shadow of the personal relation between God and us, it concludes: "Let sinners be consumed from the earth, and let the wicked be no more!" This is an exact parallel to Peter's experience, almost a foreshadowing of it.

To sum up, death is manifested at the break in the fellowship between God and us. It is not just an expression of the quantitatively dynamic distinction between time and eternity, nor is it characterized only by the autonomy of the *bios* as this is tied to development and destruction and thus to a quantitative measure. It is defined by a personal relation, namely, by our separation from living fellowship with God.

The personal relation in which we find human death embedded means that it is not just something that inevitably overtakes me by nature when my last hour comes. It is not just a law in relation to which I am a mere object. It is an event that I have caused, in relation to which I am a subject, and which I have brought about in freedom as a responsible person.

The wrath of God by which we are consumed is no mere fate, no mere shore of eternity, but God's reaction to the action that we have responsibly engaged in as persons.

In other words, a personal relation means that I must not complain against God when death comes. God is telling me something by it. In my death he is reacting to me. There is a message in it. I see God's hand and word aimed at me.[26]

We have now reached a crucial point. Everything depends on our grasping it properly. We have to show how the personal relation of guilt and death is worked out in and behind the death that limits us quantitatively.

3. Death as the Representative of a Limit

I will answer the question that is put to us in two antithetically formulated propositions:

1. Death is the representative of a limit, of the fact that life has a goal and then it is over.

2. We ourselves in contradiction, that is, concretely separated and alienated from God, are the representatives of a basic violation of the limit.

Sin in the Bible is constantly described as the violation of a limit, that is, transgression. We want to be as God (Gen. 3:5). Adam has become like one of us (Gen. 3:22). Humanity builds a tower of Babel, reaching up to God's sphere (Gen. 11). Sin in this sense is not just negative. It is not just a rejection. In our rejection we implicitly want to be more than human — we want to be divine. We want ourselves and not God to be the measure of all things, including God. According to Paul (Rom. 1:18ff.), idolatry is a truly representative manifestation of this attempt to shape the final reality in our own image and to make ourselves the criterion of all things and all values. In an impersonal mode, but with no material change, the same tendency may be seen in the service of ideas or ideologies or pleasure or mammon. The difference in idols simply derives from the difference in human types as we all of us make God in our own image. Whether or not we use the term "God" — and most people today do not — makes no difference.

When we place over against one another the fact that death is a limit and the fact that we ourselves recognize no limits, the personal character of death comes out clearly in and behind all the biological and dynamic elements. It came upon the human race the same day that Adam and Eve ate the forbidden fruit beyond the limit. A limit is set to those who know no limits.

The first limit, namely, the boundary between God and us, which we were allowed to respect in the freedom of obedience, has been wickedly transgressed in this freedom. Hence a second limit has been set before us, which we cannot get across and which involves a partition between corruptible humans and the eternal God. This boundary is death. Those who are called to living fellowship with God but who take control of their own lives are shown here that these lives of theirs are death and will fall in upon themselves.

We can trace the slope that leads from creation to the fall as follows: The divine likeness of us human creatures[27] is the privilege of living with God and not being subject to death.[28] Snatching at equality with God is an attempt to improve on this privilege, to achieve autonomy in place of commitment. But this leads to death; indeed, it *is* death: "The wages of sin is death."[29]

The terror of death, then, is not that it is the end or boundary in a quantitative temporal sense, but rather that it is the limit of that which is by nature without limits. Or, even more sharply, there is heard in death the eternal God's contradiction of finite creatures that exalt themselves to limitlessness.

This is the character of death as it appears before God. Hence we cannot isolate it again as a biological phenomenon but have to understand it in terms of the history between our I and God's Thou within which it stands. As stated earlier, we see death changed here from a fact of nature into a fact of history. I shall now expand and clarify this basic theological insight.

Death is not so much characterized by its being a limit as by the beings that it limits, namely, beings that recognize no limits but try to rise up from divine likeness to divine equality, and also by the being that imposes the limit, namely, the unique Holy One who will not tolerate any other gods.

We might formulate this insight in the following proposition. Death in the biblical sense is not our death as mammals but our death as those who want to be divine and thus have to learn that we are only human.

Since we are, of course, mammals as well as the personal bearers of hybris, death has also a biological side. But the biological end of life that it entails is not the thing that really counts, just as the fact that we are mammals does not constitute our true humanity but is only its physical basis. Our real humanity is that we are persons, and the real thing about death is that through the biological medium our person, which is limitlessness, is contradicted.[30]

Our twofold being as persons and biological creatures comes to expression in the curse that lays the sentence of death upon us (Gen. 3:19). For in it we are told that we shall have to eat our bread in the sweat of our brow and suffer various things until we return to the earth from which we are taken. This is because we *are* earth, and will become it once more.

"You are earth." This statement contains both aspects. First, it means that you are a part of nature and share the corruptibility of all creatures. Second, it means that you belong to earth, to what is below and under God, although you have tried to rise above it, and in building the tower of Babel, as a further link in the long chain of revolt, will do so again.

"You will become earth again." This means that as your death is a return to earth, it is a reminder that you will be pushed back behind the barrier through which you have burst. Your death confirms that you belong to earth and not to the heaven which you have tried to seize.

It is hard to have to return to dust because it is here that we are reminded of the fall and of God's reaction to it. This is why Paul says in 1 Corinthians 15:56 that the sting of death is sin. In the light of our present insight this means that the troubling thing about death, that reminder, that is, God's reaction, is the background of sin. Sin gives death its right to me. It is its bridgehead in my personal kingdom.

At the same time another point that emerges is the indissoluble relation between the biological and the personal event. Becoming earth involves both being thrust back into the limited zone and becoming dust quite physically, that is, decaying. The mark of living persons, their personal and biological two-sidedness, stamps their end, too. Both aspects must be seen together in both cases.

The question might be asked whether biological dying, the dessication of the cells and dissolution of the organism, can be made dependent on that process? Would the biological process be any different without it? And if so, how? But this question is looking in the wrong direction. For it introduces the inappropriate causal connection that was fatally asserted in seventeenth-century orthodoxy when a physical fact was detached from its biological sphere and made causally dependent on a metaphysical fact.

The stories of creation and the fall are not meant to be literalistic history or to derive the world and its fall from a first cause. We do not have here epochs at the beginning of the human race that can be dated chronologically. The stories are meant to describe our condition and to expound the belief that God created me. The issue is myself and not the world. I have to understand myself as the one that came from the hands of God and that is responsible to him. I have to understand myself — with Adam as an exemplar[31] or prototype — in terms of creation under God. Creation and the fall are a kind of horizon of my life and have me as their target. If we want to bring out their theological intention, we must not see them as relating to a span of time preceding my present span in the twentieth century, so that they are far outside the range of my existence, but we must depict them as a circle which is drawn around me, which forms the horizon of my personal world, and whose spokes point to me.

This forbids us to look in the direction indicated in the earlier question. In myself I cannot differentiate the personal and biological factors causally, as one can differentiate between cause and effect in a fixed entity. I do not stand over against myself in this way. As the nonmaterial subject of my responsibility, I experience the inseparable interrelation of my person and my *bios*, or, transferred to the idealistic level and modified thereby, the inseparable interrelation of causality and freedom, of the sensory world and the intelligible world. On the idealistic level Kant described a similar state of affairs when he said that on an objective view the mystery of the person is wholly incomprehensible — for we are looking in the wrong direction; on this view I necessarily see myself to be subject to the category of causality and hence cannot perceive the phenomenon of freedom or responsibility. I perceive this phenomenon only nonobjectively by facing moral decisions. Then, notwithstanding the causal derivation of things that are not "I," I experience freedom, namely, that I am the cause and not the effect of my acts.

I thus place myself on an illegal and inappropriate level (that of material and abstract thought) if I put my being as person and my being as *bios* in a relation of causal dependence, or if I do not allow the personal and biological aspects of my death to be two sides of the same thing but rather try to deduce the one from the other. This is why we used what seemed to be a suitable expression when we said that in the medium of biological death a personal act takes place that denotes the relationship between God and us, namely, the limiting of those who are unlimited. We neither can nor should try to get behind this, for we could do so only at the cost of our personal involvement, of the personal aspect. It is as impossible and impermissible to try to do this as it is at harvest-time to ask how much we owe the harvest to God and how much to the farmer. Farming is here a medium of the divine blessing that cannot be separated from it. The harvest comes through our hands — but from God.[32] Similarly, our dying is "through the hands of" the *bios* — but from God.

Biologically we die the same death as animals. Yet it is totally different for us because we are different.[33] And if, merely by way of illustration, we were to posit a human death apart from God's wrath, apart from the personal destiny that holds sway in death, it would be only a "sleep" (Luther).

EXCURSUS: HUMAN DEATH IN LUTHER

When we work out the personal character of human dying along these lines, we are in essential agreement with Luther's decisive thinking on the problem. We shall now give a brief account of the parallels, which we find particularly in his expositions of Psalm 90 and Genesis 3.

While naturally using a different vocabulary, Luther clearly perceives the difference between the personal and physical aspects of dying. He works out the distinction by illustrating the physical aspect from animals and the transcendent personal aspect from humans.

He develops the distinction from three angles: 1) The end of animal life is natural, but human dying is unnatural; 2) Human dying is present throughout life in the accompanying awareness of death; and 3) It is not permissible to despise death.[34]

1. The end of animal life is natural, but human dying is unnatural. An important quotation from Luther that we shall interpret in what follows begins by stating that death in us differs from the end of animals. Note the pregnant formulation: death "in" us. Not our death, but death that overtakes us (in distinction from animals), death that enters our sphere (the same biological death as in the case of animals) and undergoes a change thereby. Death in us is far worse than the death of other living creatures. Horses, cows, and all animals die, but they do not die under the wrath of God. For them death is temporal hardship that God ordained, not as a punishment, but because it seemed good to him in some way. (We take it that the word "temporal" here implies that the death of animals relates only to their limited span of life but has no further

ramifications.)[35] Luther can also say that the death of animals as distinct from humans is simply the fulfillment of a law of nature.[36]

Of course, Luther is not so blind to the natural world as not to recognize the fear and pain of death in other creatures or to stress the severity of human dying only by naively minimizing what it means for animals to die. When you slaughter a pig, he says, it shows its pain by resisting and squealing. And when a tree is felled, it does not fall without rustling and cracking, similar to cries of pain from the plant world. How, then, can human nature bear the thought of God's wrath (the wrath that is a special doom behind our dying) without tears and complaints and extreme resistance?[37]

This indicates why human death is so much more painful than that of animals, difficult though that is too. It is qualitatively distinguished from animal death by the relation to God that is intimated in it. Through the wrath of God, it is unending and eternal.[38] (In connection with death, "eternal" does not simply denote eternal death in hell after this present life, but relates to life here and now as well. Karl Stange is right when he says that the word "eternal" does not have a "temporal" sense in antithesis to the temporal limitation of earthly life, but death is eternal because the wrath of God expressed in it cannot be overcome by anything in the world; nothing can free us from God's wrath or lift it from us; hence it is "eternal.")[39]

Human death is unending and eternal for a specific reason. Humans, says Luther, are special creatures because they were created to live in obedience to the Word and to be like God. They were not created for death. Death has been instituted as a punishment for sin.[40] Among other things, our divine likeness means that we did not know death but had a part in God's eternal life. My image in you, God said to Adam and Eve, is that in virtue of it you should live as God lives. But if you sin you will lose this image and die.[41]

The terror of human death, then, is that it is not just a loss of physical life but a forfeiture of living fellowship with God. To use our earlier terms, it is a qualitative and not just a quantitative limit. It involves a personal destiny in our dealings with God.

If we were to think of it apart from this, apart from God's wrath, viewing it as native to us in an animal sense, death would only be a sleep, a snake that has lost its fangs, innocuous. As a dead snake still looks like a snake but has lost its poison and can no longer do harm, so death would be truly dead were it seen apart from terror (at God's wrath). This terror is, as it were, the poison of death.[42]

Thus death without its personal side would in fact be dead; it would be nothing. But in fact it still carries the poison of God's wrath. Hence it is a life that confronts us, a power that transfixes us.

We may thus say that the clearer we are about our personhood and the more seriously we take the reality of God, the greater is the burden of the thought of death. Here — as everywhere in the Christian faith — when redemption is given from anxiety, guilt, and need, when we rise with Christ, we take anxiety, guilt, and need with true seriousness and face the harsh realities of truth. The Christian faith does not give comfort by concealing the dark truths of life and death; it gives comfort by revealing them.

This is possible only because there may be seen in front of the Medusa head of terror the head of him who was crowned with thorns and who bore the threat that was meant for us. All other comfort is bought at the price of illusion, and pagan coldbloodedness in face of death derives from seeing only its biological mask, its animal aspect as a natural law, and failing to see its efficient and final cause.[43] Pagans are, as it were, as trusting and happy as children who do not notice the real danger in which they find themselves.

Luther is, of course, just as much aware as pagan thinkers that one can approach physical death in a relaxed frame of mind. As he puts it, if we consider only bodily death, we may say with Martial that one should neither desire nor fear the last day. But this death that one can approach coolly and calmly is not the real enemy, only its advance guard. And those who see the real power coming quickly lose their relaxed frame of mind. Physical death is temporal, but we are never helpless against what is temporal, nor, as in Schleiermacher's sense, are we absolutely dependent on it. We can deal with it even if only with hardiness and heroism of disposition. But the personal character of death in the medium of the biological is eternal. This means that it cannot be remedied with the help of the temporal means of outer or inner effort. No mortal is a match for God's wrath. This explains the terror of the mortal when hearing the Most High say: "Here shall your proud waves be stayed" (Job 38:11). But we Christians who have won through to knowledge and have been stripped of the pagan illusion — we endure *eternal* death, the wrath of God that cannot be conquered by us (as physical death can).[44]

2. Human dying is present throughout life in the accompanying awareness of death. The basically different evaluation of death by pagan illusion and Christian realism affects the significance of the role played by the shadow that death casts backward on days of life and health. One might put it thus: The different evaluation of death affects the actuality of death in the here and now. By way of example, Luther points again and again to the differing intensity of the awareness of death among pagans and Christians.

Although we are constantly reminded of death by cemeteries and instances of death, by nature we do not relate death to ourselves.[45] When we do this, and see that it is our death, it is usually already present. We really see it (and recognize it as our own) only when we have lived and are dying, just as we take note of sleep only when we awake.[46]

It is no wonder, then, that by nature we repress death and do not let it play any role. It is simply a matter of the last hour, Martial's final day. As purely physical death, it is for pagans analogous to what it is for animals, for whom it means something only when it is directly present.[47]

In practice the banning of death from life and its isolation to the final day means that we live as though we would not die. All our concerns and thoughts are oriented to acting as though we would live forever and could make our present life eternal.[48]

We thus live by the deception of an "as if" and not by the harsh truth of real death. We put between ourselves and death the partition of decades of life that are supposedly at our disposal[49] — which is consistent enough when death becomes acute only as the end of a span of time.

Grotesquely, then, in relation to death we struggle for little parcels of time, for wretched decades — as Shakespeare says, life is simply gaining time — and we forget the eternity that surrounds us on all sides in respect of death, and in relation to which life is distorted. In illustration of the situation indicated by Luther, we might be compared to people who in a national crisis are concerned only to protect their own property and do not consider the larger problem, forgetting in their private anxieties that they will lose their property, too, should the whole nation go down, so that it is to

the larger problem that they should devote their energy and re-
sources. Such people have lost all sense of measure and proportion,
and it is in the same absurd manner that we naturally struggle for
years when it is a matter of eternity, or seek equanimity in face
of the microcosmic death of the body when what counts is the
macrocosmic fact of estrangement from God and the dreadful fact
of the limiting of the limitless.

Only believers are healed by fear and trembling from this distortion of perspective. Only for them does death cease to be isolated to the final day and become something that puts its stamp
on their lives as lives that God has marked and put back behind
his limit. Death, then, becomes present,[50] a death that is actual
here and now: "In the midst of life we are in death."

Thus, the datable moment of physical death is not nearly as
important as the fear and trembling with whose help I relate my
present life to death. This act of anxious relating is my death in
a much more eminent sense than my physical end. For in it my
soul, my I, and not just my body, realizes that it is claimed by
death and related to it. In it, then, the personal dimension is
intimated.[51]

3. It is not permissible to despise death. On this premise Luther
naturally and logically contests the heroic pagan ideal of despising
death. To despise death is possible only when it is degraded and
the self is exalted above it. But this is both blasphemy and hybris.[52]

The trouble with it is that despising death in the strict sense
does not mean suppressing the shameful fear of death that the
physical instinct of self-preservation constantly produces in us.
Scorn of death is scorn of him that brings it upon us. It is scorn
of death as a divine measure. It is a not wanting to hear what God
is trying to tell us through it. It is possible, then, only with the
help of a degrading of God and an exalting of ourselves above
him. This is the troublesome background of the despising of death.
And where this directly blasphemous thrust against God is not
present — as in Epicurus — scorn of death is based on ignorance of
its true cause. It is thus based on a foolish security that is possible
only because one does not recognize the real danger. Monks as
well as pagans have often debated contempt for death — a sorry
affair: For in this way people become either secure or blasphemous
by setting aside the fear of God (who wills and causes death) and
thus becoming caught up in a movement against God, as though

he were acting as a tyrant (whom one should defy and oppose) and as though he were unreasonably exposing this unfortunate creation to death.[53]

As a rule the despising of death has less of the character of deliberate opposition to God and rests instead (as in Epicurus) on ignorance of God, so that it is not just an objective illusion but even subjectively it has little value as a heroic impulse, since it relates only to the biological side of death, which is the most wretched. Contempt for death, then, is possible only on the basis of an illusory security, not a realistic facing the menacing truth of death. This being so, it is no longer a clever trick or an expression of true bravery. One might call it brave only if it were facing up to the real danger. Epicurus taught us to despise death, but he did not even know that God is, nor did he know the fate of those whom God opposes.[54]

The heroism of those who scorn death rests on ignorance, on the supposed security of the rider on Lake Constance,[55] but this security suddenly crumbles when, with the real knowledge of hindsight, we have to see our being for death.[56]

We may sum up Luther's thinking as follows: Death cannot be overcome by the illusory security of ignorance nor by the degrading of God and our fearless and wicked self-exaltation above him in contempt for death. It can be overcome only by the acknowledgment of him who has ordained it, and therefore by acceptance of the counsel of his wrath. Only when I take this course and face the truth of death do I yield myself wholly to God. In so doing I agree that there is no fighting God, no remedy against his wrath. God alone can help me. God's grace alone is greater than his judgment. God alone can heal the wounds that he has inflicted.[57] All else is illusion and mad defiance. All else works with the erroneous hypothesis that there is something greater than God that can resist him, that those who scorn death, for example, are greater than God. As those who are truly called to order and addressed and awakened by God's Word, we should expect help from none other than him who has ordained affliction (and especially death) for us. For only he who has wounded us can heal us. The glory of our God is that he kills and makes alive, that he leads into hell and out again.[58] Everything depends on our relating the good and the bad to one and the same God and learning thereby how the bad (especially death) can be overcome.[59]

In connection with these thoughts on the despising of death, Luther arrives at an impressive definition of the concept of barbarism, which is worth retaining. Barbarism — stupidity, coarseness, arrogance — is not for him the mere opposite of aesthetic culture and the accompanying refinement of life-style. Real barbarism cuts across every stage in the development of human culture. Once one thinks of the attitude toward death, one finds it, for example, in the very refined cultural world of the Hellenes insofar as this involves disparagement and ignorance of God,[60] that is, the hybris and lack of awareness in ultimate things that is otherwise associated only with primitive culture and uncultivated manners and hence designated barbarism.

Clearly what Luther has in view here is his previously mentioned understanding of Epicurus. Naturally we today, with our better knowledge of how religious the Greek was, can accept this criticism only if we do not have in mind the subjective form of piety — as Luther most certainly did not — but rather the objective ignorance of the God of judgment and grace. Taking this God seriously does indeed entail a transvaluation of the concept of barbarism. As impiety and ignorance of God, as uncultivated religion, we shall find this not only on the lower stages of culture but also on the intellectual heights under the cover — which is only a cover — of aesthetic culture and refined intellectualism. And often the opposite of barbarism — final knowledge, fear, and reverence — will be found among the ranks of the despised and unworthy whom God has elected as such (1 Cor. 1:18ff.; 2:1ff.). It is a basic lesson of the NT that the great and gifted are the most in danger, and that the height of the human is no nearer God, but may be barbaric depths (in Luther's sense).

We may sum up Luther's teaching on death, so far as it is relevant to our present train of thought, in the following formulae:

1. Human death is qualitatively different from animal death because it does not represent order but disorder, namely, it is the result of the disrupted relation with God, a sign of expulsion from the life of God, and a threatening signal of his wrath.[61]

2. As death is God's judgment on our lives, it characterizes the whole life that precedes it. It is not the end of life but is its character. Hence I now live in the truth only if, in awareness of death, I relate all my life to the divine action intimated in dying.

3. Contempt for death is thus forbidden as it arises out of

defiance or ignorant security. I must not arrogantly exalt myself above death and its author, but rather place myself under them in acknowledgment. Only thus do I do justice to the fact that, myself included, there is nothing greater than God, nothing greater in virtue of which I may hope to overcome his smiting and punishment. Only God himself can heal the wound that he has inflicted; only the love of God is greater than his wrath.[62]

D. THE DIRECTION OF THE TIME-LINE AND ITS PRESERVATION BY DEATH

1. The Message of the Limit of Death in Proclamation

Thus far we have described the character of death essentially in two ways. First, there is manifested in it our loneliness in relation to things and people, which we have to leave in death insofar as this shows our person to be detachable from everything and everybody. Second, our personhood is affected in death by the fact that God imposes his limit on the limitlessness of those who rise against him. In death God's person meets us, particularly his wrath. In this way we and our death become personal. Luther developed the same idea in various directions.

We do not want to leave these aspects of the personal character of dying without a brief look at the way in which this doctrine of death is to be preached, to be proclaimed at gravesides, and to be championed in philosophical dialogue.

One cannot do this, of course, by simply playing off the personal character of death, its limiting of the limitless, against secular ideas of corruptibility, against the rhythm of spring and fall that is found in all life, and against the depreciation of the individual. This would bring to light two different worlds of thought — but it would only bring them to light and at best differentiate them. But this cannot be the task of proclamation. The understanding of death as a limit that is set by wrath can be as little demonstrated as sin can be demonstrated. For in neither case do we have an independent phenomenon that can be considered objectively like a natural phenomenon. They both involve relations. And it is to God that they are related. Sin means separation "from" God; death means being limited "by" God. The two phenomena cannot be understood apart from this "from" and "by." God stands above both as a common conditioning theme. Only because the modern world has lost sight of this theme has it lost sight of the true nature of death. Sin cannot be described as a personal thing apart from the relation to God.

Hence death can be preached only as this Lord is preached — this Lord whom by nature we do not want to have over us. The true doctrine of death radiates, as it were, from this center of the message. Proclamation becomes falsely dogmatic and peripheral — for all its apparent orthodoxy — if we play off the individual dogma too directly against its opposite outside. Doing this is the mistaken and fatal game of apologetics.[63] Proclamation must constantly retreat from the far-flung truths of the front line to an inner line of resistance, to the center of the message of the Lord who judges us and sets us up, who limits us and yet fetches us home in Christ. The other truths are credible as truths affecting *me* (and not just as dogmas) when and insofar as they are adopted in this retreat to the inner line and in essential connection with it. This is not a specific method of proclamation but part of its content.

This content and the resultant method are classically expressed in Luther's exposition of the Ten Commandments. Using our metaphor of the inner line of resistance, we might say that the frontline truths that we are not to kill, commit adultery, or lie, are not discussed as such. Luther does not try to show that they are basic truths of morality or natural law, and that violating them will have such and such consequences (which is no doubt true as well, but only in terms of frontline truth). No, he argues for their truth in connection with the inner line of resistance, that is, the first commandment, and therefore the relation to the Lord (and author) of the law. The truth of the detailed commandments follows from the fact that we are to fear God and love him. Conversely, when we fear God and love him, when the center is in order, the norms of attitude and conduct will arise "of themselves."

The same applies to sermons on death. Here, too, we must observe the principle of the inner line of resistance, for death is a subject for both church and world, for the Christian message and secular myth. Yet the church's preaching of it as an actual message is particularly disputed, and is thus in special danger of becoming an abstract topic of frontline discussion. It is not good enough to oppose to the thesis that death is a transition in the rhythm of life the counter thesis that it is a result of sin. Put thus, the message is dogmatically correct but still false because it is delivered at the wrong point and on the wrong level. Petty polemics, pamphleteering, and the like suggest that the church is constantly letting its proclamation be forced on to this level and is losing sight of the connection with the center, with the inner line.

Since working out from this central position could determine the discussion of the question of death in our own and every age, we must not let slip the opportunity to make this homiletical observation. With it we now return to our interrupted train of thought.

To the extent that we understand death personally, in taking it seriously we not only achieve a new relation to the *world*, over against which we are isolated and forsaken by its gods; we also achieve a new relation to *God*, who limits us in our dying. And finally, through these two relations, our relation to *time* as our own life-time becomes new and different. We must now discuss this.

2. The Transforming of the Sense of Time in Face of the Limit of Death

We may briefly recall what we discussed in the first chapters (mainly from a phenomenological standpoint).

Our life consists of a steady movement toward a frontier, or, one might say, it is a steady approach to this frontier without a single pause or even a temporary backward movement (Ps. 39:4ff.).

The clock, as we have already shown, is a poor symbol for this stretch of time that hastens toward its end. The movement of the hand on a clock is in a circle; it comes back to the beginning and starts again. The hour that it measures is not a unique span of time in one direction. It may be, and is, endlessly repeated. Time as represented by the clock is cyclical or bent; as Leopold Ziegler has shown, it forms the background for the great year or the world time of the myths.[64] This concept of time is dominant, then, in the intellectual sphere in which human personality is down-played, in which it is a nonunique and repeatable specimen of the species, or a representative of suprapersonal forces.

We have to liberate ourselves from the symbol of the clock. It is certainly significant that those who are bound to a cyclical view of time usually find it hard to perceive the flow of time at the moment when the hour strikes, but do so only at such decisive

points as birthdays and perhaps New Year. But here the message
of the circling hand is obviously deceptive, for while the hours of
the day return, the years that have gone do not. Here it is suddenly
apparent — and so terrifyingly apparent that those who have no
consolation resort to stupefying means of forgetting — that we are
not marching in a circle in which everything will go on indefinitely
but in a span of time that will come to an end. Cyclical time is the
temporal form of the processes of nature in which everything
moves in a circle and comes back according to the seasons. As
Homer put it, the generations are like leaves. The wind blows them
off and others come. The forest blooms again with the new life of
spring. So it is with the generations; one grows and another decays.

The recurrence here is that of generations; individuals do not
return. Individuals have no part in eternal recurrence. Even though
individuality is not given a special sense in virtue of the alien
dignity conferred in the gospel, the irreversibility of this exclusion
and loss is also felt by those who dwell in a landscape of cyclical
time. The saga of Orpheus and Eurydice shows this, and Catullus
can sing of the pain of pitiless extinction and thus hint at the
irruption of linear time into the human sphere: Suns can go down
and return, but we, when our brief light dies, have only the permanent night of sleep.[65]

In the movement toward the end of our span of time as the
Bible understands it, two things may be seen that very profoundly
affect my existence. First, I always take myself with me. I am
always my past, for I can never give up my identity. Second, I
cannot posit myself afresh and begin again from the beginning as
in cyclical time. My time-line is irreversible. It is directed straight
to its end. It is "soon gone, and we fly away" (Ps. 90:10). These
are the two statements that the reality of death produces in relation
to our time.

The two truths — which are in reciprocal relation — are both
held open and protected against repression only as we take seriously
the Lord from whom that irreversible line comes and to whom it
hastens. For only in relation to him do I become a person, that is,
unique, incapable of being represented, responsible for myself (as
I have undoubtedly been loaned this self by him). It is of a piece
with this that I cannot give up my identity, that I cannot put
myself away from myself and change my identity into something
else in order to start again, but that I always have to stand before

him as one who is called by name — the sign of identity — and is meant to be God's. The directed time-line of my course derives from this existence of mine as a person before God. "Directed" means two things. It denotes orientation to an end. But it also carries with it the sense of standing in the judgment (German *gerichtet*).

The point is, then — and we must stress this to safeguard ourselves against the onset of natural theology — that I cannot speculate on cyclical time or stretches of time — rather along the lines of New Year's experiences — and rise from that to awareness of my uniqueness and existence as a person before God. All our natural knowledge of God is held down in unrighteousness, so that, although it is present, it cannot break forth. As we have seen, it is repressed.[66] Hence the New Year's experience and the resultant sense that our time is oriented can lead only to the illusion, which represses the truth, that we live only once, that after us comes the flood, that we should eat, drink, and be merry, for tomorrow we die.

This example shows us that we cannot grasp on our own the thought of uniqueness as it has been worked out here. The concept remains a grotesquely distorted fragment that can lead only to an inverted personal uniqueness, namely, to dispensation from responsibility on the ground that death brings everything to an end. The uniqueness of the godly, of those who are called by God and named by him, is not even formally similar. There is a qualitative difference. In the first case death becomes the preacher of uniqueness in its quality as meaninglessness. In the second it becomes the preacher of the *kairos*, of the unrepeatable span of grace and calling: Now is the accepted time. It also becomes the preacher of the truth that God's history with us does not end, but we stand in the sphere of power of the resurrection and life. But this is understandable only in terms of personal fellowship with God. For it is not our own life, nor the power of our own resurrection, that bursts death open; rather, it is the history of God with us into' which we have been taken up and become persons, and which continues.

Personal uniqueness and the implied orientation of our span of time thus may be perceived only on the condition of death, which is itself understood as an event in our history with God, a personal limitation and not just a formal boundary.

3. A New Delimitation over against the Mythical Character of Time

If the orientation of our span of time is manifest in this sense, we can perceive an important connection between sin and death. We note that death is a watcher over the guilt of our life, keeping this guilt open and preventing it from being suppressed.

The two statements I had to make about my time in view of death as its end were 1) that I always take myself with me, and 2) that I cannot begin again in the sense of cyclical time. Both statements imply that I cannot take back my guilt. The moment my open future becomes the present and my decision is taken, there is no going back. To put it pointedly, I as a person am the sum of all my decisions, including those already taken. I continue to be this. But since we have to understand our personhood strictly in terms of God and his calling, this means concretely that before God my past life has not vanished but is still present. Hence "my sin is ever before me" (Ps. 51:3). It is still here in the present because it falls in the same span as that on which I still move. This explains the prayer in Psalm 25: "Remember not the sins of my youth" (v. 7). The time when they were committed has not vanished but is still my present time. (Pastoral counselors and psychiatrists know the concreteness of this truth.) I cannot escape myself. I cannot leave my path, my time-line. I have to pursue it to the very end. I stay identical with myself. I must confess that the phase between my beginning and my end is part of me. "I am my time" (Rudolf Hermann). Death is the pitiless watchman over this inexchangeable course of life, this irreversible time-line[67] — naturally on the assumption that I understand death personally. The sting of this irreversible and inexchangeable time-line is sin.

We may make at this point some important philosophical observations. It is not by chance that the following two phenomena always come together and hence give evidence of a material inner connection.

A perception of the supraindividual dimension into which my personal uniqueness is taken up, and which makes me immortal, always crops up in connection with a cyclical concept of time.

On the other hand, it is not by chance that in biblical thinking the personhood that arises with calling is connected with an irreversible time-line and therefore with serious wrestling with death and finitude. This relationship might be much more rewarding than our limited subject allows. For the oriented time-line applies not merely to the microcosm of individual life but also to the macrocosm of the whole world and its destiny, which is determined by the last day and therefore by the end, by its eschaton. This macrocosmic time-line is manifest in the light of the summons of the Word, for it is the time in which God's message is set forth, the accepted time, the time of patience. Awareness of the end and death of the world is oriented strictly to this summons. The end comes when the time appointed for the call is at an end and human responses and the related woes of the world have filled up their measure. The end in its form as the last judgment is simply the sum of the call and its results, the harvest of history when the grain is separated from the chaff.

Thus the orientation of the time-line is evident from the standpoint of the death of the world, too. God's call rings out, and by it the world is characterized as something that has a time and must reach an end. The aeon has a kind of macrocosmic personhood. Related to this is the fact that the world's death and judgment are already anticipated in some sense here and now. Already part of the world — a nation or an area — has neglected the call and come to an end, dying the world's death in advance by missing the showers of the gospel and remaining unblessed. Luther constantly advocated this apocalyptic idea — with his own people, Germany, in mind as this part of the world. Johann Walter took it up in his powerful chorale: "Wake up, wake up, O German land" (1561).[68]

Death, both personal and cosmic, is the pitiless watchman over the time-line as this moves on to its end. In the story of the rich man and Lazarus (Luke 16:19– 31),[69] the uniqueness of our time-line is made unmistakably clear. This story also shows unmistakably that awareness of this uniqueness cannot arise simply by contemplating one's end in death, but only through the summons of God and his Word. The five brothers who are still alive are not listening to Moses and the prophets. They are deaf to the call. Hence it will be of no use to them even for someone to come back from the dead. In other words, even a manifest demonstration of death and what comes after will be of no value to them.

The watchman over the uniqueness of our span of time is not just death as such; rather, it is only the death whose mystery I have accepted in the summons, the death that is indeed itself this summons as limit and judgment.

E. THE IGNORING OF DEATH AS SECURITY

1. Security and Repression

In a second train of thought we shall consider some further phenomena that now appear in a new light. We encountered them first when we were simply noting the everyday experiences of death.

Ignoring death, or, better yet, trying to forget it, means biblically refusing to see one's limit and finally, in fact, missing it. This gives rise to security. When Psalm 39:4 prays: "Lord, let me know my end, and what is the measure of my days; let me know how fleeting my life is," this petition is equivalent to asking God to break my security. This is the false and deceitful security of those who walk about like "shadows," dancing and eating and drinking and flirting like the passengers on the *Titanic* just before it hit the iceberg.

Now it is important to note that security always involves disquietude: "Surely for nought they are in turmoil." What is this relationship? Security is when we see ourselves in the light of the goods and values of this world and cling to the support we think they offer. We are defined and secured by what we heap up (v. 6), or, as the singer of Psalm 49 says with reference to those who persecute him, "Their houses abide for ever, their dwelling-places to all generations, they named their lands their own. Yet man cannot abide in his pomp, he is like the beasts that perish. This is the fate of those who have foolish confidence, the end of those who are pleased with their portion" (vv. 11ff.). The inner fate of security, then, is that it is founded on that which does not have abiding worth.

This is why the security that is sought is permeated by secret disquietude (paradoxical though this may seem at first). This disquietude expresses itself in constantly choosing anew and amassing this world's goods, in piling up money and honor and power, which seems to be identical with achieving more security. But as this disquietude is constantly inspired by the hope that the acquisition of goods brings satisfaction, it is unrest on the soil of security. For this reason Faust's unrest is security when viewed from this angle. It is a supposed ability to live without dying.

Now we have to remember that there is no security either in

an objective sense or a subjective psychological sense. The unrest indicates this precisely because it is unrest and lives on as such, destroying security. It lives on because there is in fact no true ignorance of the threat of death. The NT shows that there is no complete ignorance of the divine truths that determine our existence; there is only a suppressed knowledge. The classical example of this is to be found in Paul's depiction of the wrath of God on the Gentiles and their idolatry (Rom. 1:18ff.). We have often referred to this passage and must now look at it more closely.

There is here a wholly similar attempt to gain security as in the case of death except that on the part of the Gentiles it now applies, not merely to security against death, but to security before God in general. The apostle notes that people outside of faith pray to human and animal images and finally sink into self-worship. The theological question here is whether unbelievers do this because they do not know about the true God (whether because he is hidden or because they are too irreligious or unreceptive to perceive him), or whether they go to false gods because they do know something about the true God but for some reason they repress this knowledge and do not want it.

In the first case the Gentiles would not be responsible because a deficient cognitive function or a hidden subject of knowledge can never produce guilt. But in the second case, that of repression, we have to speak about guilt because a latent act of protest gives rise to the ostensible ignorance.

With a clarity that leaves nothing to be desired, Paul stresses that the denial of God falls into the second category, and that this is why God's wrath is kindled against this intentional idolatry. How does Paul come to see it this way? (We shall expound the relevant verses in an attempt to understand this.)

Paul proves the guilt of the Gentiles by referring to the clear knowability of God in his works. All creation is a manifestation of God in which one can see and grasp him. The Creator can be seen through creation. If this does not occur, it is not because God dwells in a darkness that no one can penetrate, but because the human heart — the subjective part of the knowledge of God — is "darkened." The origin and nature of this darkness are described exactly, in order to avert the misunderstanding that we have here a general dogmatic judgment on human wickedness that is open to debate.

The explanation is that objectively we can see the Creator in his creation, but we do not praise and thank him. In other words, our attitude toward God is wrong. We do not want to be dependent on him or to see ourselves as creatures. In terms of the biblical thinking in which Paul has his roots, it is easy to see why this is so. Being a creature means being under God, seeing our limits, and recognizing our debt to God as those who are made by him. We do not want to understand our existence as that of stewards who have to give an account. We do not want to be under an obligation to obey God and to "acknowledge" him in judgment and in grace.

Because we do not want this but prefer to be independent, we lose sight of God. When a wrong idea of God is present, we cannot see the true God. Only those who *are* of the truth, that is, who in their life and actions take their existence under God seriously, hear his voice and accept his manifestation. In the knowledge of God the question is not whether our organs of knowledge are intact or deformed but whether we have a right existential attitude toward God. In other words, knowledge of God rests always on acknowledgment of God.

It is not so, then, that I have first to be convinced about God by a proof of God, an epistemological process, and will then acknowledge him. The exact opposite is the case. This is why Blaise Pascal refuses to try to bring anyone to a knowledge of God by way of proofs. We can achieve this knowledge only by coming into the truth with our existence, that is, by letting God bring us into this truth. Hence Pascal says in his *Pensées* that we should not try to achieve conviction by augmenting proofs but by diminishing passions.[70] Elsewhere, he notes that people say that they would give up excesses if they had faith, but he tells them, conversely, that they would have faith if they gave up their excesses.[71] Knowledge of God is based only on acknowledgment. It is thus through and through an existential affair.

2. Repression and Guilt

Because we feel threatened by God, because we know we are in his hands — for the Creator is also the judge — we do not want him and we will not have him. We repress him and resort to other gods which are made in our own image and by which we feel confirmed and accepted and believe we are secured.

It is a mistake, of course, to suppose that this is a conscious process that takes place in the upper level of the consciousness. When the Gentiles repress the fact of God, they really think they are worshiping true gods. As there is no sequence of first knowledge, then acknowledgment, so there is no sequence of first knowledge, then nonacknowledgment. Nonacknowledgment is not a subsequent act of protest or a categorical declaration against God with the deliberate Promethean gesture of a raised fist. It is a secret protest, an inner apostasy, which initiates the movement from a wrong attitude to a mistaken knowledge, providing the attitude with the corresponding cognitive superstructure.

We all know how such repressions occur in other areas of life. A sick person will not accept the idea of a feared illness and hence refuses to recognize it for a time. The eyes are closed to it and arguments enough are found or invented to produce a different explanation and thus to recognize anything but the real state of affairs. The more highly developed our cognitive organs are, the more skillful they are in the art of concealing truths and talking us out of them. For example, the medical training of fatally ill doctors places at their disposal all kinds of associations and arguments to make their condition seem less serious and thereby to conceal the truth. They have an interest in not being dying people. They will not acknowledge that they are dying, and therefore they refuse to know it. What we desire, we easily believe or think, and *vice versa*.

It is the existential attitude, then, that shapes our knowledge. The Gentiles do not know God because they do not want either him or their related creatureliness, because they hold down the truth in unrighteousness. Kierkegaard expresses this insight when he states that it is conviction that sustains reasons, not reasons conviction.[72]

To this extent the security that the Gentiles seek in the shadow of the innocuous gods of their own choosing is not based on real ignorance. (If it had been, they would have found real rest — like children who are not aware of dangers.) Their security rests in fact on a repressed but ultimately present knowledge which obscurely attests itself in the restless bubblings that constantly boil up from the depths.

A striking example of the repression that arises out of not wanting to know may be found in the frequent assurances that Germans gave after 1945 to the effect that they had had no knowledge of Nazi atrocities. But they could in fact have known a good deal — if not all — of what was going on if they had not intentionally looked the other way. To have admitted the truth would have made demands that they did not feel they could accept, but whose nonacceptance would have brought severe pangs of conscience.

Jesus illustrates this refusal to look and accept in the parable of the Good Samaritan (Luke 10:30ff.). The priest and the Levite draw near to the man who is lying wounded and helpless by the roadside. They would have felt obliged to help him but would thus have exposed themselves to the danger of falling into the hands of the robbers themselves. They did not categorically refuse to offer help and then pass by on the other side. They did things in reverse. Jesus uses the Greek word *antiparelthon* to describe this, which means that they went round, or passed by on the other side, so as not to see anything. In this way they repressed the fact with its demands and maintained their moral security, not losing a clear conscience.

This is exactly how we must understand the security that is sought, with the help of carnal forces, in face of death. A non-acknowledgment or repression that is the result of fear is what is involved here, not a true ignorance of death. And precisely as the Gentile gods seem to be the objects of genuine knowledge — for the protest against the true God is not an open one but is concealed in that knowledge — so the philosophical reinterpretations of death seem to be the object of real knowledge but in fact are simply a repression of our true fate in death, a refusal to accept it.

We hope that something of this has already come to light in our exposition of the secular handling of death, and thus will simply repeat here our theological point that, when I understand myself in terms of immanent goods and entities that are supposedly of value, I repress the knowledge of death and I hold it down in unrighteousness. Or I suppress it when I depersonalize myself after the manner of the Germans or Faust or Hegel and transfer my true I to such supraindividual and apparently permanent entities as the tribe or earthly achievements or spirit, or when I simply do not relate death to myself at all, as in Tolstoy's story.

What we have here is not knowledge but repressed knowledge. What we have is not truth but a refusal to accept truth. What we have is not a real perception of the reality of death but the perception of some interest in face of this reality. This is how the philosophical approach looks from the biblical standpoint. A new light is thus shed on the first part of our presentation.

3. Guilt and Lack of Peace

A sign that this attempt to secure ourselves against death by repressing it does not bring real peace or mastery over death or the world is that we constantly have to find fresh security against worry, and are beset by the anxiety that underlies both.

When death actually comes it shatters absolutely the illusion of security because it is an unmistakable reality. There are two possible attitudes toward this reality when it comes. The first is one of *open* despair such as one sees at many secular funerals or when the *Titanic* sank. People are awakened out of sleep by the last enemy as by a murdering robber — and they do not know what to make of it.

The second attitude is one of *repressed* despair — the despair of clenched teeth — which becomes as such the testimony to a new kind of holding down or nonacceptance, except that now this relates to the subjective state that arises when the objective reality of death comes as the end. This repressed despair is usually called "bearing up." It is vividly described by Spengler in terms of the soldier of Pompeii, and finds its most consistent interpretation in Ernst Jünger as a being borne by nothing in face of nothing.[73] The knowledge of God and death that is held down in unrighteousness is what the Bible calls security. The despair that is held down in unrighteousness it calls defiance.

Plainly to be seen here is the difference between what is called security and what is called peace. If we were to begin mistakenly with the psychological fact and therefore with the mere reflection of what is really at issue, we might suppose that these two terms are both meant to express the "rest of the heart" in face of threatening forces. But behind what seems to be the same psychological state there lies a completely different objective basis. Peace means that things are in order with God, and among other things — many others — it entails a "border arrangement" on the basis of reconciliation in Christ. Peace is thus a personal thing; it is peace between persons, the bridging at the cross of the gulf that had opened up between them. The peace of the heart is only a reflection of this objective reality. But there can be this peace in face of threatening forces such as death. Or, more exactly, when this peace is given by God as new fellowship between God and us, it is plain that only he who has dealt the wounds can heal them: God himself gives us the confidence that the history begun in Christ will not be broken off in death but we will continue to be companions of the risen Lord. Hence peace in face of death is granted only by him who is the source of the lack of peace that comes with fear of death. Only he can lead us out of hell who has thrust us there. This is the objective basis of peace that lies outside us.

In contrast, security is an inner, subjective thing. It arises when the ultimate cause of insecurity and terror has not been faced and dealt with. It is a looking the other way. Concern for it is, medically speaking, a mere therapy of symptoms that cannot prevent the real trouble from constantly breaking out afresh. We examined the process when we dealt with security on the ground of disquietude and brought to light the despair that inspires it. We can expound the two phenomena with the help of the doctrine of justification, although we can present this only in outline.

To be secure is to hold down the truth in unrighteousness, to repress the reality of death. To have peace, however, is to be established in new righteousness by God. For the righteousness of faith means saying Yes to God in judgment and grace and thus accepting both the border of death and the faithful history of God that helps us across it. To be secure is to be of untruth, while to have peace is to be of the truth.

4. The Connection between Person and Death in the Biblical Understanding
Concluding formulations

Before closing this consideration of person and death, we should look at the biblical concept of the person from a concluding angle. We do so in order to give final sharpness to the concept that really underlies our understanding of death.

The uniqueness of the person comes to particular expression when it is viewed from the standpoint of the law and the gospel. We have already looked at it from the standpoint of the law, and a sentence or two will be enough to recall what was said. When God as legislator and judge issues the summons "Adam, where art thou?", Adam cannot shelter behind Eve nor Eve behind the serpent. Both must answer for themselves: "No one can redeem his brother"

(Ps. 49:7). It is in this dimension, where we are on our own, that death takes place.

Personhood is no less plain from the standpoint of the gospel. We are led to a new and important insight here. We are helped first by the gospel of the image of God. The *imago* means that we are addressed and addressable and thus responsible. This lifts us above other creatures and calls us to a particular encounter with God. The *imago* simply means that we are summoned into the history with God. This is what is meant when the Sermon on the Mount says that we are "of more value" than lilies and birds (Matt. 6:26). "Of more value" does not have the quantitative sense of more highly bred or developed. It implies difference. In contrast to the lilies and birds we may say "Father" to God (6:32) and seek first his kingdom (6:33). We are called to personal fellowship with him.

The ultimate theocentric sense of this personal character first comes to light, of course, only in the cross of Jesus Christ. Paul tells us in Romans 14:15 and 1 Corinthians 8:11 that we should not be irritated by people who make a fuss about certain things (cultically prohibited foods, eating idol meats, etc.) for the wrong reasons. We might be tempted to ignore these small people with such limited horizons. What role can they have except, perhaps, that of being an obstacle to fellowship and acting as a cultural brake. They are not outstanding leaders who cannot be replaced. They represent the average mass. It is not by chance that none of their names has been recorded. Yet we should not be irritated by them, for Christ died for them, they are bought with a price. They may be nobodies from a social or cultural standpoint. They may be easily replaceable. They may be a liability to the community. Yet each of them is of infinite worth and should be left unmolested. These nobodies, however, do not have worth or dignity in and of themselves nor because of some immanent quality. They have worth and dignity outside themselves as an alien righteousness, namely, because someone died for them. This is the alien dignity or worth of which we spoke and it is the background of their personhood, their uniqueness, their infinite value.

Luther works out the same thought in his teaching on baptism when he says that the parents often look just like other people, like Turks or heathen, and are thus replaceable or exchangeable; nevertheless, they have a unique dignity that makes them persons whom none other can represent ("represent" is our own term). For they come under the protection and acknowledgment of the saying that we are to honor father and mother. Hence I suddenly see another person adorned and clad with the majesty and glory of God. The commandment, I say, is the golden chain that he wears around his neck, the crown on his head, that shows me how and why one should honor this flesh and blood.[74]

The personal concept is here given its most pregnant form from the standpoint of the gospel. In this light we can look again at our own train of thought. Parents are flesh and blood like other people — and even animals. But they are lifted out of the ranks of similar creatures by the Word of God that is spoken regarding them, and that confers on them an alien dignity that is strictly and exactly illustrated by the metaphor of the golden chain of office. They are unique and irreplaceable only under the Word, which is both the Word of the law and the Word of the gospel. Human death has special significance because it has reference to those who are persons in this sense.[75] It impinges upon an infinite and irreplaceable value. Something unique comes to an end.

If the Christian faith teaches us to see life in the light of its end and thus to consider its vanity and destructibility, a remarkable contradiction arises. Bernard Groethuysen draws attention to this in his analysis of the secular experience of death in France, namely, that this last moment of life, when we have to set aside every concealing illusion, and when the ending and vanity of life are manifest, achieves significance precisely because of the value that we attach to life.[76] But the sense of this value is greater, and its basis is apparent, only when we are viewed from the standpoint of the law and the gospel and therefore as personal members of God's history, that is, as the bearers of an alien dignity. Purely immanent definitions of dignity lead logically only to nonuniqueness, to the possibility of being reperesented by others.

From all this it follows that personal uniqueness is connected with the summons of God and the history with him. This does not mean that nothing can be known of it — although in a different way — in the non-Christian sphere. In discussing the problem of time we have seen already that secular thought has some awareness that time is a span and that it comes to an end (in contrast to cyclical time). But since the boundary of time is not seen as one that is set by God, it takes on a different character from that of the end in death that is understood personally. This different character comes to expression in the inference that since the end is coming, we should eat, drink, and be merry, for tomorrow we die; whereas the biblical awareness that time is a span that has an end leads to the conclusion (if one wants a pregnant contrast) that we should repent, for the kingdom of heaven is at hand. If God is banished from the picture, the analogous phenomenon of the "span" of time at once has a different quality.

The same applies to the uniqueness of the human person. This uniqueness can be experienced in some sense even apart from the summons of judgment and grace. But in spite of the apparent parallel the uniqueness is quite different when it is simply a fact of experience and is not constituted by the encounter with judgment and grace, by fundamentally becoming a person. One might take Greek tragedy as an example.[77] Everywhere experience of the uniqueness of life underlies this. Yet it is striking that in distinction from the biblical deduction on the basis of a totally different understanding of uniqueness, the Greek conclusion is a tragic view of life. Curt Langenbeck is profoundly right when he says in this connection that the Greeks were convinced that personal life is unique and cannot be repeated, but the result was that they had to produce tragedy. They had to come to terms with life as a whole within this life that is given only once. For once Hades receives us, there is no going back, no more possibility of action.[78]

F. THE ANTITHESIS OF DEATH AND ETERNAL LIFE

1. The Altered Understanding of Life

If our main interest thus far has been in the personal character of human death, we must now discuss the concept of life that stands in antithesis to death as thus understood.

Biological life certainly cannot adequately express the antithesis to human death, no matter whether we take a biblical or a secular view of the latter. In the secular sphere death, as we have seen, is part of the rhythm of life itself, but it is the down beat. Or, if we have the myths of immortality in mind, it is the transition of one form of life into another. An absolute antithesis to natural *bios* cannot arise along these lines.

153

On the other hand, physical life, *bios*, is not the antithesis of human death on a biblical view, either. For what takes place in the framework of the laws of biological life, as secular thought is well aware, is only physical dying. I have in mind here the OT accounts of the deaths of the patriarchs, which repeatedly say, as we have seen already, that the patriarchs were old and full of years when they died. Even the idea of death as the wages of sin, as we have come to realize, cannot bring liberation from the laws of natural life and death.

Everything depends, then, on finding the strict antithesis to the biblical concept of death, for only thus can we give final precision to the personal character of human dying.

To find this antithesis, we do best to begin with the assumption that a personal concept of life will necessarily correspond to the personal character of death. Such a concept may in fact be found in the Greek term for human life, the word *zoe*. For in the vocabulary of the NT this term refers strictly to the history that God enters into with us. To be sure, *zoe* has a great breadth of meanings in the NT. But all the nuances are held together by the basic thought that life of this kind relates to stages and forms of that history with God, of a history, then, to which we are called.

In a particularly emphatic way *zoe* can be understood as eternal life, and as such it is most clearly differentiated from the biological life for which death is a definitive end. But *zoe* can also be present life (1 Tim. 4:8), this life (1 Cor. 15:19), or life in the flesh (Gal. 2:20). Even then, however, the privilege of human life is unmistakably apparent. For this present life is related to eternal life and represents a time of decision in which the latter is gained or lost. It is the *kairos*, the today when we hear God's voice and are required — as Hebrews exhorts us[79] — not to harden our hearts. We *can* harden them. For our present life can in fact be lived outside fellowship with God and without claiming his turning to us in Christ. It can thus become a lost life. It is the more lost and wasted the more it builds on the self and thus inevitably reaps corruption from the flesh on which it builds (Gal. 6:8).[80] For the end of flesh is dust. Hence the ungodly and self-centered life is already dead under its perhaps attractive mask of life.[81]

Death cannot be regarded as the antithesis to this kind of life because this life is itself characterized as "dead." But dead though it may be, it is still related to the real life to which we are oriented. Its relation to this life has an indelible character. *Zoe*, too, can say

No to God. In so doing it does not become a life *without* God but a life *against* God. It continues to be a life with God, but in the negative mode. Atheism has to be interpreted theologically along these lines.

If we analyze the concept of *zoe* a little more closely, we find confirmation of our thesis that it always expresses the privileges of *human* life, that is, life that is oriented to God. For even when we read about living (*zen*) in the flesh, which comes to an end in physical death, we can clearly detect a nuance that denotes human life. Even our span of existence in the flesh, our physical life, is meant to produce fruit (Phil. 1:22). Its point is that, in distinction from the animals, we should take our lives in hand and orient ourselves to something.

This is why it can be an open question for Paul whether it is better to depart and be with Christ or to live on in the service of others (Phil. 1:23f.). Even the fact that during this present life we are still bound to the law, and escape its onslaught in judgment only when we die, or are dead to it as new creatures (Rom. 7:1–3), gives evidence of an understanding of life that is proper to humans alone (and to Christians as such). *Zoe* can thus be referred to spheres that affect the spiritual life (again human). We can offer ourselves as *living* sacrifices (Rom. 12:1). *Living* oracles were given to Moses at Sinai (Acts 7:38). The *living* word is like a two-edged sword, piercing joints and marrow (Heb. 4:12). A *living* spirit fills the word (John 6:63, 68), and there is a *living* hope (1 Pet. 1:3).

We are speaking, then, about the privileged human life that is sheltered against natural death. Although bread (representing natural nourishment) is a condition of our physical life, we do not live by bread alone but by every word that proceeds out of the mouth of God (Matt. 4:4). Thus our human life, our *zoe*, transcends the physical *bios* that we share with animals. It does so exactly as Christ, the bread of life, transcends lifegiving earthly bread (John 6:35, 41) and takes us through death to eternal life (6:50f.).

Human life as *zoe* is no more restricted to the physical realm than human death. Since we exist in our relation to God, life and death are both defined by this relation. Only in this light can we understand death as the limitation of the limitless by God's wrath, as exclusion from the life of God. *Zoe*, then, is something that comes only from God.[82] A life that is led apart from this life of God, being focused on the self, on this life, apart from Christ or in a wrong relation to him, is "lost" and makes us the most to be pitied of all creatures (1 Cor. 15:18f.). Such a life is dead even before it comes to a physical end (Luke 15:24, 32; Eph. 2:1, 5; 5:14, etc.).

Life in the flesh (Gal. 2:20), which is subject to death even though it points beyond it, is not, then, *true* life.[83] The true life is the future one that has left death behind and is really eternal life.[84] At issue is not the immortality of the soul but participation in the resurrection of Christ (1 Cor. 15:20ff.).

What does this mean?

Paul tells us in Romans (6:5– 12). His point may be summed up in the statement that participation in fellowship with Christ is unbreakable and cannot be interrupted or broken off by death. This fellowship means that in solidarity with Christ we ourselves die and rise again. This is not imitation in the sense that we "die and become" on our own (as in Goethe's idea of personality). This dying and rising again happen to us. They take place as we are taken up into Christ's dying and rising again, as we are incorporated into this saving event, as Christ our exemplar (or prototype) reproduces himself in us.[85]

This may sound abstract and dogmatic at first, but it becomes intelligible and commends itself for acceptance if we differentiate the processes at issue.

1. Paul first says that the crucifixion of the *Kyrios* works itself out in the lives of those who belong to him. The old man is crucified with him; the body of sin receives a mortal blow. This does not mean, as Calvin points out,[86] that sin ceases at a stroke, that it no longer plays any role for us, that it is ontically erased from our lives. (Luther's slogan that we are righteous and sinners at the same time expresses our common experience here.)[87] What *is* meant is that the dominion of sin comes to an end when we hand over our old lives for crucifixion with Christ, that a change of government takes place in our lives, that we are "transplanted." If, rightly, we still call ourselves sinners, this is no longer a complete definition, nor does it touch the core of what we now are. Sin, having lost its dominion, has been robbed of its point, which involved separation from God, Nothing now separates us from God (Rom. 8:31ff.). Sin does not come to an end, but its divisive function does. We are no longer cast back on our isolation from God. We are no longer left on our own as we were before. Sin is no longer an abyss that divides. A bridge has been built and a

Mediator stretches out his hands across it.

This does not exclude — but rather includes — the initiation of a process of ontic renewal. If the dominion of sin is broken, necessarily its ontic elements are increasingly diminished and there is progress in sanctification.[88] A process begins, though it has not yet reached its goal. It is not as though all sin were immediately at an end (Calvin).[89] But we live in the name of the promise that we shall eventually win the victory. God's work will not be completed the first day it begins on earth, but it develops gradually and reaches its goal by daily augmentation.

That renewal is a *process* and means a *comprehensive* struggle with sin, although under the banner of a victory that has already been won, is something that Paul makes clear by means of the many imperatives that he links with the indicative of the promise of victory and pardon (Rom. 6:7). Now that the dominion of sin has been broken, we are not to let it reign over us any more. We are to resist it. We are not to let our members be weapons or instruments or openings for the sin that still seeks to dominate us (6:12f.). We are pardoned and set in a new field of force, but this is no reason for taking our ease or for indifference (6:15).

2. This change of government has a direct bearing on the problem of death. If the dominion of sin is undermined, death necessarily ceases to be the wages of sin. To explain this, we need to refer back to our interpretation of the story of the fall. We showed there that sin is to be understood as limitlessness, as wanting to be like God, as the perverting of the divine likeness into arrogant equality with God. The passing of the sentence of mortality on the human race meant that a limit was set to the limitless. We were compelled to experience the fact that we are *only* human, *only* dust, and separated from God by an infinite qualitative distinction. But when the old, rebellious man in us is crucified and the force of the revolt is broken, when there is that "transplanting" in faith with all that it entails, the desire for limitlessness is ended and death as the sign of limitation is no longer needed. The wages of sin, then, will no longer be paid.

In this sense death takes on a different meaning. The sting is withdrawn which made it a painful reminder of the fall (1 Cor. 15:55f.). It is included when the divisive forces are all robbed of their power. It can no longer be a divisive force that excludes us from the life of the living God (Rom. 8:38) and causes us to put our trust in perishable things, in things that are overshadowed by death — in short, in the flesh. For when Christ awakens us out of death and leads us to a life that no longer knows death (Rom. 6:9) but is life in and with and for God alone (6:10), he keeps us here and now in fellowship with himself and makes us his companions not only in his crucifixion but also in his resurrection life.[90]

This is no mere matter of looking at ourselves and fixing statistically what we have done to overcome death and the fear of death, and to make spiritual progress. Every form of introspective "looking back" (Luke 9:62) can lead only to error and open the gate to disquietude. Psychological attempts to examine our own experiences cannot possibly be a standard for spiritual orientation. This type of procedure is merely unstable and unreliable "flesh" in the biblical sense, albeit *religious* flesh. The real point is that we should count on the fact that lies beyond all our subjectivity,[91] the fact of our once-for-all pardon in the death and resurrection of Christ and the consequent breaking of the dominion of sin and opening of the pathway to life. This means no less than that death is altered and changed in substance. From a divisive force it has become a transition to life. It no longer thrusts us into the alien territory of finitude but brings us home from the hut of transitoriness to the eternal dwelling that is prepared for us (2 Cor. 5:1f.).

The figure of Christ is always present where the border *once* existed but is now removed. He is the prince of life who leads me through the barrier of death. Though I may depart from him, he will never depart from me. This fact shows us that the overcoming of the boundary is from above and not from below. The movement from below to above by which Adam proudly tries to leap over the border is precisely what *causes* the border to be set up and power to be given to death. No movement of life from below to above can surmount the frontier of death. All such movements will simply make it deeper and stronger and more impregnable. They will simply make us trust more in transitory things and focus on them. Precisely in the secular culture of life and the apparent triumph of vitality, does not death become more frigid and puzzling and terrible and the lie become more daring with which we conceal it — conceal ultimately the nothingness and annihilation of life itself? The victory comes only from above to below. It takes place only in the condescension, the incarnation of the Word, the acceptance of comradeship in death at the cross.

The secret of the frontier lies in the apotheosis of humanity, the denial of its mere creatureliness. The secret of the removal of the frontier lies in the incarnation, in God's condescension to the crib and the cross.

2. Eternal Life Present and Future

A look at what has already happened, opening up the prospect of what abides after death in eternity, brings before us once again the question of eternal life as both present and future. The initiation of eternal life by Christ's resurrection gives a new quality to past, present, and future.

The individual stages in the span of time are no longer divided by a radical break,[92] for the decisive thing has already happened with the resurrection on the third day. Paradoxically, we have our future not only ahead of us but already in the past behind us. We go toward it as we come from it. In the Christ event eternal life has already dawned. It is among us; it is our present (Luke 17:21; 2 Cor. 6:2). As thus qualified, the Now differs from both past and present. It differs from the past event of the resurrection in which the change of aeons took place and which takes present form in our new birth, in the beginning of the "new creature." It differs from the coming life of fulfillment which is prepared today and whose first installment is given us here and now by the Spirit (2 Cor. 1:22; Eph. 1:14). Hope itself is already a sign of this coming life, a form of its presence (1 Pet. 1:3). The tension between "fulfilled already" and "still to come" is a structural mark of what the NT has to say about time.

From this angle death loses its character as an absolute break, so that the distinction between this side of death and the far side is relativized. This is a further indication that power is wrested from death[93] and that those who are touched by the lifegiving Spirit have already broken through death to life (John 5:24). Faith is the place of this breakthrough and the newly given capacity for love is its seal and sign (1 John 3:14f.). In this sense "now" is the accepted time, "now" is the *kairos*.

God has entered into a history with us that can never end. For the saving event that the lifegiving Spirit initiated does not rest on the self-development of our spirit, which would come to an end, but rather is an event that befalls us as God's Spirit acts upon us, and will continue to do so to all eternity. A point of all the promises is that we can no longer be separated from him who has accepted us and taken us up into Christ's resurrection life, and that all the powers — including death — break on the power of this fellowship and have to confess that they are robbed of their power by it (Rom. 8:31ff.).

What remains, then, is only the biological side of dying, the fading *physis*, which no doubt has significance as *anamnesis*, but has now lost its sting and poison. All that remains by way of the fear and anguish of death — even in the train of the prince of life! — is simply a reflection of the instinct of self-preservation, the universal creaturely mark of a physical shrinking from destruction. This has nothing whatever to do with the personal destiny of death and its sting. It is to be regarded as part of our creaturely constitution, which contains the instinct of self-preservation as a kind of protective mechanism.

With reference to the robbing of personal death of its power, Hebrews can say (2:14) that what Christ has overcome in relation to death is not physical death — there will still be death, just as in the case of birds and flowers — but the one who had the power of death, the *diabolos*, the demonic destroyer.

We must be careful here not to refer to the *diabolos* as a mythical figure. The Bible never makes the devil a cause — thus excusing us — in a mythological explanation of evil. The role of the serpent in the story of the fall is a striking paradigm in this regard. Everywhere there is extreme restraint in the ontological description of the devil, which corresponds in many ways to similar restraint in the NT in the ontological description of the person of Christ. If Melanchthon says in his *Loci* that to know Christ is to know his benefits, one might reverse the statement in relation to the devil and say that to know the devil is to know his ill effects. (Cf. EF III, 448ff.)

This *diabolos* usurps the power of death by saying that everything ends with death, so that the goods of this world are ultimate values and therefore idols that we must serve and reverence. (Even Goethe's Mephistopheles has traits of this kind.) Did not this *diabolos* suggest to the solitary Jesus in the wilderness that these goods are gods: the world's riches and kingdoms, and bread as the staff of life and a means of achieving dominion? And did he not make the point that if Jesus would cleave to these gods he would then be the Son of God with recognizable power?

But this power to slay is now taken away from death. It can no longer make those who are in living fellowship with Christ into slaves of the fear of death and therefore slaves of idols. Death is not set aside, but it is deprived of its power (cf. Col. 3:3, 5). Hence the real point of death is no longer parting from, but homegoing to.

As death is deprived of its sting and poison, as it is no longer a personal fulfillment of God's wrath, it is only a biological mask that has no bearing on fellowship with the risen Lord.[94] Those who believe in him who is the resurrection and the life will live even though they die, and those who have this life and believe in him will not die eternally (John 11:25f.). This means that we can die "in peace" — we die only in quotation marks, in an improper sense. For the one in whose hands death was a weapon and device can no longer harm us. Even with the help of death he can no longer hand us over to the gods of this world and therefore tear us out of the hand of God. The fear whose slaves we were can no longer overcome us because there is no longer any reason for the fear of God, which comes disguised as the fear of death. God has stooped down and come to us in love.[95] If we believe, we have already passed from death — from being for death and determination by it — to life (John 5:34; 1 John 4:18).[96]

3. Immortality and Resurrection Again

We now put for the last time the self-critical question whether this eternal life might not be a new form of the immortality and survival after death that we had to reject so definitely in the name of taking death seriously, and that we had to describe theologically as a "flight" and a "holding down in unrighteousness" (Rom. 1:18). Is there really any alternative?

This fellowship with the risen Lord, this living even though we die, differs in two ways from the theories of immortality that we discussed earlier. First, these theories always work with an immanent quality in humans, with a suprapersonal substance that indwells them and by the sharing of which they themselves survive as specimens. In contrast, the overcoming of death in fellowship with the risen Lord is a historical event, not a timeless substantial affair. *Zoe* is a quality of divine life to which I am recalled and in which I participate in the described personal manner of obedience and love. This *zoe* is not a quality of my own but a quality of God. It is extrinsic to me, not intrinsic.

This brings us to a second factor, which displays a strong analogy to the doctrine of justification. The righteousness that counts before God, making me certain of his unmerited turning to me and of my fellowship with him, is not a quality of my own in virtue of which I am righteous, but a quality of God in virtue of which he makes me righteous, or, in modern terms, in virtue of which he accepts me. Luther described this in both its aspects with the aid of the concept of the mathematical point. As the subject of the faith that grasps God's righteousness, we ourselves (1) are a mathematical point, that is, we are not extended in such a way that our righteousness occupies a specific physical space that we can claim as our own possession and attribute. All that we can do is simply place ourselves in confident trust under God's quality of being gracious. Our righteousness, then, is the quality of another; it is an alien righteousness.[97]

The same applies (2) to the whole length of our life, at the end of which stands death. Even if we live to be a hundred, this life is like an unextended mathematical point. It thus has no substance of its own but is constituted only by him who causes it to be lived and died. Hence the life that endures, *zoe*, is not to be understood as a quality of my own but as that of another.[98] Neither quality, neither righteousness nor *zoe*, becomes conditionally or secretly a possession of my own, as the doctrine of the infusion or substantial impartation of grace would have it. If impartation of this kind is postulated, there necessarily arises at the same time the postulate of a possible substantial or habitual righteousness of our own. An impressive ideal of holiness then follows, and this leads to the thing that called forth Luther's protest, namely, the advancing of a claim on God on the basis of some quality that is our own even if it is given.

This view then entails a partnership between us and God which, in spite of the ongoing recognition of God's authorship of the righteousness, is an extremely refined form of blasphemy, since it sets God in analogy to us.

With the same inevitability — for the root is the same — the idea of infusion produces a new doctrine of immortality that necessarily works with the postulate that when the soul is filled with the substance of divine grace and enriched with *zoe*, it cannot fall victim to death but will survive it.[99]

In contrast, the biblical faith that Luther rediscovered realizes that, like righteousness, *zoe* remains exclusively under God's control, and that I have a share in it only insofar as I am made worthy, without cause, of fellowship with God in Christ.

The personal character of this fellowship stands in the sharpest contrast to every form of substantial participation, for personal fellowship means that in faith, love, and hope I may live under God as one who expects *everything* from him and thus prays that he will hold fast to me, as one for whom Jesus Christ has become a brother and who may ascribe to the self all that is his because God is prepared to accept his vicarious work[100] (but not a mystical transfusion of quality from Christ to us).[101]

In keeping with this, my death — even as a biological mask — can never be understood as something that is not literal because of some immortality of my own that means that my soul is spared and passed over. No, I sink into death as a totality, and nothing gives me the right, when I confront death, suddenly to split my biblically proclaimed totality into a body and a soul, into a perishable and an imperishable part of the I. I sink into death, however, in such a way that I know that I shall not stay in it, for God has called me by name and will call me again on his day. I am under the protection of the risen Lord no matter what anxiety the long night of death might cause.[102] I am not immortal, but I am one who awaits the resurrection. God has begun to speak with me. He will not break off the fellowship that he has started with me nor let it be annulled by death. This is the certainty of victory over death that has its ground outside me in God. When God speaks with us, whether in wrath or in grace, we are immortal, for the person of the God who speaks, and the Word of God, show that we are creatures with whom he wills to speak eternally and immortally.[103] The biblical, Reformation insight into justification comes to a climax here. As we always stand with empty hands before God and can only beg him to accept us all the same, so we go down into death with empty hands, with no substance of the soul that is sheltered from death, and can only beg God to hold us fast.

In death I approach with confidence him who has life as well as judgment in his hands. I need not rely on my own good works or on my immortal soul. I may not do so, for the works are not good and the soul is not immortal. I am righteous by grace alone, and it is by grace alone that I share in the resurrection (2 Cor. 4:7). I will remain in the fellowship of him who is Alpha and Omega. With this knowledge I go into the night of death, which is a real night. I know who is waiting for me in the morning.

In this light, death obviously undergoes a transformation. As what is not my own, but is taken from me by Christ, seizes me, I may confess that I am not dying my own death as it is defined by my Adamic existence. Instead, I am making the death of Jesus Christ my own death. I can apply to myself all that Christ has done, just as he bore on his own shoulders all that afflicted me. As Luther said, Jesus Christ is my righteousness, and I am his sin; he has taken what is mine and given me what is his.[104] Faith demands that we rely on what Christ did and suffered as though we had done and suffered it ourselves.[105]

I thus live in the fellowship of the Lord who cannot be held, nor his companions, by death. This participation in Christ's own dying comes to concrete expression in the way that I fulfill death. Its first mark is that I no longer experience death merely as a fate to which I am subject, but that I really do fulfill it, which means voluntarily and affirmatively grasping it. By saying "Yes, Father," I grasp the *anamnesis* of my fall and put myself under the judgment that God pronounced, or expose myself to it. But in so doing I also place myself under the cross of Christ and Christ's death, which I appropriate and make my own along the lines that Luther suggested above. For Jesus Christ did not just suffer death. He was outside its dominion and claim. He was not one of those limitless people who had to be limited. He fulfilled death freely. He accepted the judgment that is passed on us in death. He let himself be smitten by it. Dying for him was far more active than passive.

When I for my part insert myself into this action, *my* death is changed into Christ's and bears the mark of the second Adam, not the first. I have changed the prototype in terms of which I exist. Obediently affirming the God who speaks to me in the destiny of death, I loose myself from bondage to the world and self and give myself to my new definition in Christ. This is the inner, supremely factual and supremely concrete change that death undergoes by reason of my participation in the death of Jesus Christ. This is the true overcoming of death that the risen Lord imparts to his companions, not merely reducing death to a biological mask but making our death his and his death ours.

We will now gather together our findings regarding the robbing of death of its power. They take two directions. First, death is robbed of its power as we are set in the sphere of God's life and in fellowship with the risen Lord, as we are set, therefore, in what John's Gospel calls "eternal life." Second, death is robbed of its power as the limit that is set for me in death is removed, as the cherub with the flaming sword — to put it symbolically — no longer stands at the entrance to the garden of God in which there is life.

For Christians, then, death is only what I have called a biological mask. That which defined it personally and gave it its sting (our limitation and the reaction of the divine holiness proclaimed therein) has been taken away.

To be sure, death is still there, as the sinner in fact is still there, but only as a mask with no authority or power, like a snake that has lost its fangs, so that it is still a snake but has no power as such. The power of death was that it kept us behind that boundary that we could not cross and thus caused us to make life an end in itself and to deify our goods, for after us comes the flood.

What does it mean to stand instead in the sphere of the risen Lord (if we may add a few strokes to our existing sketch)?

1. To stand in the sphere of the risen Lord is to stand at the point of breakthrough where Christ shattered the front of death. It is to be embraced by his life in which our own life now is only a fragment, a pilgrim state, in which it is only the span of time — what a transformation! — in which I can only believe and see the glory of God in a dark mirror, whereas one day I shall see him face to face and thus know him as I am already known by him (1 Cor. 13:12).

2. To stand in the sphere of the risen Lord is to be embraced by his life in such a way that we may confidently die daily for his sake, for if we live, we live to the Lord, and if we die, we die to the Lord (Rom. 14:8). To the Lord! We are in his living hand — only his hand is living! — and we can die only into this hand, falling into the hand of him who lives. Disciples have the promise that they will win life if they lose it for the Lord's sake. For this is the living Lord who has burst the fetters of the prince of death. The time of this world perishes, but the Lord abides.

3. To stand in the sphere of the risen Lord is finally to have

fellowship with God in Jesus Christ and hence to have no more fellowship with death. It is to have a Lord and hence not to be able to be ruled by death or by the gods and goods of this life.

I am a companion of Jesus. Where he is, I shall be. Is he not in life? Then I shall live, and death cannot separate me from the love of God. I might depart from him, but the prince of life will lead me. I will cling to him as a member does to its head, and where the head goes he will take me with him. He moves through death, the world, sin, need, and hell, and I am his constant companion (Paul Gerhardt).

•Appendix I •

FURTHER REMARKS ON THE PROBLEM OF DEATH IN GOETHE

Apart from the concept of the entelechy, which we took as normative for the discussion of the problem of death in Goethe, the question of death arises in various other connections. Thus in the *Prometheus Fragment*[1] we find it in the Promethean proclamation of an identity of death and life. In an extreme feeling of joy and pain, of vitality, such as the experience of love encloses and discloses, death announces itself as the moment that fulfills everything, everything that we have dreamed and yearned and hoped for; Pandora, that is death. In the great convulsions of life we seem to perish and sink into night even as we embrace a world. Then we die. Death and extreme life are closely related.

And after death? Death is only a blissful sleep in which everything dissolves and will finally live again, bringing new fears and hopes and longings.[2]

In the Divan poem *Selige Sehnsucht* this proximity of the mystery of love and life to death is symbolized in the butterfly that is singed in the flame. A strange spring comes, which causes us to sense a higher mystery of life behind the reproductive experience as the act of a mystical disclosure of life. New desire leads us on to new mating. But the mystery is also the mystery of death. For only here do we see the mystery of "Die and become," of change through the fiery death. This is the perishing of which the *Prometheus Fragment* spoke, but on a higher level. As long as we do not have this "Die and become," we are only melancholy guests on earth. In the new form of religious philosophy the same slogan recurs in the symbol of the cross of roses in the fragment *Die Geheimnisse*.

In Goethe's conversations, however, especially those with Eckermann, the concept of the entelechy is always the basis of the indestructibility of life and the conquest of death. "The idea of death does not disturb me at all. For I have the firm conviction that our spirit is an entity of a wholly indestructible kind. It moves on from eternity to eternity. It is like the sun, which seems to go down to our earthly eyes, but does not really go down but continues to shine unceasingly."[3] To the same effect is the passage already quoted from the "Bekenntnisse einer schönen Seele" in the *Lehrjahre*, which says that though the body may be torn like a garment, the I, the well-known I, I am.[4] But we are not immortal in the same way. To show ourselves to be something in the future, we have to be something.[5] Those who have no hope of another life are dead for this one. But such incomprehensible things are too remote to be a subject of daily contemplation and speculations that disrupt thought. Solid people who are trying to be something good already, and are thus engaged in daily struggle and battle and action, will let the future world alone and be active and useful in this one.[6]

The look "beyond" that is thus called into question gives to many of Goethe's statements on the theme the character of a meditative and fragmentary experiment in thought that can hardly be accorded thetic rank. Some sayings from Ottilien's diary in the *Wahlverwandschaften* are typical. "When we consider the many sunken gravestones on which churchgoers walk, and even the churches which have collapsed on the gravestones, life after death can come before us as a kind of second life into which we enter in a picture or superscription and stay even longer than in real life. But sooner or later this picture, this second existence, fades. Time does not let its right to men, any more than to memorials, be taken from it" (c.2).

• *Appendix II* •

THE CONCEPT OF PALINGENESIS
IN ROMANTICISM

A typical but more remote attempt to master death with means of thought similar to those just described may be found in the concept of palingenesis in Herder, Novalis, and Kleist. This concept is characterized especially by the abolition of what we have called uniqueness and irreversibility. The following passage from Herder may be taken as an example:

> The old man must die in us, in order that a new youth may come forth. But how does this happen? Can a man go back into his mother's womb and be born again? No answer can be given to this doubt of Nicodemus of old but that of palingenesis! Not revolution, but a happy evolution of the rejuvenating forces that slumber in us. What we call outliving ourselves, or death, is in better souls only a sleep with a new awakening, a relaxing of the bow with a view to new use. The field is fallow in order that it may bear the more richly; the tree dies in winter in order to sprout and thrust forth again in spring. Destiny does not abandon the good so long as they do not abandon themselves or give way to ignominious despair. The genius which seemed to have departed from them will return at the right time and with it will come new activity, happiness, and joy.[7]

Historically considered, the thought of reincarnation, which does not allow our unique time to end but brings it back again, achieved "a reconciliation of the vitality and cosmic thinking of monistic and pantheistic immanence with the core of historical Christianity on the further field of the problem of immortality, and in contrast with prior answers along dualistic and transcendental lines."[8]

To be compared are similar concepts of palingenesis in Lessing's *Erziehung des Menschengeschlechts*.[9] Typical versions may also be found in Kleist's letters to his bride Wilhelmine (3.22.1801), to Karoline von Schlieben (7.18.1801), and to Rühle (8.31.1806).

• Appendix III •

DEATH IN THE COSMOS

It is a mistake to deduce the biological death of plants and animals causally from human sin. Some biblical passages are adduced in favor of this, such as Romans 8:19, 22; 2 Thessalonians 2:6; the story of the flood, Genesis 6:7; and the story of the fall.[10] The following points may be made concerning these.

The Bible regards human sin as a cosmic event, just as in eschatology redemption far transcends the human sphere and has universal significance. We can only state this here without giving a full account of the existential experience expressed therein. Dogmatic statements must be avoided for this reason. Extreme attempts to make such statements may be found in Edgar Dacqués's well-known works *Urwelt, Sage und Menschheit* (1938) and *Das verlorene Paradies* (1940). At the most it seems that we cannot say more than as follows.

1. Humanity is the crown of creation. This may be seen from the depth of its fall. Nature is drawn into its sinful plight, and this shows that nature is not an end in itself but a means to display humanity's kingly position. The light of human existence is mythologically lit up by the shadow of creation. This may be caught from the inner accents of what is said about nature. It is shown especially by the orientation of creation to the human race (cf. Gen. 1 and 2). Similarly, in the intimation of the flood that will engulf all living things, the animal world is merely a background for humanity (Gen. 6:7), and the animals that are saved with Noah in the ark are not presented as independent participators in the fall and salvation, but simply as representatives of the living things whose head is Noah. The human story casts a shadow on the cosmos, probably not merely in the sense of a direct relation of humanity to the animal kingdom (ruling with fear and trembling, Gen. 9:2), but in the sense of the sharing of a common creaturely fate. But we must not try to say how this happens. The orientation of all the statements to humanity and its fall forbids this. Nature has its own right to life, for the world has to remain intact with

all its laws of life in order to make possible for humanity the age of the covenant of grace, the accepted time (Gen. 8:21f.; 9:11).

2. Thus, the concept of vicarious representation, which runs through the whole of Scripture, applies positively only to Christ as the suffering Servant of the Lord, yet it also appears negatively as responsibility for others. Thus Adam commits "my" sin vicariously and is "my" representative (inclusively). Again, God visits the parents' sins on the children, who are in this sense represented by their parents. Again, later generations have to suffer for the murder of Abel (Matt. 23:35). "The fathers have eaten sour grapes, and the children's teeth are set on edge" (Jer. 31:29). In the same way the human race, as the head of the cosmos, is also its representative, and by sinning in its official capacity (and not just privately) it plunges the cosmos represented by it into the abyss.

3. Regarding the dependence of cosmic death on the human race, compare Genesis 3:17ff.; 5:29 (also 8:21); in these passages the earth is cursed because of us. Similarly in many parts of the law the ungodly's property, especially in the form of animals, is drawn into the judgment that is meted out on them.

According to Romans 1:18ff., God's wrath is revealed from heaven on all ungodliness. Heaven, the cosmic order, is the organ of the forces of destruction released by the just God. According to Romans 8:20 the nonhuman creation (*ktisis*) is dragged by the human into the bondage of perishable being and subjected to vanity because of it.

There is no question of any alteration of nature in a demonstrable sense. The important thing to recognize is that we do not have here biological speculations nor any simple causal relation between personal guilt and biological effects. The relation is one of representation to the extent that humanity is the head of the cosmos and its position is expressed in mythical symbols.

With due dogmatic caution I would explain cosmic death as a consequence of sin along the following lines. Conflict and death are natural laws. While these laws find exact parallels in human life, and are strengthened by our biological character, we experience their reality differently in regard to both conflict and death. Looking back on the cosmos, with our extra knowledge we view natural events in analogy to human experience. Is this reading something into nature, or is it a disclosure of its ultimate secret, that is, the radiating of human guilt? Who of us can seriously question the biblical view—fumbling though we are in our attempts to work it out—when we look into the eyes of a dog and we have at our command the biblical insight into guilt and redemption? The cry for redemption runs through the cosmos. Its forces of death and destruction are due to a curse that lies upon it and that the Bible connects with human guilt. Who of us does not discern these metarational relations? As Schlegel says, a universal weeping extends to the stars and runs through all the veins of nature. In an agony of love, creation sighs and yearns for the granting of transfiguration.[11] The statements of Scripture seem to me to be much too restrained for us essentially to say more or even to ask more along these lines. No dogmatic pronouncement may be made here, but the *problem* can certainly be taken seriously. We at least cannot and will not do more; it might be that others think they can, and some really can.

THE INTERMEDIATE STATE[12]

This is the place to allude to the question of the intermediate state between death and the resurrection. Strictly speaking, of course, this eschatological problem is not part of our remit, since we were trying to study death simply in relation to anthropology.

If we still have to look at the question, it must be particularly because our previous trains of thought have implications for the intermediate state on which I should like to express my position.

These implications are determined primarily by the principle of personal totality. If there is in fact no division of the I into body and soul, and death affects the totality of the person, it seems to me that the intermediate state falls away with the immortality of the soul, and the total I, both body and soul, sinks into the nothingness of the night of death. The resurrection is then a new creation out of nothing on the day of God.

I myself am too strongly impressed by the consistency of this approach not to feel affected here by a distrust in principle of all theological consistency. Might it not be that the consistency entails a restriction of the wealth and fullness of the biblical statements, that it is possible only in the monologue of reflective thought, and that it is attained only at the cost of a constant readiness to listen? A law that is often illustrated in the history of theology is that the illumination brought by one theological insight — and our recognition of the death of the whole person may be such an insight — often brings obscurity in some other respect.

More precisely, the question is this: Are we justified in using our thesis that the total person is extinguished in death as a criterion by which to measure scriptural statements about the intermediate state and thus to disparage these as heterogeneous elements (possibly Hellenistic remnants), or must we bring our thesis under the criticism of the richer fullness of biblical thinking and make it more flexible?

No solution to this problem is possible unless we deal with certain material questions. Perhaps it would be as well to put the most decisive of these in their *popular* form, which is drastic but clear. Does death mean a direct transition to eternal life, a simultaneous raising up again to this life? Do we not have something of this in mind when we refer on gravestones to resting in God or being at peace? But what is the relation of an immediate resurrection of this kind to the eschatological resurrection of the dead? How are we to understand the interval between the two forms of resurrection? What is the ontic state of the dead during this interval? I shall try to answer these questions in a series of steps.

1. As noted earlier, the NT distinguishes between the victory that Christ has won over death[13] and the definitive destruction of the last enemy on the last day. We came across this distinction when it was a matter of seeing that the "victory" refers to the robbing of the power of personal death, to the withdrawing of its sting and poison, whereas physical dying and death will continue to the end of the age, during which period death will still be the last enemy. In elucidation I might refer again to the example of Stalingrad. The decisive battle was fought there, the victory was proleptically won, but the defeated enemy would still engage in rearguard actions; similarly, the snake will continue biting even though its fangs have been taken out and it has lost its power to kill.

2. This gives rise to the question of the state of the dead, especially those who sleep in Christ. Their death is overcome, but not set aside. They are still waiting for the hour when death will be no more (Rev. 21:4). "How long?" the martyrs who sleep under the altar cry (Rev. 6:9f.).

3. These quotations refer to the intermediate state, which is at issue here. We nowhere find any speculations concerning its nature, obviously because NT thinking relates soberly to our existence and to salvation, and speculations on the *how* necessarily are irrelevant for this type of thought. The only standpoint from which the interval is viewed is that of those who are still alive in time. This standpoint directs our attention not to an ontic state, but to a relation, namely, that of those who sleep in Christ to their Lord. These deceased believers are sheltered in Christ and even set in especially close proximity to him. The souls (we shall say a word about this) of the martyrs are under the altar at the heart of the sanctuary. God through Jesus will bring those who are asleep with him (1 Thess. 4:14). Both the living and the dead are in immediacy

to him, neither having the precedence (1 Thess. 4:15– 18). Lazarus, when he dies, is carried to Abraham's bosom – sheltered in the same way (Luke 16:23). Paul confesses that he would like to depart and be with Christ (Phil. 1:12), denoting in this way the basic relationship of believers that death cannot disrupt and that climaxes in immediacy. The crucified (and not yet risen) Lord says to one of the thieves: "Today you will be with me in Paradise" (Luke 23:43). Nothing mythical is here being said about this Paradise and its nature. For the point of the saying is the promise that the malefactor will be with him when his execution is complete. One might almost say that being with him *is* Paradise. Here, too, Paradise can only be described as a relation, a personal union and link.

The most impressive statement of this view is made by Paul in 2 Corinthians 5:1– 10. Prior to death, while we are at home in the body, we are distant from the Lord. We walk only by faith, not sight. We thus live in a stage of mediacy. "Now we see in a mirror dimly" and not yet — "but then" — "face to face" (1 Cor. 13:12). For this reason we want to leave our present home in the body of death in order that we may find our home in the Lord (2 Cor. 5:8). Death is viewed here as a going home – no matter what anxiety the long night of death may cause. Even before our rising again on the last day, so long as the intermediate state continues, we are taken up into the shelter of that relation that is promised to the faith of the living: we are "with Christ."

Paul's statements in 2 Corinthians 5 are the basis of the verse of the chorale that speaks of the long night of death causing us anxiety. Paul is referring here to the creaturely anxiety that he experiences in face of death even though he knows and says that death is defeated. For him this anxiety comes to – very non-Greek – expression in a fear of the loss of the body. The bodilessness of the inner person – or whatever else we may call our surviving substratum – is for him a state of nakedness (5:3). He thus longs not to be left unclothed at death, but to be clothed with the spiritual body.

In relation to the intermediate state, what is said about death amounts to this: Death is defeated, but it still remains and its definitive destruction is still awaited. A fear of nakedness in death is confessed, but so, too, is the confidence that after the present finite span of time we shall find shelter in Christ, even during what we call the intermediate state and what we mean by the "night of death."

4. The questions that arise relative to this state are to a large extent analogous to those that are raised by another interim period, the time between Christ's resurrection and his *parousia*. In both cases we have a problem of time and temporality, though differently put. Regarding the second interval, we have seen what is involved in imminent expectation of the end of the world. After the victory of Easter, which brings about the change in aeons, the temporal interim is transparent to the definitive end, so that the end of the world seems to be close. We have referred in this regard to a prophetic foreshortening of perspective.

The intermediate state also — although naturally in a modified way — confronts us with this problem of time. This is palpable when we consider some of the ways in which we speak about death. Thus we say that a person was called away from the temporal sphere. Within the schema of Kant's philosophy, one might put the problem thus: Time and space are epistemologically constitutive for us. Hence death is a transition to an inconceivable mode of being. Our cognitive apparatus cannot cope with a state outside time. The attempt to penetrate it epistemologically necessarily leads to the fatal consequences of a metaphysics entangled in (what Kant would call) antinomies.

Connected, perhaps, with this problem of cognition and expression is the fact that many theologians, for example, Carl Stange and Paul Althaus, have adopted Luther's idea of soul sleep to try to overcome the epistemological problem of talking about the intermediate state.[14] Luther could say of the dead that they sleep a painless sleep ... they rest in peace and will not be afflicted by any more suffering (Sermon on Matt. 9:1ff.).[15]

This has two implications for the intermediate state and its inexpressibility. First, sleeping means that there is no reflection on the nature of this state. The dead are at peace — that is all. Second, the metaphor of sleep indicates that the dead are called out of time (as those who are asleep lose a sense of time in dreams). Thus the interval between dying and the resurrection at the last day no longer presents a problem of time. The person who comes back into time after being asleep can think that the sleep has lasted only an hour or two when many hours of the night have actually passed.[16]

The resurrection at the end is, then, an awakening out of sleep.

The removal of a sense of time means for those who are awakened that the long night of death is reduced to a mathematical point, and they are thus summoned out of completed life.

The problem of time exists, then, for those of us who are alive and tied to the form of time, but not for those who sleep. This sleep is also one of peace. It is protected. After death the soul finds rest and peace, and in its sleep does not feel any pain, and yet God keeps the waking soul (*loc. cit.*).

This thought is finely expressed by Sir Thomas Browne (*Religio medici*, 1642). He prays that the hour will come when all sleep will be past and we shall rise up forever. For him this is the sedative that he takes when going to bed. He does not need any other opiate, but peacefully closes his eyes and would not be averse to saying farewell to the sun and sleeping until the resurrection.

To sum up, we may say that all the relevant passages in the NT — they were deliberately taken from different sections — display the same certainty that there is a being at home with Christ and a being distant from him. This state is certainly not to be regarded as a form of immortality on the basis of the potential energy of the soul, nor as a state analogous to that of the resurrection. One is to view it instead in terms of Paul's metaphor of being unclothed and waiting (2 Cor. 5:4ff.). Positively it is best described as being with Christ (Phil. 1:23).

From neither standpoint is one led to the thought of immortality. Both suggest a communication with Christ that cannot be broken off. It is not my soul, nor some part of me, that is with Christ. I myself am with Christ as one who shares fellowship with him. The head takes its members with it. In his promise to the dying thief Jesus says that "you," not "your soul," "will be with me in Paradise."

If, nevertheless, I cautiously use the term "soul" for this relationship with Christ after death, and if it is to be found in our chorales and elsewhere,[17] this is because the term is unavoidable. With its help we can inadequately express something negative, namely, the I insofar as it is no longer corporeal.

The emphasis, however, is not on qualities of my own that survive after death but on the attribute of my Lord that he will never leave me. (This is why the words "with me" are so important in the promise to the dying thief.) The form in which I am with him (in body or soul, for an interim or forever) is no more to be investigated than the state of the I, the subject of faith, is to be analyzed psychologically. For faith does not live by the subjective state of the believing I, but by the alien righteousness of its Lord, by its object.

Similarly, the intermediate state of believers who have gone home is not characterized by the state itself but by him who will not allow the fellowship to be disrupted. And as Luther called the subject of faith an extended mathematical point, and often described progress in faith as annihilation, so one may view existence after death, as regards the how or what of the form of existence, as an annihilation that lives in virtue of the extension of the Lord who does not abandon us in death. We may apply 2 Corinthians 4:7 in this sense: "We have this treasure in earthen vessels, to show that the transcendent power belongs to God and not to us."

Precisely when the intermediate state is thus defined, not in terms of the subjective structure of what lives on, but in terms of personal fellowship with Christ, one can understand why the state of those who are apart from Christ is characterized with even greater restraint. It simply consists of a lack of communication (in distinction from rejection in judgment). The puzzling saying in 1 Peter 3:19 agrees with this when it speaks about preaching to the spirits in prison. The state of these spirits is that they have no relationship to Christ. Such a relationship has yet to be established.

Finally, there may be an indication of the inexpressibility of the subjective structure after death in the fact that there is no fixed term for the continuing element; rather, there is vacillation between *psyche* and *pneuma* (cf. Rev. 6:11 and 1 Pet. 3:19).

The upshot is that we have to respect, in all their indirectness, the hints that Scripture gives about our personal state; and insofar as these hints do not emphasize the subjective state but rather personal fellowship with Christ, they fit very well into the framework of personal totality with which we have been working. At any rate, the statements do not produce in any sense a doctrine of immortality or the hypothesis of a division of the I. Biblical anthropology is thus confirmed rather than contested by what is said about the intermediate state.

• Appendix V •

LETTER TO A SOLDIER ON DEATH

[This letter was sent to Hans Felix Hedderich, who soon afterward was shot down over the Mediterranean. He was one of my earliest students and doctoral candidates. His dissertation, *Die Gedanken der Romantik über Kirche und Staat* (Gütersloh, 1941), was banned at home even while he was fighting as a soldier abroad. The ideas expressed in this book occupied me even then. They found their first expression in the lectures that Hedderich attended. This letter may perhaps be of help to some readers because it applies to a particular situation — an extreme one — that is discussed in the book theoretically.]

You remind me in your letter of many a pre-war prophecy that should the apocalyptic horseman of war ride through our land, a storm of inner awakening would inevitably be unloosed. People would have to awaken out of all their illusions and idolatries and human states to the final realities of death and God.

And now, writing from hospital as one who is gradually convalescing, you say that this plausible expectation has not for the most part been realized. In spite of every expectation, truly apocalyptic encounters with death — with death in its most horrible forms and with a sadistic disclosure of human nature — have not usually served as preaching of the law or as visitations. All these things seem instead to have made the hardening even harder. One might have thought that the divine tocsin would have wakened up everybody to hear, but the almost over-loud force of events has had the very opposite effect. Consciously or unconsciously, most people find in all that is happening merely the revelation of pure struggles for power, which we can endure like the soldier of Pompeii and in which we must protect our souls with a thick hide. "The play of forces, and our related personal destinies, are in the hands of fate." This usually closes the discussion.

Why is this so, dear H.?

You write about our fathers who fought at the front in the First

World War: "No matter how dead their Christianity might be, no matter how conventionally or liberally distorted ... they had learned off a few hymns by heart, they knew some psalms, they knew a few Bible verses which in case of need or danger or death suddenly began to ring out in a wonderful way. The hidden seed sprang up when the hard plow of war broke up the ground. But has there been today any winter sowing anywhere in our soul? ... But without this sowing events are unintelligible, and we get through best if we close our ears and with the part of our soul that is at our command trust in luck or fate."

I believe you have rightly hit on the core of the matter even though it is hidden in God's hand and remains mysterious.

We find analogous situations in God's history as it is narrated in the old covenant. Events as such — terrors, wars, and natural disasters — did not open up the way to God. Nor did God's famous march through history necessarily force people to listen to him. Listening and fellowship with God came because there were prophets and patriarchs who explained that march and those events through the Spirit of God that was given them. The promise is connected only with God's Word, not with the march, or with the march only insofar as God must speak if it is to be distinguished from the logical unfolding of events and from the apparent wonders that his human instruments work when their iron march resounds across our planet. The moving of God's mantle, whose tip we may catch, can leave people quite indifferent if God does not grant the moving of his Spirit. Bismarck knew this when he made his famous remark about God's mantle. He knew the Spirit as well as the mantle. Otherwise it would have been madness and arrogance to describe the little bit of cloth in his hands with such ardor. Those who do not recognize the same Lord behind the poor robe of the Crucified and the rustling cloak of the apocalyptic horseman, those who do not do so in such a way that they see in both robe and mantle the garments of eternal majesty, their eyes will remain closed.

In saying this I have already expressed my conviction that we should present the poor robe of the Crucified to people in such a way that we also expound the rustling of the mantle of God in our day. God does not only speak; he also marches. And why should we not venture, why do we not have to venture, to speak about this marching too when we have put ourselves under the discipline of his words? Everything depends upon whether we and our comrades will live and go through all that God may send with the familiar lamps that he has given us on our path. And you theologians out there are perhaps summoned even more today than the preachers in the pulpits to hear the command of the hour and to become socratic theologians going through the markets and foxholes and guard rooms and lonely command posts, visiting one person after another, speaking and answering, and often being silent while others talk, and causing this Word to shine in the darkness of events.

God's march through events cries out for those who can explain it, for even the most stupid people can see the footprints of something extraordinary, but they do not suspect who it is that is passing by, nor do they perceive whether we make history or history makes us, or whether it is fate that rules or the Lord of history.

One thing is clear; you will agree with me in this. Everything uplifting or terrifying that happens to us, particularly death, confronts us all with a question. Consider only how people constantly find themselves questioned by the symptoms of our mortality, such as in war. Consider how some stop their ears and cry out noisily: "Let us eat and drink, for tomorrow we die," while others spend this symbolic hour of destruction in prayer and put it in the light of eternity. Consider both these groups and note that at a time like this all people can hear the grass of time growing and all are confronted by the question of what path they are on and how far they are from its end. It is only the answer given by the two groups that differs. They are all asked the same question.

And now I ask how socratic theologians whom God has set among their comrades in destiny should tackle the question of death as this is put by the New Year's Eve of war.

I will outline my thoughts on this.

When the question of death shouts at them, many people pack it in cotton-wool, no matter whether the shout comes when they themselves are in mortal danger, or when their comrades fall beside them, or when they face the enemy massed in solid ranks on the battlefield. Two gags are thrust into the jaws of death when it cries to us.

The one is that it is "part of nature." The rhythm of developing and decaying comes to expression in the inevitability of death.

There is no more to it! We have this rhythm even when the fury of war unleashes it to a wild beat.

Let me tell you the following story, not simply as an anecdote, but because it is vividly before me at the moment and has symbolic force. An eighteen-year-old in a Panzer division, a gifted student unknown to me personally, wrote to me about one of my writings that had reached him. The letter gave signs of the storm and stress of the age of development: very well-read, genuinely seeking, only half understanding many things, in many matters high-flown and speculative, as is often the way with intelligent young people whose minds stretch further than their experience of life can help them. I imagined him as a lanky fellow whose "inner organs" had not kept up with the growth of his intellect. In my answer I tore down his thoughts and referred him to the simple *doing* of the truth in relation to his comrades, whether in service or in danger; only thus, and not by abstract speculation, would he come to know whether "this teaching is of God." He wrote back a few sentences, agreeing with me and telling me he would let me know later when he had worked along these lines and made headway; he sensed that he was only at the beginning. The next news I had was that he had been killed, but then I heard that in his pack was a half-written letter to me in which he told me of his first halting progress in the matter, but also how violently and even aggressively — at odds with himself — he was struggling against it. Before he could finish his letter, even while he was writing it, the fatal bit of shrapnel hit him.

Why do I tell you this, dear H.? Because I saw overpoweringly here that it was not the rhythm of life that carried off this boy when he was only just getting started. The rhythm of life was violently and shatteringly interrupted in the middle of his letter. We surely have to feel — and the many who have similar experiences must surely do so — that death is here an enemy and an adversary, that death ought *not* to be. Does not death invade the relationships of life and friendship as a destroyer? Does it not take the very best? Does it not reduce the life of thousands to a fragment? Is it not really unnatural, a breach of order, as the Bible presents it? I believe that much would be gained if we would uncover its unnatural character in forceful phrases. Even the greatness of an object for which a sacrifice is made should not blind us into thinking that something unique has to perish when it is full of promise and designed by God.

Something unique — that leads us to the other gag used to choke the cry of death. We can only die alone even though we may be surrounded by comrades to the very last. Each of us must go to join the ranks of the dead alone in his narrow bed. Companionship drops away from us here like May blossoms. Lonely dying in hospitals perhaps shows more clearly than death on the battlefield that death is a narrow barrier through which we must each of us pass alone and on which it is written that life cannot be transferred but concerns only the self and ends with the self. When I myself realized, learning it as a soldier, that even in the midst of companionship there is this isolated individual to which death relates so emphatically, I began to look on each company that marched past with new eyes. There is compressed force in their step, and their singing forms a single body of sound. We can experience this only when we are among them, surrounded by the striding and singing on every hand, so that private existence is erased. Nevertheless, I often consider that all those who march live in a dimension in which they cannot be represented and are fully alone, all of them bearing their own guilt and care and death. And I think of the end of a young soldier whose death I had to live through in a hospital who shortly before he died said: "We die here all alone" — even though his relatives were gathered around him.

I believe, dear H., that when we consider that death strikes us in this dimension in which we are alone, and where something falls away and threads are snapped that cannot be joined again — much of the rosy make-up with which we conceal the deepest messages of God is stripped away.

If we see this, then we suddenly understand why death has such tremendous seriousness in the world of Holy Scripture. Nietzsche could think that the "corruption of the hereafter" is what leads Christianity to its "misuse of the hour of death." We know better. The people of the Bible realized that we are called to a life in fellowship with God and that death is thus real disorder, the last enemy. They realized that we cannot be represented but are alone in the decisive things of life — in guilt, in "the most powerful hammer-blow of suffering." Hence they did not conceal by any collective fantasies the dimension in which dying affects the self, in which I stand alone before God, and in which, notwithstanding all the love that cries out for "deep, deep eternity," every living thread is snapped.

But I hear you ask: Should we really make hard things so hard? Do not those who heroically despise death, believing in fate, tread a way that is perhaps easier for the masses, ignoring the abysses, and doing what is done on New Year's Eve?

You are right, dear friend. Despising death is the easier way, for the same reason that many times the way without God is the easier way because there are fewer obstacles. Luther contended against the scorners of death (who were very impressive to him at the human level) because they were also scorners of him who permits death, and because in blind defiance they lifted themselves up above the message that he holds in his bony fingers: the message that here a limit is set for the limitless, that a wall separating us from God's eternity is set up, a wall that will not accept the rebel in us, a wall that in wild Titanic defiance this rebel constantly tears down.

Nevertheless — and now I am asking with you — what will your comrades say if you accept the seriousness of the truth, the seriousness of the truth of *death*, simply because it is the truth? Is not that alone the truth which serves life? And is not life served only by that which conceals its abysses, conferring on us the foolish boldness and productive ignorance that does not see dangers, and for this very reason invincibly overcomes them?

I was speaking about this recently with a young man who had fought against the soldiers of Soviet atheism. We discussed how it was that they died so easily and apparently enviably, letting tanks roll over them rather than surrendering, and still throwing grenades even when they were reduced almost to bloody pulp. Is this greatness, is it heroism, is it madness, or what is it? The young soldier, with what I thought to be the sure instinct of youth, explained it as follows. They died so easily because they had nothing to lose — that is all. What do they really lose when they lose themselves? They do not know the Lord who makes them solitary and non-representable, independent selves. They do not know the "infinite value of the human soul" possessed as the soul of a creature and child of God bought with a price. They feel perhaps that they are only units in a great collective. What do they lose, what do they think they lose?

Dear friend, here we come up against the ultimate mysteries of

our faith. Dying takes on the greater seriousness the more we have
to lose; that is, the more we know the true destiny to which we
are called, the more we recognize the uniqueness and dignity of
our person that is hit by death.

I believe, dear H., that I hardly need issue to you the warning
that this dignity is not native to us and should not be misconstrued
along the lines of an empty individualism with its cult of personality. We refer to the "infinite value of the human soul" only
because we are so infinitely loved and dearly bought. God does not
love us because we are of value; we are of value because God loves
us. It is because God's love rests on us, and one died for us, that
we have that golden chain around our neck and that crown on our
head of which Luther speaks in his Larger Catechism. This crown
makes us kingly, not *vice versa*, as though we were given the crown
because we are kingly. The Reformers spoke about an alien righteousness that is ours through Christ. In the same way we might
speak about an alien worth that is granted to us. This and nothing
else is meant by the infinite value of the human soul. And mark
you, it is wholly against nature that we have to die as people of
this kind. It is not *something* that dies, the body, or the individual
in me; it is the *person* who is loved in this way and has this destiny.
No one and nothing has thought and spoken so highly of the
human race as the message of the Bible. This is why no one and
nothing has taken death so seriously or given it such full and
unrelieved weight as the Bible.

I will not close this long letter, dear friend and brother, without
a final insight. Luther says in several places that only he who
inflicts and permits the wound of death can heal it. No one else.
Certainly not illusions or silence. The atheistic method of cheap
death is no cure. It simply teaches bleeding without looking. It
teaches the end of an anonymous unit in a collective but not the
end of a human person that is taken out of anonymity and called
by name and is his. No, only God can heal the wound, because it
is he who inflicted it. Only he can heal it whose love reveals with
such pain but also with such blessing and promise the infinite value
of the human soul. For we know that it is not an *it* in me that
dies; I die, and I cannot be represented by the fellowship that ends
at my grave. I am truly and pitilessly and realistically at an end;
but I am also one whose history with God cannot cease because
I am called by name and am a companion of Jesus. I stand in the

victorious force field of the risen Lord — and it is with his alien life that I have fellowship, and it is this alien life that carries me through everything and receives me on the other side of the dark tomb. My quality of soul, my supposed disposition for immortality, will not carry me through; this traveler who marches at my side as my Lord and Brother, and who can as little abandon me on the other side as he will let go of me here on this side of the grave, will carry me through.

Should we not interpret in this way the march of God through the woes of history and the thousandfold death of battles? Must we not expound it thus? May God grant us the grace not to fail to pass on to our neighbors the message of this march!

• Appendix VI •

EPILOGUE FOR
THEOLOGICAL READERS

During the last few years when many were trying to change theology into practology and to throw away the rubbish of dogma, the slogan often appeared: "There is a life *before* death." Its purpose was to correct the interest of theology in the hereafter and to direct attention to concrete action and the improvement of this world. What we had here was a timebound yet seriously meant attack on the ghetto mentality of the pious, which supposedly — or in fact — was rejecting all responsibility for the world. Yet the slogan has a significance that goes beyond the actual situation. It can remind us of certain fundamental problems of theological thinking.

No theological statement can claim to be binding as a mere dictum, for example, because it is taken positivistically and out of context from the Bible. All theological statements are enmeshed in a network of correlations. Thus what the NT says about redemption cannot be understood apart from the gospel of creation in which God already makes himself known — in the fine saying of Luther — as the God who wants to be "my" God, God for us humans. Again, the gospel of the forgiveness of sins can be understood only against the dark foil of the law, the message of God's claim and my defaulting on this claim. Only this polarity protects theology against presenting God as a statically indulgent God and impels it to display his love as a miracle, as a historical act, as the confession of a Nevertheless to us. Hence a web of richly related statements integrates each statement into a totality and makes it understandable only in this framework — or "context," as we usually call it today.

In this light the hereafter, the question, popularly put, of where we are to seek the dead, cannot be understood or find an answer unless we relate it to the situation *before* death. If there are no signs here that death is more or other than a mere conclusion of our physical and mental activity, if this life does not constantly give evidence that it transcends itself,[19] then at most eternal life after death and the message of the resurrection of the dead can be based only on the assurances of spiritists or certain conventions of religious life that are accepted without question or argument. And obviously this will then produce such results as, for example, the Marxist interpretation of the idea of the hereafter as mere consolation and palliation, the opium of the people. A statement about the hereafter that does not give intimation of itself here, and is not grounded in the faith of the living, cries out for other explanations, whether primitive or psychological (as in the projection theory of Feuerbach).

This is why in this book I have tried to understand this present life of ours in terms of the boundary of death. I have done so first from a phenomenological standpoint. The question here is how thinking contemporaries understand this life that is limited by death. I have consulted poets and philosophers for their views on human finitude and set them in contrast to my own interpretation with its Christian orientation. In this attempt we have been led from many different sides to the same question of why our self-understanding as those who are going to die constantly transcends purely biological categories, why it is inadequate to interpret dying as a purely natural event. Symptoms of this inadequacy become apparent at once when we consider the qualitatiative difference between animal and human death and when we realize why death is experienced as an alien guest, even an absurdity, and is thus repressed or banished from our eyes by flight into dreams of immortality.

It might seem, then, that for long stretches this book is devoted to purely immanent phenomenology. In reality, however, the Easter mystery is the center of its perspective. Hence my concern has been to show that the final point of the repression may be seen only in this light.

The Easter mystery, however, is not presented as a dogmatic decree, but as the goal of several insights, so that it is first accorded only an indirect role in which light is shed on the phenomenology but the source of this light is not yet directly visible. In this regard we are following the NT tradition. For here the earthly life of Jesus,[20] his coming in history, is already set in the light of the resurrection even though his messiahship is secret and the eyes of his disciples are "held" in face of the risen Lord, as on the road to

Emmaus.[21] The earthly life of Jesus is a prophetic life which, like any prophecy, is opened up only by its fulfillment.

In sum, the transcendent content of the awareness of our mortality is investigated in the light of the Easter mystery, and a point of contact[22] is thus opened for the message of the resurrection; a bridgehead is established for this message in our consciousness. We are thus guided by a hermeneutical concern. What is ultimately at issue is that the Easter message should be understandable.

I realize that the objection might be brought against this procedure that I am moving in a hermeneutical circle and trying to prove something that I have already smuggled into my premises (like the conjurer who can produce a rabbit out of his hat only when he has first slipped it in).

I have two arguments in reply to this objection. First, there is obviously no question here of a "proof." It would be absurd, and contrary to the intention of the NT, to objectify the kerygma of the resurrection, to try to turn it from an object of faith into an object of sight and obvious plausibility. For all the differences, the presentations of what took place on the third day have one thing in common. They definitely avoid the style of objective recording that is proper for neutral witnesses. Encounter with the risen Lord is granted only to those who walked with him on earth and who were his committed disciples, so that they were "biased," if one will.[23]

Second, the phenomenological part of the book on the modern view of death does not move in a hermeneutical circle, for the conclusion that death is found to be inconceivable, and is thus repressed, is not a theological finding and is certainly not "read in" apologetically. The inconceivability of death is to be found in a secular self-understanding. The only theological component of this phenomenology lies in the interpretation of this self-understanding and the working out of the importance and meaning of what it expresses.[24]

NOTES

CHAPTER 1

[1] ThE III §§ 2730f.

[2] Cf. the papal encyclical "Casti connubii" (1930).

[3] For this problem of identity cf. especially Max Frisch and the thinking of Sartre on essence and existence.

[4] Quoted in Choron, *Der Tod im abendländischen Denken*, 61f.

[5] *Philo. Bemerkungen* (1964), 149.

[6] Cf. H. F. Steiner, *Marxisten-Leninisten über den Sinn des Lebens* (1970), 305.

[7] *Als wär's ein Stück von mir*, 380f.

[8] *Ibid.*, 240.

[9] For details cf. c.2, 6.

[10] Cf. Jacob von Uexküll's *Nie geschaute Welten. Die Umwelt en meiner Freunde. Ein Erinnerungsbuch* (8th ed., 1939).

[11] Alfred E. Hoche, *Jahresringe. Innenansicht eines Menschenlebens* (1936).

[12] E. Jüngel in his book *Tod* (2nd ed., 1972, 145f.) interprets death as "the event of relationlessness that totally breaks off all human relationships," ET 115ff.

[13] 80 d f.

[14] Cf. Harald Braun, ed., *Dichterglaube* (1931).

[15] WA 40/III, 550, 1: Fear of death, despair, terror, is itself death (LW 13, 115: the text differs here).

[16] E.g., J. C. Hampe, R. A. Moody, and others. E. Kübler-Ross, *Interviews mit Sterbenden* (3rd ed., 1977) is on another plane.

[17] Cf. Anouilh's *Der Reisende ohne Gepäck* for a similar problem.

[18] Leopold Ziegler, *Überlieferung* (1936), 173ff. Cf. EF I, 72f. (EG I, 77f.).

[19] Cf. Heidegger's *Analyse* and Tolstoy's *Death of Ivan Ilych*.

[20] Heidegger, *op. cit.*, 254.

[21] "It takes all of life to learn how to die," but we busy ourselves with other things; Seneca, *De brevitate vitae*.

[22] "Gird up the loins of your mind," 1 Pet. 1:13; Eph. 6:14; 1 Thess. 5:8.

[23] Cf. the chapter on distraction in Pascal's *Pensées*.

[24] Cf. Pascal. There are some percipient people like E. Jünger, especially in his early writings, who face up to shades, but the situation of adventure into which they plunge is really only a sublime way of evading them. Their basic attitude is less one of facing up to horrors than enjoying their own fortitude: a remarkably narcissistic therapy.

[25] Cf. Pascal, *op. cit.*

[26] *Sein und Zeit*, 251.

[27] Cf. E. Jünger, *Das abenteuerliche Herz*, 91ff. Jünger notes that the modern city bears the marks of anxiety in movement and dreaming in rest. Street-corners and bridges are infinitely oppressive. In the supreme insecurity of a crisis like today's no satisfaction is possible; all that remains is bravery. The rigid, narcotized state of modern man at rest is astounding. Such lostness would hardly be found in a Chinese opium den, What is expressed is the ineluctability

and decisive sameness of processes. Vigilance and bravery are needed on our banners.

²⁸ Novalis, Fourth of the *Hymnen an die Nacht*.

²⁹ O. Spengler, *Jahre der Entscheidung* (1933), notes that it may be the weakness of advanced people today to be cut off from the earth and the natural experiences of destiny, time, and death. There is a flight from history (including, we might add, their *own* history and therefore their finitude) into artificial systems alien to the world.

CHAPTER 2

¹ I might add for theological readers that the basic epistemological scheme here is that of the analogy of faith. We are not pursuing immanent anthropology with a view to finding later that the message of the resurrection fits it. On the contrary, in the light of this message it is clear to us in advance that human death is not just a natural process. This provides our categories.

²According to Gen. 1:29 humans and animals are all vegetarians.

³ I have discussed this further in my work *Wer darf sterben? Grenzfragen der modernen Medizin* (1979); ET: *The Doctor as Judge of who shall Live and who shall Die* (1976).

⁴ *Wer darf sterben?*, 25ff., 49ff. (ET 21ff., 26ff.).

⁵ The eternal life of the cell does not contradict this, for it depends on constant renewal of laboratory culture for its vitality.

⁶ Cf. the similar process with cancer cells under laboratory conditions.

⁷ *Tod und Fortpflanzung* (1906), 37ff.

⁸ K. Eissler, *Der sterbende Patient*, 195.

⁹ Cf. W. Wickler, U. Seibt, *Das Prinzip Eigennutz*.

¹⁰ Cf. the use of the term "nature" in Aristotle and Scholasticism; cf. ThE §§ 972ff.; 1880ff. (ET I, 198ff., 400ff.).

¹¹ Cf. E. Jüngel, *Tod* (2nd ed., 1972), 145, ET 115.

¹² Epicurus characterized this destruction as a kind of atomic disintegration. Human life is a conjunction of two atomic masses, the body and the soul. Each holds both the other and itself together. At death the union and each mass disintegrate. The bodily atoms, being heavier, hold together longer; the soul, having left the body, "evaporates."

¹³ For all our linguistic reservations, we shall use the term "soul" here for "life"; cf. EF III, c.XXXI, 2.c. (EG III, 527ff.).

¹⁴ From a sermon for Invocavit (1522), WA 10/III, 1ff., LW 51, 70ff.

¹⁵ On the significance of the individual in Israel cf. H. W. Wolff, *Anthropologie des AT*, 41ff. Cf. the exclusive "I" in the prophets as compared with the collective "I" earlier; G. von Rad, *Theologie des AT* II (1960), 66ff., ET 54ff.

¹⁶ *Gott ist nicht ganz tot*, 229.

¹⁷ *Ibid.*, 227.

¹⁸ *Monologen* (1800) in H. Gerdes and E. Hirsch, *Schleiermacher. Kleine Schriften* I (1970), 65.

¹⁹ Cf. R. Kautzky, ed., *Sterben im Krankenhaus*, esp. 75ff.; also "Die neue Weise vom Tod des Jedermann," *Spiegel* 6.26.77.

²⁰ Cf. A. Dorozynski, *Der Mann, der nicht sterben durfte. Das Leben des russischen Nobelpreisträgers Lew Landau* (1966).

²¹ A. D. Holl, *Tod und Teufel* (1973), 40. Sociologically this means that "the

question of personal compensation of living individuals remains imperfectly solved" (Talcott Parsons, *The Social System* [London, 1964], 372).

22 Heb. 3:7, 15; 4:7.

23 2 Cor. 6:2, cf. Luke 4:19.

24 Heidegger, *op. cit.*, 264.

25 Cf. Anthrop. 433– 472.

26 *Jenseits des Lustprinzips*, XIII, 40.

27 A. Görres, *Kennt die Psychologie den Menschen* (1978), 248; also "Physik der Triebe — Physik des Geistes" in H. Vorgrimler, ed., *Gott in Welt* (Rahner Festschrift) II (1964), 556ff.

28 *Briefe* 1873– 1939 (1960), 429. Cf. Anthrop. 443ff.

29 *Makrobiotik oder die Kunst, sein Leben zu verlängern* (1796).

30 F. Hoff, *Von Krankheit und Heilung und vom Sterben* (1975), 280.

31 One might note that a philosopher of the absurd like Albert Camus emphatically doubts the supposed existence of a transcendent future. This is not a confession of hopelessness but a shifting of hope to this life. The hope now is that the flame of life will shine the more brightly and burn the more intensively within our limited span and the horizon of the absurd.

32 Hoff, *op. cit.*, 272.

33Luther has something similar in mind in discussing the doctrine of predestination (Rom. 9– 11) in his *Preface to Romans,* where he says that for beginners in faith (or unbelievers) this is too strong drink and milk would be more suitable. We cannot solve the mystery of predestination by speculation; we must begin with justification (Rom. 1– 8). The inquisitive will turn to predestination too soon and discuss it to no effect. Predestination is not a presupposition; it is a consequence of justification, at least noetically. Every doctrine has its own time and age and hour.

34 Cf. Sophocles' "Antigone"; G. Nebel, *Weltangst und Götterzorn* (1951), 179ff.

35 *Iliad* 9, 457.

36 *Odyssey* 11, 218ff. (cf. W. Otto, *Die Götter Griechenlands*, 183, ET: *The Homeric Gods*, 140ff.).

37 The totally different existence of the dead as compared with the living, the alien character of death, comes to expression in Homer in "Ate" as this may be seen in the case of Hector (*Iliad* 22; cf. W. Schadewaldt, "Das Gedenken der Toten in der Antike," *Hellas und Hesperien* [1960], 60ff.). "Ate" is subjugation to death through the wrath of the gods, a predisposition for approaching disaster to which the hero is blind. Those afflicted by it, and therefore subject to hybris, follow their course in a blind search for fame or revenge; their madness conceals the fact that they will inevitably die.

38 Cf. M. Bartels, ed., *Mensch und Tod. Totentanzsammlung der Universität Düsseldorf* (1976); on this concept in the new humanism cf. H. Weinstock, *Die Tragödie des Humanismus* (1953), 229ff.

39 *Zufall und Notwendigkeit* (1970).

CHAPTER 3

1 The Platonic doctrine of immortality is only one aspect of the Greek struggle with death. (Another is the idea of Hades.) On death in the tragic dramatists, cf. Josef Sellmair, *Der Mensch in der Tragik* (2nd ed., 1941); W. F. Otto, *op. cit.*; W. Jaeger, *Paideia* I (Berlin and Leipzig, 1934), 207ff., 419ff.; Schadewaldt, *op. cit.*; G. Nebel, *op. cit.*; H. Thielicke, *Schuld und Schicksal. Ge-*

danken eines Christen über das Tragische (1935). Plato's thinking may be found especially in the *Phaedo, Gorgias, Politicus,* and *Phaedrus.*

[2] *Phaedo* 18 and 41.

[3] *Ibid.,* 23.

[4] The child in us does not fear death; *ibid.,* 24.

[5] *Ibid.,* 54f.

[6] *Ibid.,* 55.

[7] Lambert Schneider edition, II, 436ff.

[8] *Phaedrus* 9.

[9] *Politicus* 10.

[10] Yet it can be said that mutually acquainted souls will "greet" one another in the hereafter, which would hardly be possible if there were no individuality. This is stated only in passing.

[11] There are analogies to Plato's view in Schopenhauer when he says that death affects only our phenomenal side and not our substantial core or *"Ding an sich" (Werke,* ed. J. Frauenstädt, VI, 287). Life, or the objective world with its medium of presentation, the intellect, perishes, but this has no bearing on the continued existence of the real I, for this life is only a dream and death is an awakening to what is originally proper to us (VI, 287), that is, to the independent will (VI, 290). Cf. also *Über den Tod und sein Verhältnis zur Unzerstörbarkeit unseres Lebens an sich* (III, 528).

[12] In what follows we shall deal with examples in which the division of the I is harder to recognize.

[13] *Werke,* ed. E. Förster-Nietzsche, XIV, 217. Cf. K. Jaspers, *Nietzsche. Einführung in das Verständnis seines Philosophierens* (1936), 198ff., 285ff.

[14] *Werke* VIII, 144.

[15] V, 149.

[16] IX, 144.

[17] VIII, 144.

[18] VI, 106.

[19] VI, 108.

[20] VI, 105ff. Cf. Zarathustra on Free Death.

[21] XVI, 315.

[22] Cf. VI, 106–108.

[23] III, 294.

[24] *Loc. cit.* (cf. Jaspers, *op. cit.,* 287).

[25] A similar act of thinking that transcends death may be found in the idea of eternal recurrence.

[26] In the excursuses that follow I shall be taking up many of the points dealt with in my *Wer darf sterben? (The Doctor as Judge).*

[27] *Hand an sich legen* (1976).

[28] Lorenz, *Das sogenannte Böse* (1963), 361f.

[29] As a basis I may refer to what I have said, and will go on to say, about alien worth or dignity.

[30] Cf. Bonhoeffer's *Ethik* (1949), 114f., ET 125ff.

[31] K. Binding and A. Hoche, *Die Freigabe der Vernichtung lebensunwerten Lebens* (1920), 29.

[32] *Die Euthanasie und die Heiligkeit des Lebens* (1935), 106f.

[33] W. Grönbech, *Kultur und Religion der Germanen* (Hamburg, 1937).

[34] W. F. Otto, *op. cit.,* 342, ET 263ff.

[35] *Ibid.,* 176, ET 140ff.

[36] *Ibid.,* 340ff., ET 263ff.

[37] Hölderlin to Neuffer (who died as a bride), Jena, May 8, 1795.

[38] On the Greek view of death cf. also R. Bultmann, "Thanatos," TDNT III, 7ff. (TWNT III, 7ff.).

[39] Grönbech, *op. cit.*, 251.

[40] Only on the margin may I refer here to the remarkable phenomenon among both Greeks and Germans that two forms of individual immortality may be seen — first, supraindividual survival in the welfare and honor of the overarching community, and second, survival in Hades or Valhalla. The latter is a shadowy continuation of individual existence, a dreamlike, evanescent afterform, and thus implies a distant sense of the problem of personal individuality and uniqueness with some survival of individual identity.

[42] A clear echo of this Christian awareness may be heard even in very secular writings; cf. W. Kessler, ed., *Und eines Tages öffnet sich die Tür. Briefe zweier Liebenden* (Berlin, 1940), 224f., which refers to an inner solitude that not even love can share, much though one would like to believe that the love of someone can. But there has to be a summons and obligation in this final solitude at the point where human claims cannot penetrate, and if there is no place or stillness where this can be heard, there will always be an empty core within us and we can find no footing.

[43] *Encyclopädie* § 370 (Meiner, 327).

[44] *Op. cit.*, 331.

[45] Frauenstädt III, 547f.

[46] For an analysis of the change from Hegel to Marx, cf. my essay on Marxist anthropology in *The Hidden Question of God* (1977), 35ff.; German *Die geheime Frage nach Gott* (4th ed., 1978), 41ff.

[47] H. Rolfes draws attention to this in his *Der Sinn des Lebens im marxistischen Denken* (1971), 124.

[48] K. Marx, *Die Frühschriften*, ed. S. Landshut (1953), 239.

[49] F. Engels, *Dialektik der Natur. Notizen und Fragmente*, in K. Marx and F. Engels, *Werke* (East Berlin, 1956ff.) XX, 554 and 559.

[50] K. Marx, *Zur Judenfrage*, in *Frühschriften*, 199.

[51] *Nationalökonomie und Philosophie, ibid.*, 241.

[52] *Der Mensch ohne Alternative* (1960), 207.

[53] H. F. Steiner, *Marxisten-Leninisten über den Sinn des Lebens* (1970), 288.

[54] Adam Schaff, *Marx oder Sartre* (East Berlin, 1965).

[55] Cf. L. Kolakovski, *Der Mensch ohne Alternative*, 206f. For Communists the world is something to be changed, not contemplated. Their consciousness is one of active coexistence with history.

[56] (1958), 284.

[57] Steiner, *op. cit.*, 276f.

[58] Kolakovski, *op. cit.*, 211.

[59] *Ibid.*, 212f.

[60] *Die Zeit* 42 (1973), 24.

[61] *Herder-Korrespondenz* 10 (1977), 501ff.

[63] Cf. the letter to Zelter, March 19, 1827: "Let us go on working until we are summoned into the aether by the world spirit! May the living one not withhold from us new activities analogous to those in which we have already proved ourselves. The entelechic monad must keep up restless activity; to all eternity it can never cease to be busy in some way. Pardon these abstruse expressions." And in a letter to Chancellor von Müller, Jan. 26, 1825, we read: "I should not know what to do with eternal felicity if it did not offer me new tasks and problems to overcome."

[64] To Eckermann, Feb. 25, 1824.

[65] To K. G. von Brinkmann, Sept. 3, 1792.

[66] To the same, Oct. 23, 1792.

[67] To Johanna Motherby, March 7, 1810.

[68] This reminds us of the young Schleiermacher, who found the universe reflected and symbolized in the microcosm; cf. *Die Reden*, 61 (ET: *Speeches on Religion*, 70).

[69] Goethe's letter to K. F. Zelter, May 11, 1820.

[70] *En-telos-echeia*, "what bears its basis, goal, and meaning in itself."

[71] The devil is given to us to spur us on because we so easily give up working. Schiller has the similar thought that the fall was the most fortunate event in history because it opened up the possibility of freedom. It is typical that André Gide has to alter the parable of the prodigal son to bring in the teleology of evil: the returned prodigal has a younger brother whom he sends off into the far country to gain maturity and to experience it as a productive transition.

[72] Cf. the more poetic expression of the same view of infinity in the *Sprüche*, although in spatial imagery: "If you want to go into the infinite, simply explore every side of the finite; if you want to refresh yourself with the whole, you must consider the whole in the smallest part."

[73] To Falk on the day of Wieland's funeral, Jan. 25, 1813.

[74] *Wanderjahre* I, 10.

[75] Venice, Oct. 12, 1786.

[76] March 11, 1828.

[77] *Lehrjahre* 6.

[78] The saying of Panthalis in the Helen Scene of Faust (Part II), that fidelity as well as merit confers personhood, is no proof to the contrary in view of the autonomy of the mythical scene and the true scope of the saying (both merit and fidelity). There is also no emphasis on personhood here. The saying is to be understood in the light of the analogous but clearer statements to Knebel on Sept. 3, 1781: "It is an article of my faith that only through steadfastness and fidelity in our present state shall we be able to enter upon another one, whether in time or eternity," and the famous statement to Eckermann on Feb. 4, 1829 that nature commits us to unceasing activity in continued existence after death.

[79] To Falk, Jan. 25, 1813.

[80] Cf. palingenesis at the end of Lessing's *Erziehung des Menschengeschlechts* and in the *Jacobi-Gespräch*. On both passages cf. my book *Offenbarung, Vernunft und Existenz. Studien zur Religionsphilosophie Lessings* (5th ed., 1967).

[81] To Eckermann, Feb. 4, 1829.

[82] *Sprüche in Prosa*, 1028.

[83] Goethe from Naples, May 17, 1787. There is a parallel to this thought of the merging of the core of the entelechy into universal life in a remark of Albert Einstein recorded by Antonina Vallentin in her book *Das Drama Albert Einsteins* (Stuttgart, n.d.). Once when sick, he was asked by the wife of the physicist M. Born whether he was afraid of death. He answered: "Why should I be? I feel such solidarity with all that lives that it is all one to me where the individual begins and ends."

CHAPTER 4

[1] Cf. EF III, c.XXXI, 2.c.

[2] *Romans Commentary*, Ficker 12, 15, LW 25, 11.

[3] EF III, 412ff.

[4] In this section I am indebted to U. Kellermann, *Überwindung des Todesgeschicks in der alttestamentlichen Frömmigkeit vor und neben dem Auferstehungsglauben*; also to H. W. Wolff's *Anthropologie des AT*.

[5] Gen. 35:29; 1 Chron. 29:28; Job 42:17.

[6] Thus Thomas Mann can say that Jacob died content that there is a limit to everything (*Joseph und seine Brüder* III, 1978, 1265, 1309).

[7] Sex in Gen. 19:31, death in 1 Kings 2:1f.

[8] Kellermann, 260.

[9] L. Köhler, *Der hebräische Mensch* (1953), 97ff., ET: *Hebrew Man* (1956).

[10] 2 Sam. 14:7; Kellermann, 266.

[11] Cf. W. Eichrodt, *Theologie des AT* III (1939), 152.

[12] Cf. the metaphors of the hot wind (Ps. 103:15f.; Job 14:2; Ps. 90:5f.) and the fleeting breath (Ps. 78:39; Job 7:7) (Kellermann, 263).

[13] G. von Rad, *Theologie des AT* I (1957), 385, ET 387f.

[14] L. Köhler, *op. cit.*, 100.

[15] Cf. E. Jüngel, *Tod* (1972), 99, 138, ET 77, 108f.

[16] Eichrodt III, 161ff.

[17] On later Wisdom literature and the Greek view of immortality, cf. Kellermann, 278ff.

[18] Cf. Bultmann's view of resurrection and my debate with him in EF I, 57ff., and II, 440ff.

[19] It will be seen that the subject-object relation is inadequate there, and it is thus to be taken with a pinch of salt.

[20] Cf. the story of the rich young ruler in Mark 10:17 − 27 and the author's exposition of this in *Und wenn Gott wäre* ... (1970), 135ff.

[21] Ficker 12, 15, LW 25, 11.

[22] On the theological use of the term "soul," cf. EF III, 411ff.

[23] "For we are consumed by thy anger; by thy wrath we are overwhelmed. Thou hast set our iniquities before thee, our secret sins in the light of thy countenance" (Ps. 90:7f.).

[24] Cf. Augustine, *Confessions* 11.

[25] Cf. Kant's view of immortality, which is worked out characteristically and consistently in the name of an ideal demand of this kind. The qualitative gap between what is and what should be leads to a quantitative prolongation in order to close the gap (*Critique of Practical Reason*, Part II, Book 2, Section IV).

[26] This view of the penal connection between sin and death is indirectly confirmed by the central Pauline teaching that Christ's death is a vicarious expiation for our sin (Rom. 8:3f.; 2 Cor. 5:21f.; Gal. 3:13; Heb. 2:14f.; 9:27). John's Gospel also relates wrath and death, for the death of Jesus "takes away the sin of the world" (1:29), and the *archon tou kosmou* is at the same time *anthropoktonos* (8:44).

[27] On the divine likeness cf. ThE I §§ 774ff., 843ff. (ET I, 152ff., 194ff.) and EF III, 393, 401, 452.

[28] We intentionally avoid the term "immortality," not just because it is metaphysically freighted and points in a different direction, but also so as not to fall into a dogmatic metaphysics. There is plainly in the biblical statements (Gen. 3) a profound material difference between the original destiny of life on the one hand (3:3ff.) and the immortality that was grasped after on the other (v. 22).

[29] Cf. Luther's interpretation in his exposition of Ps. 90, WA 40/III, 513, 18ff., LW 13, 94ff.

[30] Cf. Michael Schmaus, *Katholische Dogmatik* III, 2 (1941), 493. By physiological law dominion is stretched to the point of destruction. Though neither experiment nor experience can prove this, faith says that we have here the fulfillment of divine judgment.

[31] In such contexts Luther likes to use the idea of the *exemplar*, especially with reference to Christ, whose righteousness and humanity are mine. Cf. his

Sermon on Matt. 11:25ff., Feb. 24, 1517, Cl. 5, 246. All that applies to him can be said of those who believe in him; WA 2, 531, 10, LW 27, 282. We have to trust in what he did and suffered as if we had done and suffered it; WA 2, 140, 7; 40/I, 278, 6; LW 27, 163. Cf. also his lectures on Hebrews (German E. Vogelsang [Berlin-Leipzig, 1930], 40). Only in this light can we see the full scope of the "for me." Adam is also my *exemplar* — his creatureliness, fall, and sin being mine, too (1 Cor. 15:21ff.). Cf. my analysis of identity with Adam in *Geschichte und Existenz* (2nd ed., 1964), 239ff.

[32] Matthias Claudius.

[33] Cf. Appendix III.

[34] Those aspects of Luther's thought in which death is related to spiritual processes, such as the death of the old man and rising again with Christ, are irrelevant here, and are thus omitted.

[35] WA 40/III, 513, 18; LW 13, 94: Death for us is a greater calamity than for other living things.

[36] WA 40/III, 513, 28; LW 13, 94: Animals die by a law of nature.

[37] WA 40/III, 537, 12; cf. 535, 15ff.; 536, 23ff.; LW 13, 107 (cf. 13, 105, 106): Human nature cannot bear God's wrath without tears, murmurings, and objections.

[38] On the concept of eternal death in Luther cf. the list of different forms of death in his *Romans Commentary* (Ficker II, 153, 12ff.; LW 25, 310f.): Death is of two kinds, temporal and eternal, and eternal death is of two kinds, one good, the death of sin and death, and the other terrible, the death of the damned.

[39] Karl Stange, *Luthers Gedanken über die Todesfurcht* (Berlin-Leipzig, 1932), 15f. Cf. WA 40/III, 487, 18–22; LW 13, 76f.: Death is eternal because God's wrath is.

[40] WA 40/III, 513, 23; LW 13, 94: We were created for obedience to the Word, not for death.

[41] *Ibid.*, 513; LW 13, 94: It is shocking news that he who had been created good and perfect for life is now destined for death.

[42] *Ibid.*, 549, 27–550, 12; LW 13, 115: If there were no fear of death, it would be a kind of sleep.

[43] *Ibid.*, 485, 487; LW 13, 75ff.

[44] *Ibid.*, 487, 18–22; LW 13, 78: We need not fear purely physical death, but we are subject to eternal death, which no one can overcome.

[45] Cf. the quotations from Tolstoy adduced in the first part.

[46] WA 40/III, 526; LW 13, 102: Life is like a dream; before we discover we are living, we have ceased to live.

[47] *Ibid.*, 537, 11ff.; LW 13, 107.

[48] *Ibid.*, 524, 15; LW 13, 100: People plan as though they were going to live forever.

[49] *Ibid.*, 524, 21ff. (cf. also 561, 22); LW 13, 100 (cf. also LW 13, 128f.): People die today who yesterday hoped for another forty years, and if they had had it, would have wanted more.

[50] *Ibid.*, 572, 18; LW 13, 128.

[51] *Ibid.*, 550, 1.

[52] *Ibid.*, 537, 18; LW 13, 107: Reason, to escape God's wrath, proposes the way of disdain or blasphemy.

[53] *Ibid.*, 520, 10; LW 13, 98: Gentiles and monks talk about scorning death, but wrongly. They become either sinners or blasphemers, not reverencing God, but angry at him as a tyrant who for no reason abandons us to death.

[54] *Ibid.*, 544, 25; LW 13, 112: Epicurus, when he dies, knows neither the existence of God nor his own misery.

⁵⁵ *Ibid.*, 485, 13ff.

⁵⁶ Cf. E. Bälz, *Über die Todesverachtung der Japaner* (1936), for an impressive modern example.

⁵⁷ WA 45, 472f.; LW 24, 15: Christ comforts those whom the devil frightens and vice versa, for the two are always opposed to one another.

⁵⁸ WA 40/III, 518, 20; LW 13, 97: He who has torn will heal. He kills and restores to life. He brings down to hell and brings back again.

⁵⁹ *Ibid.*, 517, 23: Unlike Epicurus, Moses does not try to mitigate inescapable evil, but teaches us to refer both good and evil to the one God, and thus to overcome evil.

⁶⁰ *Ibid.*, 459, 22f.

⁶¹ Cf. 1 Cor. 15:21, 26, where there is distinction, but not division, between purely physical suffering in death and the personal sense of guilt and experience of God's judgment. Death as we experience it derives from sin and the law, and no human death worthy of the name is without this sting.

⁶² Cf. EF II, 185ff.

⁶³ Cf. my book *Zwischen Gott und Satan* (5th ed., 1978), 49ff., ET (1958), 26ff.

⁶⁴ Leopold Ziegler, *Überlieferung* (Leipzig, 1936), 343ff.

⁶⁵ I owe both these quotations to G. Nebel, *op. cit.*, 153.

⁶⁶ As with all repression we have "complexes" here, of which the gods and substitute religions are an ideological expression.

⁶⁷ Although the term "irreversibility of the time-line" comes from Karl Heim, who uses it constantly and impressively with reference to the experience of guilt, I sense a difference from Heim in that he views this inexchangeability as a phenomenon of existence that forces itself upon us and can thus be demonstrated. I emphatically deny this. The natural evaluation of what I call the New Year's experience may be very different. Everything depends upon insight into the personal structure of existence and the boundary of death, and this derives only from the self-disclosure of the God who encounters me and makes me personal. Cf. my debate with Heim, "Jesus der Weltvollender," in *Theologische Blätter*, June/July 1938.

⁶⁸ *Evangelischer Gesangbuch* No. 390.

⁶⁹ Cf. the exposition of this parable in my book *Das Bilderbuch Gottes* (1957), 47ff.

⁷⁰ Guardini ed., 44.

⁷¹ *Ibid.*, 51.

⁷² S. Kierkegaard, *Der Einzelne und die Kirche* (1934), 31.

⁷³ Cf. *Das abenteuerliche Herz*, esp. the first version of 1929. The older Jünger outgrew his earlier nihilism. Cf. my book *Fragen des Christentums an die moderne Welt* (4th ed., 1947), 60ff.

⁷⁴ Larger Catechism, Part IV: Baptism.

⁷⁵ In his *Christentum und Selbstbehauptung* (Frankfurt, 1940), W. Kamlah has worked out the relation between awareness of death as a limit and awareness of the self as a theologically qualified individual (cf. pp. 47ff.).

⁷⁶ B. Groethuysen, *Das Bürgertum und die katholische Weltanschauung* (1927), 83.

⁷⁷ Cf. J. Sellmaier, *Der Mensch in der Tragik* (2nd ed., 1941); also my *Schuld und Schicksal* (Berlin, 1937).

⁷⁸ C. Langenbeck, *Wiedergeburt des Dramas* (Munich, 1940).

⁷⁹ Heb. 3:8, 15; 4:7 (on the basis of Ps. 95:8).

⁸⁰ Cf. again the parable of the rich farmer.

⁸¹ Matt. 8:22; Luke 15:24, 32; Col. 2:13; Eph. 2:1, 5.

⁸² "... *Zōē* is proper to God as the *zōn*, i.e., as not only the One who has

life originally in Himself (Jn. 5:26), who lives eternally and who alone has *athanasia* (1 Tm. 6:16), but above all as the One who can both make alive and kill. . . . Thus God is Lord of life and death, as He is also Judge of the quick and the dead" (Bultmann, TDNT II, 862; TWNT II, 863).

[83] 1 Tim. 6:19 calls this true life *ontōs zōē*, to which *ontōs thanatos* corresponds as definitive death; TDNT II, 863, n. 268; TWNT II, 865, n. 268.

[84] E.g., Matt. 19:16, 29; Acts 13:46, 48; Rom. 2:7; 5:11; 6:22f., etc.

[85] On Luther's use of *exemplar*, cf. EF II, 195ff., 404 (EG II, 232ff., 499).

[86] Cf. Calvin's *Commentary on Romans*, on Rom. 6:6.

[87] Cf. R. Hermann, *Luthers These: Gerecht und Sünder zugleich* (1930).

[88] Cf. EF III, 68ff. (EG III, 97ff.).

[89] Calvin's *Commentary on Romans* (6:6).

[90] Paul Gerhardt, *Gesangbuch*, 86, 6.

[91] Cf. Paul's *logizesthe*, "reckon yourselves," "consider yourselves" (Rom. 6:11).

[92] Cf. the impact of OT promise and fulfillment on this gap, EF III, 151ff., 172ff. (EG III, 201ff., 230ff.).

[93] 2 Tim. 1:10; cf. Rom. 8:38; 2 Cor. 1:10.

[94] M. Schmaus goes far beyond this idea of the biological mask when he says that bodily death fulfills the death died in baptism (*Katholische Dogmatik* III, 2, 2, 494). This seems to me to be unbiblical and dogmatically hard to defend, for on this view death loses the oppressiveness it still has as a biological mask. It no longer threatens us as the last enemy (which it still is). Hence the defiance with which we go to meet it in the name of the risen Lord makes no sense. In fact, death is still a reminder of the fall. It stands in opposition to the life of God even though it can no longer separate us from fellowship with him. As the redeemed we can never be on the same wavelength or move in the same direction as death. Even Paul's joy at his approaching end (Phil. 1:23) is not joy in the fulfillment of the baptismal blessing, but joy in the ending of his divided existence, his walking in the shadow and in exile.

[95] Cf. the Apology for the Augsburg Confession, Art. III (IV) (Tappert, *Book of Concord* [1959], 124ff.).

[96] Only on one condition does death retain its definitive character, namely, when fellowship with God is rejected. In this case the Bible speaks of the second death. Already in this life there is a death in sin, Luke 15:32; Rom. 7:10; Eph. 2:1; 1 Tim. 5:6; 1 John 3:14; Rev. 3:1.

[97] Cf. Luther's exposition of Ps. 45, WA 40/II, 527, 9. The concept of active righteousness is also apposite here.

[98] WA 40/III, 572, 23, LW 13, 128: The Holy Spirit is to teach us to equate even a hundred years of this life with a mathematical point and the briefest moment.

[99] On the Roman Catholic side cf. B. O. Karrer, *Der Unsterblichkeitsglaube* (1936).

[100] In the concept of vicarious representation, another is something that we are not and never can be and do not even become through this representation. For this reason Christ's vicarious righteousness is always "alien." Only in this sense can I apply what is Christ's to myself. Only in this way am I by faith taken up into Christ's humanity and justified. Cf. WA 2, 490, 25.

[101] The concept of infusion is found on Protestant soil, but not, I think, with the same consistent tying of the doctrine of justification to a materially corresponding doctrine of immortality. Cf. Osiander's idea of the imparting and indwelling of Christ's essential righteousness in contrast to Melanchthon's forensic view, EF III, 35ff. (EG III, 54ff.).

[102] See Appendix IV.

[103] See Luther's *Commentary on Genesis*, WA 43, 481, 32ff., LW 5, 76.

[104] From a letter to Spenlein, 1516, Briefe I, 35.

[105] WA 2, 531, 10; 140, 7; 40/I, 278, 6, LW 27, 282; 27, 163.

APPENDICES

[1] Act 2, Cotta ed., 3, 177.

[2] *Ibid.*, 778.

[3] From the conversation on May 2, 1824.

[4] Cotta ed., 6, 481.

[5] Eckermann, Sept. 1, 1829.

[6] In the conversation on Feb. 25, 1824. Cf. the earlier discussion of the term "activity."

[7] *Werke*, ed. Suphan (1877ff.), XVI, 122, quoted in R. Unger, "Herder, Novalis und Kleist," *Deutsche Forschungen* 9 (1922), 23.

[8] Unger, *loc. cit.*

[9] On the implied concept of time cf. my *Offenbarung, Vernunft und Existenz* (5th ed., 1967).

[10] Cf. the passages from later Jewish apocalyptic in E. Stauffer, *Theologie des NT* (1941), 56ff.

[11] Quoted in F. W. Weber, *Gott in der Natur* (1936), 46.

[12] I may refer theological readers to EF III, 411ff. (EG III, 548ff.), where the debate with Roman Catholics on the intermediate state is discussed.

[13] Cf. the term *katargeō* in 1 Cor. 15:26 and 2 Tim. 1:10. This word means "to triumph" in the sense "to put out of action," "to deprive of power," or, in the passive, "to have no more concern with." According to 2 Tim. 1:10 Christ has conquered death in this sense (robbed it of power) and brought life and immortality to light.

[14] See the Bibliography.

[15] WA 37, 174ff. (not in LW).

[16] Cf. what Luther says about the sleep of the righteous in his exposition of Gen. 25, LW 4, 309.

[17] We recall the last chorale of Bach's *St. John's Passion* with its prayer that God will let his angel take my soul at the end to Abraham's bosom (M. Schalling, c. 1570).

[18] Cf. EF III, 411ff. (EG III, 549ff.).

[19] This self-transcending is the sustaining note in my anthropology, *Mensch sein — Mensch werden* (3rd ed., 1980).

[20] EF II, 445f. (EG II, 550).

[21] Luke 24:13ff.; cf. *ibid.*, 450 (558).

[22] In my rather dubious use of the term "point of contact" I differ from both E. Brunner in his unequivocal endorsement of the term and K. Barth in his no less unequivocal rejection of it, as I have shown in ThE I, 321ff. (§§ 1643–1690) and EF I, 140f. (EG I, 179–181).

[23] EF II, 432 (EG II, 533).

[24] As regards the mystery of the resurrection, which can appear here only in an indirect light, I may refer to my chapters on the theme in EF (EG) II and III.

BIBLIOGRAPHY

Ahlbrecht, A. *Tod und Unsterblichkeit in der evangelischen Theologie der Gegenwart* (1964).

Althaus, P. *Die letzten Dinge. Entwurf einer christlichen Eschatologie* (3rd ed., 1926; 6th ed., 1956).

—————. *Der Friedhof unserer Väter* (3rd ed., 1928).

—————. *Die christliche Wahrheit. Lehrbuch der Dogmatik*, 2 vols. (1947/48).

Améry, J. *Hand an sich legen. Diskurs über den Freitod* (1976).

Andrae, T. *Die letzten Dinge* (1940).

Ariès, P. *Studien zur Geschichte des Todes im Abendland* (1976).

Baden, H. J. *Literatur und Selbstmord* (1965).

Baetke, W. *Art und Glaube der Germanen* (1934).

Bally, G. "Das Todesproblem in der wissenschaftlich-technischen Gesellschaft," *Wege zum Menschen* (1966), 129ff.

Balthasar, U. von. *Apokalypse der deutschen Seele. Studie zur Lehre von den letzten Haltungen*, 3 vols., no date.

Bälz, E. *Über die Todesverachtung der Japaner* (1936).

Barbarin, G. *Der Tod als Freund* (1938).

Barth, C. *Die Errettung vom Tode in den individuellen Klage- und Dankliedern des AT* (1947).

Barth, K. *Church Dogmatics* III,2 (1960), 587ff. (KD III,2, 714ff.).

Baum, S. *Der verborgene Tod. Auskünfte über ein Tabu* (1979).

Beauvoir, S. de. *Ein sanfter Tod* (1965).

Behnk, W. "Vom Mythos der 'Leben-nach-dem-Tod' Literatur," *Zeitschrift für evangelische Ethik* 3 (1979), 221ff.

Bonhoeffer, D. *Widerstand und Ergebung* (1951ff.), ET: *Letters and Papers from Prison* (1972).

Bovet, T. *Die Ganzheit der Person in der ärztlichen Praxis* (no date).

Bultmann, R. "The Concept of Life in the OT," TDNT II, 849ff. (TWNT II, 850ff.).

—————. "The Concept of Life in the NT," TDNT II, 861ff. (TWNT II, 862ff.).

Bürkle, H. "Der Tod in den afrikanischen Gemeinschaften," in Lohse, *Leben*, 243ff.

Choron, J. *Der Tod im abendländischen Denken* (1970).

Cullmann, O. "Unsterblichkeit der Seele und Auferstehung der Toten. Das Zeugnis des NT," *Theologische Zeitschrift*, Basel 2 (1956), 126ff.

Dehn, F. *Das Gespräch vom Tode* (no date).

Dirschauer, K. *Der totgeschwiegene Tod* (1973).

Dorozynski, A. *Der Mann, der nicht sterben durfte. Das Leben des russischen Nobelpreisträgers Lew Landau* (1966).

Ebeling, G. *Dogmatik des christlichen Glaubens* III (1979), c.11.

Ebon, M. *The Evidence for Life after Death* (1977).

Eissler, K. R. *Der sterbende Patient. Zur Psychologie des Todes* (1978).

Elze, M. "Spätmittelalterliche Predigt im Angesicht des Todes," in Lohse, *Leben*, 89ff.

Engisch, K. *Euthanasie und Vernichtung lebensunwerten Lebens in strafrechtlicher Betrachtung* (no date).

Fohrer, G. "Das Geschick des Menschen nach dem Tode im AT," *Kerygma und Dogma* 4 (1968), 249ff.

Freud, S. *Das Ich und das Es* (1923), ET: "The Ego and the Id," *Major Works*, 697–717.

Gardavsky, V. *Gott ist nicht ganz tot* (1968).

Goppelt, L. "Geschichtlich wirksames Sterben," in Lohse, *Leben*, 61ff.

Grönbech, W. *Kultur und Religion der Germanen* (1937), ET: *The Culture of the Teutons* (1928, expanded).

Grote, L. R. "Das Problem des Todes unter dem Gesichtpunkt der biologischen Zeit," *Synopsis. Studien aus Medizin und Naturwissenschaft*, ed. A. Jores (1949), 25ff.

Groethuysen, B. *Die Entstehung der bürgerlichen Weltanschauung in Frankreich*, I (1927).

Haas, R. "Zum Todesmotiv im Werk Hemingways," *Die neueren Sprachen*, 10 (1959), 455ff.

Hampe, J. C. *Sterben ist doch ganz anders* (1975).

Heidegger, M. *Sein und Zeit* (3rd ed., 1931), ET: *Being and Time* (1962).

Heinz-Mohr, G. *Jetzt und in der Stunde des Todes* (1963).

Hengstenberg, H. E. *Einsamkeit und Tod* (1938).

————. *Tod und Vollendung* (1938).

Henry, M. L. " 'Tod' und 'Leben' im AT," in Lohse, *Leben*, 1ff.

Hengstenberg, H. E. *Einsamkeit und Tod* (1938).

————. *Tod und Vollendung* (1938).

Hildebrandt, B. "Die theologische Bedeutung des Todes," *Theologische Versuche* VI (East Berlin, 1975), 193ff.

Höfer, W. *Leben müssen, sterben dürfen* (1977).

Hoff, F. *Von Krankheit und Heilung und vom Sterben* (1975).

Hornung, E., ed. "Das Totenbuch der Ägypter," *Bibliothek der Alten Welt* (1979).

Hunzinger, C. H. "Die Hoffnung angesichts des Todes im Wandel paulinischer Aussagen," in Lohse, *Leben*, 69ff.

Husserl, E. *Vorlesungen zur Phänomenologie des innern Zeitbewusstseins*, ed. M. Heidegger (1928).

Jaspers, K. *Philosophie* II. "Existenzerhellung" (1932), 220ff.

Johnson, A. R. *The Vitality of the Individual in the Thought of Ancient Israel* (1949).

Jores, A. "Der Tod und der Arzt," *Synopsis* (1949), 3ff.

Jüngel, E. *Tod* (2nd ed., 1979), ET: *Death* (1974).

Kasper, W. "Gespräch über christliche Eschatologie," *Herder-Korrespondenz* 3 (1977), 130.

Kautzky, R. "Der ärztliche Kampf um das Leben des Patienten 'bis zum letzten Atemzug,' " *Hochland* (1961), 303ff.

————, ed. *Sterben im Krankenhaus* (1976).

Kellermann, U. "Überwindung des Todesgeschicks in der alttestamentlichen Frömmigkeit vor und neben dem Auferstehungsglauben," *Zeitschrift für Theologie und Kirche* 3 (1976), 259ff.

Klempnauer, G. *Wenn ich nur noch einen Tag zu leben hätte, Aussagen von Jugendlichen* (1977).

Köberle, A. *Die Theologie der Gegenwart und das Leben nach dem Tod* (1970).

Koch, K. "Der Schatz im Himmel," in Lohse, *Leben*, 47ff.

Kraus, H.-J. "Vom Leben und Tod in den Psalmen," in Lohse, *Leben*, 27ff.

Kretschmar, G. "Auferstehung des Fleisches," in Lohse, *Leben*, 101ff.

Kübler-Ross, E. *On Death and Dying* (1969), GT: *Interviews mit Sterbenden* (1979).

―――――. *Death: The Final Stage of Growth* (1975), GT: *Reif werden zum Tode* (3rd ed., 1977).

Lehmann, K. *Der Tod bei Heidegger und Jaspers* (1938).

Leipold, J. *Der Tod bei Griechen und Juden* (1942).

Lohff, W. "Theologische Erwägungen vom Problem des Todes," in Lohse, *Leben*, 157ff.

Lohse, B. "Gesetz, Tod und Sünde in Luthers Auslegung des 90. Psalms," in Lohse, *Leben*, 138.

Lohse, B. and Schmidt, H. P., eds. *Leben angesichts des Todes* (1968) (= *Leben*).

Margull, H. J. "Tod Jesu und Schmerz Gottes," in Lohse, *Leben*, 269ff.

Martensen-Larsen, H. *An der Pforte des Todes* (1955).

Mauder, A. *Die Kunst des Sterbens* (3rd ed., 1976).

Moody, R. A. *Life after Life* (1975), GT: *Leben nach dem Tod* (1978).

Müller-Schwefe, H. R. "Tod und Leben in der modernen Dichtung," in Lohse, *Leben*, 223ff.

Nebel, G. "Platon und die Unsterblichkeit der Seele," *Griechischer Ursprung* I (1948), 11 – 219.

Neill, S. "Die Macht und Bewältigung des Todes in Hinduismus und Buddhismus," in Lohse, *Leben*, 283ff.

Nikolainen, A. T. *Der Auferstehungsglaube in der Bibel und ihrer Umwelt* I (1944).

Otto, W. F. *Die Götter Griechenlands* (1934), esp. 175ff., 189f., ET: *The Homeric Gods* (1954), esp. 140ff., 263ff.

Pannenberg, W. "Tod und Auferstehung in der Sicht christlicher Dogmatik," *Kerygma und Dogma* 3 (1974), 167ff.

Poelchau, H. "Bewusstes Sterben (vor der Hinrichtung)," *Synopsis* (1949), 19ff.

Quell, G. *Die Auffassung des Todes in Israel* (1967).

Rad, G. von. "Life and Death in the OT," TDNT II, 843ff. (TWNT II, 844ff.).

―――――. *Theologie des AT*, 2 vols. (1957ff.), ET: *Old Testament Theology* (1962/65).

Rahner, K. *Zur Theologie des Todes* (2nd ed., 1958), ET: *On The Theology of Death* (1961).

Rehm, W. *Der Todesgedanke in der deutschen Dichtung vom Mittelalter bis zur Romantik* (1928).

Röhricht, R. "Der Name 'Gott,'" in Lohse, *Leben*, 171ff.

Rudolf, R. *Ars moriendi. Forschungen zur Volkskunde* (1957).

Schadewaldt, W. "Das Gedenken der Toten in der Antike," *Hellas und Hesperien* (1960), 60ff.

Scheler, M. *Vom Ewigen im Menschen* (1923).

Schmidt, H. P. "Todeserfahrung und Lebenserwartung," in Lohse, *Leben*, 191ff.

Schrötter, K. and Wüst, W. *Tod und Unsterblichkeit im Weltbild der indogermanischen Denker* (1942).

Schur, M. *S. Freud. Sein Leben und Sterben* (1973), esp. 436 – 444.

Seneca, *De brevitate vitae.*

Simmel, G. "Metaphysik des Todes," *Logos* I (1910), 57ff.

Stange, K. *Luthers Gedanken über die Todesfurcht* (1932).

Thielicke, H. *Theologische Ethik* I-III (ThE), ET: *Theological Ethics.*

―――――. *Der evangelische Glaube* I-III, ET: *The Evangelical Faith* (EF).

―――――. *Mensch sein — Mensch werden* (Anthrop.) (3rd ed., 1980).

Tillich, P. *Systematic Theology* II (1954), 66ff.

Tolstoy, L. *The Death of Ivan Ilych* (1960).

Valentin, F., ed. *Die Euthanasie* (1969).

Bibliography

Wach, J. *Das Problem des Todes in der Philosophie unserer Zeit* (1934).

Wächter, L. *Der Tod im AT* (1967).

Wehrung, G. *Der Mensch und der Tod* (1950).

Wickler, W. and Seibt, U. *Das Prinzip Eigennutz* (1977).

Wiesenhütter, E. *Blick nach drüben. Selbsterfahrungen im Sterben* (1974).

Wolff, H. W. *Anthropologie des AT* (2nd ed., 1974), esp. § 12.

Ziegler, L. *Überlieferung* (1936).

INDEX OF SUBJECTS

206